The Key to the Universe

THE KEY TO THE UNIVERSE

or a Spiritual Interpretation of Numbers and Symbols

BY

HARRIETTE AUGUSTA CURTISS

AND

F. HOMER CURTISS, B.S., M.D.

Founders of "The Order of Christian Mystics"

With many diagrams and tables.
Also ten full page plates.

Sixth and revised edition

NEWCASTLE PUBLISHING COMPANY, INC.
1983

ISBN 0-87877-068-2

A Newcastle Book
First Printing October 1983
Printed in United States of America

NEWCASTLE PUBLISHING COMPANY, INC.
NORTH HOLLYWOOD, CALIFORNIA
1983

TABLE OF CONTENTS

TABLE OF CONTENTS

FOREWORD

These are days of great unrest in all walks of life. Many are running to and fro seeking a firm foundation on which to erect their Temple of Truth. These are the days foretold by the prophet Amos: "Behold, the days come, saith the Lord God, that I will send a famine in the land, not a famine of bread, nor a thirst for water, but of hearing the words of the Lord."[1] It takes but little insight to see in present day conditions the literal fulfillment of the prophecy: "For many shall come in my name, saying, I am Christ; and shall deceive many. * * * Then if any man shall say unto you, Lo, here is Christ, or there; believe it not."[2] But that we may not be deceived there must be some firm foundation on which we can rest assured and build. Where shall this be found? This is the question which this volume seeks to answer through the interpretation of the spiritual meanings of the unchanging symbols handed down to mankind in the only exact science, numbers. It does not profess to be the 1 and only Book of Wisdom, the only true and satisfying solution of the world's problems, but it does strive to set forth an exposition of the framework on which the cosmic philosophy of the ancient Wisdom Religion was based (subject to the human limitations of the transmitting personalities), together with such inspirational Light as has been vouchsafed to the authors, who make no claim to aught save the office of transmitters and distributors of the spiritual food especially stored and preserved in the storehouse of the King, in readiness for this time of famine.

Today many are striving to appease this Soul-hunger. Many well-intentioned teachers who have had a

---

[1] *Amos*, viii, 11.

[2] *St. Matthew*, xxiv, 5-23.

realization of a phase of Truth strive to fill the need, but because they have not a cosmic and all-inclusive philosophy, they can give but a few crumbs to an hungry 1 here and there, while the great mass—those who are not content to take any single phase of Truth—still seek, hungering, starving or feeding on the husks of materialistic conceptions. Others, in an effort to be less personal, are telling the hungry ones to cease seeking for help from teachers and look only to the Within. In fact, we have in our hands a little circular which voices, in the following words, the note of almost universal despair and disappointment with teachers: "To you, who thought you had found in some great teacher, who was perhaps the acknowledged head of some Society, Fraternity or Religion, and who appeared to you to be a 'Master,' so marvelous was the wisdom he taught and the works he performed; only to awaken later to the realization that that 'Master' was but a human personality, with faults and weaknesses, and secret sins, the same as you, even tho' that personality may have been a channel thru which was voiced many beautiful teachings, which seemed to you the highest 'Truth.' * * * To *you,* I AM come. * * * For I AM your *real* Teacher, * * * and the *only* MASTER."

This idea that all wisdom, comfort and help can be found within is but a further fulfillment of the prophecy as given in *St. Matthew* (xxiv, 26): "Wherefore if they shall say unto you, Behold, he is in the desert [of mere intellectual learning]; go not forth: behold, he is in the secret chambers [the Within]; believe it not." Here we find the 2 opposite poles of teaching, as common in the days of the Apostles as today, anticipated and provided for. Where then shall we find rest, peace and spiritual food?

Foreword

Dear Reader, long ere the famine was sent into the land the preparation for it was made. Joseph was sent into the darkness of Egypt to prepare for the 7 years of famine by gathering up the over-plus of corn and wine during the 7 years of plenty, and preserving them in the King's granaries and storehouses, so that when the lean years came there should be food a-plenty for all who asked it of the King. So the Spiritual Teachers of the Race, the Masters of Wisdom and Elder Brothers of humanity, have for our sakes dwelt in Egypt that They might store up in the granaries of the King of Kings the spiritual philosophy which alone can bring satisfaction when the days of famine of the Word are upon us. They it is who have marked out the Way which leads direct to the storehouse of the King of Kings.

Think you in the days of famine in Egypt, those who came seeking the food so lavishly furnished them by Joseph caviled at his personality? Did they say, "This man is a Canaanite. He has served time in prison. He has been sold as a slave. He is but human like ourselves, with faults and weaknesses and secret sins, even as we ourselves. He cannot feed us. We will have none of him. The same God who gave him the forethought to store up the corn and wine is our God. We will find Him within, and He shall feed us, for all things are ours?" It is obvious that such an 1 would have gone hungry and been forced to prove the fallacy of his doctrine. And so must it ever be. For while the I AM is The Christ within every Soul, there is no greater sin—if by sin we mean mistake—than the great "heresy of separateness." It takes all humanity to complete the expression of the Divine, hence, since the wisdom of no 1 man has ever evolved a complete science or formulated a philosophy without the aid of his predecessors, so no 1 Soul can unaided find the whole Truth within himself. All a Soul can find within is its own Truth, the Truth that shall make it free. The voice of The Christ within giveth testimony unto Truth, *i. e.*, the I AM tells us unmistakably what is Truth and what is not. Also it should be remembered that all Truth comes to man through an human intellect, either through your own or that of another, while *the I AM simply knows and recognizes Truth,* witnesses to and affirms it. Therefore, as long as we listen to this Voice within no personality, teacher or teaching can deceive or disappoint us; for we will "take, eat" only from The Christ the bread that He has broken and given to His disciples to be distributed to the multitude; we will drink only from the Cup that He has blessed and filled with His own spiritual life-force. This is the basis on which we ask you to consider the teachings of this volume. If you hear the assenting Voice within or feel the thrill of Truth confirmed, then partake of it to the upbuilding of your spiritual life. If not, then pass it by until a riper understanding reveals it to you.

The Wisdom Religion is the accumulated wisdom, 1st of Revelation; 2nd of Inner Assent by The Christ within; and 3rd of Experience, not of any 1 man, but of many men in all ages who have struggled, sinned, suffered, triumphed and finally *mastered* the problems and forces of life. These have left behind them a well trodden Path leading to the very door of the storehouse of the King, where They ever stand ready to pass on to soul-hungry, starving humanity the life-giving food; for They have eaten of it and found it utterly satisfying and will neither hunger nor thirst any more. Some morsels are offered herein. Take, eat, if you will, and be satisfied.

PREFACE

> "The twenty-two sounds and letters are the Foundation of all things. Three mothers, seven doubles and twelve simples." —*Sepher Yetzirah,* II, 1.

Our great desire in presenting this work to the public is that it shall be a practical treatise; that it shall explain to the student the reason for and the nature of the many mysterious experiences which he encounters as the Path of Attainment unfolds before and within him, to the end that he may understand their significance, learn their lessons and avoid the mistakes and discouragements which result from ignorance of the Law. In other words, we shall endeavor to show that all personal experiences are expressions of the 1 Great Law manifesting according to mathematical principles, demonstrating that the unfoldment of the godlike possibilities inherent in each Soul follows, step by step, the same order of events that is followed in the evolution of the Cosmos, and that such steps are symbolized by the first 22 numbers—the Signature or Name of God. This signature is impressed upon the Cosmos through the Divine Trinity, the 7 Sacred Planets and the 12 signs of the Zodiac.

"In fact, in the 'Sepher Yetzirah,' God considered as the Infinite and consequently the indefinable Being, extended throughout all things by His power and existence, is while above, yet not outside of numbers, sounds and letters,—the principles and general laws which we recognize!"[1]

Our effort throughout will be not to compile a work for scholars only, but to popularize occult philosophy by presenting in a form easily comprehensible by the

[1] *La Kabbale,* Franck, quoted by Westcott in *The Sepher Yetzirah,* 8.

average intelligent reader, the philosophic principles symbolized by the 1st 22 numbers. These few numbers, as we explain herein, truly form the key to the evolution of both man and the Cosmos, or *The Key to the Universe,* for they symbolize and illustrate the cosmic principles back of all manifestation, and prove mathematically the relationship between the microcosm and the macrocosm. They also mathematically demonstrate the principles of Christian Mysticism as expounded by *The Order of Christian Mystics (Order of the 15).*

In addition to giving the spiritual interpretation of the 1st 22 numbers, we also include an explanation of the esoteric meaning of the 22 letters of the Hebrew alphabet which correspond to them, together with the symbology of the 22 Major Arcana of the *Tarot* cards.

"The alphabet of the Hebrews is composed of 22 letters; these letters, however, are not placed by chance, one after the other. Each of them corresponds with a number according to its work, with a hieroglyphic according to its form, with a symbol according to its affinities with other letters."[2]

While accepting many of the more spiritual interpretations of other writers on numbers and the *Tarot,* by the presentation of a great mass of original material derived from inspirational sources, we shall avoid making this work either a mere compilation of the statements of others presented without elucidation or a dry mathematical treatise.

Another feature of this work is the liberal quotations from that wonderful mine of information and the foremost authority on occultism in the Western world, *The Secret Doctrine,* by Helena Petrovna Blavatsky. This work is so large and expensive that it is possessed only by a comparatively few scholars. Hence, for the benefit of the great mass of occult students who would

---

[2] *The Tarot,* Papus, 94.

otherwise never partake of its riches, we will quote extensively from it, as well as paraphrase other portions whenever they will either elucidate or substantiate our point or interpretation. That these quotations may be easily distinguished from the original matter, and for convenience in reference, they will be placed in a special style of type.

The Secret Doctrine and *The Voice of Isis* will be referred to so frequently herein that their titles will be abbreviated in the footings to *S. D.*, vol., etc., and *V. of I.*, respectively.

We regret that the monthly lessons referred to in the footnotes are now out of print, but they will probably appear in subsequent volumes.

San Francisco, Cal.,
Sept. 15th, 1915.

THE KEY TO THE UNIVERSE

CHAPTER 1

THE ORIGIN OF NUMERICAL SYSTEMS.

"Every cosmogony, from the earliest to the latest, is based upon, interlinked with, and most closely related to, numerals and geometrical figures."—*The Secret Doctrine,* Blavatasky, III, 69.

"So teach us to number our days, that we may apply our hearts unto wisdom."—*Psalms,* xc, 12.

"God is a Number endowed with motion, which is felt but not demonstrated."—*Balzac.*

Mathematics is the only exact science; the only 1 whose propositions are capable of conclusive proof and demonstration. All other so-called "exact sciences" are based upon assumptions, deductions and "working hypotheses" which are more or less useful until further investigation and discovery proves them to be but partial truths. And in these days of rapid progress, the changes of base in the "exact sciences" are so frequent that the scientific text-books have to be rewritten every few years, so rapidly are the materialistic conceptions of matter and the universe outgrown. Only 3 centuries ago the "exact science" of the day was unanimous in the opinion that the earth was flat, and opposed the idea of the infinity of the universe and the plurality of worlds to such a degree that its leaders burned Giordano Bruno at the stake for daring to oppose their dictum. Within a decade or 2 "exact science" ridiculed the possibility of the transmutation of metals, classing it as a mere vagary of unbalanced mystics, yet today we have the transmutation of metals going on in many laboratories as a matter of course. Only a few years ago we were taught that the atom was a particle of matter, but today the same "exact science" asks us to believe that it is not "matter" at all, but the union of 2 units of force called "electrons." The facts as taught by the mystics of all ages remain; modern interpretation of them evolves and expands.

Words are symbols of ideas, but numbers are symbols of divine realities; spiritual verities eternal in the heavens, which express themselves periodically in the worlds of objectivity. "If as Pythagoras said: 'The world is built upon the power of numbers,' then numbers must be the key to the understanding of the world." "They are a key to the ancient views on cosmogony, in its broad sense, including man and beings, and the evolution of the human race, spiritually as well as physically."[1]

> "Hence we find numbers and figures used as an expression and a record of thought in every archaic symbolical scripture. They are ever the same, with certain variations only, arising from the first figures."[2]

Following Prof. Max Müller, it is commonly accepted that our present numerical system was invented by the Arabs, for he tells us that, "The two words *cipher* and *zero,* which are but one, are sufficient to prove that our figures are borrowed from the Arabs."[3] As a matter of fact the system was introduced into Europe by Pythagoras, who found it already fully developed in India. It is true that later the system was widely spread by Arab traders, but they also obtained it from India. Prof. Müller later admits this origin himself when he says elsewhere: "Cipher is the Arabic *cipron,* which means simply, *a translation of the Sans-*

[1] *Isis Unveiled,* Blavatsky, II, 407.
[2] *The Secret Doctrine,* Blavatsky, I, 341.
[3] *Our Figures,* Müller.

krit name of nought."[4] Among the Hebrews the kabalistic word *Sephiroth* also corresponds to the word cipher, not in the sense of nothing, but rather in the sense of containing within itself the powers of creation by number and degrees of evolution, altho as yet unmanifested, hence a void.

The Hindus, however, do not claim to have originated the science, for the sages declare that it was *revealed* to them by the Devas (the Gods). Also, "The Pythagoreans asserted that the doctrine of Numbers, the chief of all in Esotericism, had been revealed to man by the Celestial Deities; that the World had been called forth out of Chaos by Sound or Harmony, and according to the principles of musical proportion."[5] These are but confirmations of the occult teaching that the science of numbers was not slowly evolved by primitive man learning to count on his fingers—which is deduced as the *probable* origin by exoteric investigators—but *was a fully elaborated system* of computation *revealed* to the priesthood of the early Races by the Elder Brothers and Spiritual Teachers of mankind.[6]

"The symbol was the origin of measures, shadowing forth *creative law* or *design.* * * * Reflection becomes more involved when it is considered that the power of expression of the law, *exactly,* by numbers clearly defining a system, was not the *accident* of the language, but was its very *essence,* and of its *primary organic construction;* therefore, neither the language, nor the mathematical system attaching to it, could be of man's invention, unless both were *founded upon a prior language which afterwards became obsolete.*"[7]

No matter how far back into the night of time archeological or other investigations are extended, high stages of civilization are found, each having an elabo-

[4] *Chips*, Vol. II, 284 (1873).

[5] *S. D.*, I, 467.

[6] A volume might easily be written substantiating this statement, but its truth is so self-evident to all who have investigated the subject that we do not consider it necessary to present further evidence than is contained in this volume.

[7] *The Source of Measures.* Skinner, 204.

rate numerical system, where, according to modern scientific theories, only the most primitive conditions might be expected. Even today we find primitive systems existing side by side with the most advanced. They are found, however, only among the sub-races which are not in touch with the highest civilization of their age. Relics of so-called primitive people—the so-called "cave-man" and other *degenerate remnants* of the earlier sub-races—are no more an index of the stage of development to which mankind as a whole had reached in those bygone days, than the development of the present Bushmen of Australia or the Ainos of Japan are an index to the height to which civilization has reached today. The 2 extremes exist at the same time, if not side by side.[8] The almost incalculable antiquity of elaborate astronomical and numerical systems is sufficiently indicated to sustain the occult teaching by the following quotation:

> "Diogenes Laërtius carried back the astronomical calculations of the Egyptians to 48,863 years before Alexander the Great. Martianus Capella corroborates this by telling posterity that the Egyptians had secretly studied Astronomy for over 40,000 years, before they imparted their knowledge of the world. * * * Mr. Proctor shows, in his *Myths and Marvels of Astronomy*, that the ancient Astronomers had acquired a system of the most accurate Astronomy 2,400 years B. C.; the Hindus date their Kali Yuga from a great periodical conjunction of the Planets *thirty-one centuries B. C.* * * * Simplicimus, in the sixth century, A. D., writes that he had always heard that the Egyptians had kept astronomical observations and records for a period of 630,000 years. This statement appears to frighten Mr. Gerald Massey, who remarks that: 'If we read this number of years by the month which Euxodus said the Egyptians termed a year, *i. e.*, a course of time, that would still yield the length of two cycles of precession (51,736 years)'."[9]

[8] For the occult teaching on the origin of **Races** see the *Voice of Isis*, Curtiss, Chapters xiii, xv, xvii.

[9] *S. D.*, I, 712-3.

Herodotus tells us that the Egyptians founded a system of a 12 god theogony. Hence we find in Egypt the duo-decimal system, or method of reckoning by 12, in common use. And it is to the use of that system in the construction of the pyramids, that the origin of the English foot of 12 inches has been traced. Among the early Races the decimal system, or reckoning by 10, was esoteric and known only to the higher Initiates among the priesthood.

> "Now, if, on the one hand, the most ancient Indian MSS. show as yet no trace of decimal notation in them, and Max Müller states very clearly that until now he has found but nine letters, the initials of the Sanskrit numerals; on the other hand, we have records as ancient, to supply the wanted proof. We speak of the sculptures and the sacred imagery in the most ancient temples of the Far East."[10]

The decimal system was held sacred because the priesthood, having received it directly from the Divine Teachers of mankind and having been taught its sacred significance, understood that in the numbers from 1 to 10 the whole evolution of the Cosmos and of man, the descent of Spirit into matter that matter might be redeemed, together with man's At-one-ment with the Divine, were portrayed and revealed to those who had eyes to see and hearts to understand.

> "*We know* that the decimal system must have been used by mankind of the earliest archaic ages, since the whole astronomical and geometrical portion of the secret sacerdotal language was built upon the number 10, or the combination of the male and female principles. * * * The 10, being the sacred number of the Universe, was secret and esoteric, both as regards the unit and cipher, or zero, the circle."[10]

The priesthood knew the dire results of the misuse, perversion, debasement or reversal of any symbol, hence

---

[10] *S. D.*, I, 386.

would have saved mankind from all the degradation and suffering which has resulted from the fraudulent manipulation of these sacred symbols by man to acquire personal advance or power at the expense of his fellow men; for example, the acquiring of individual wealth at the expense of the community and mankind in general (*i. e.*, the worship of the Beast), in contradistinction to the creation of wealth through agriculture, mining, manufacturing, etc.

We may here mention that 1 of the most common ways of perverting the potencies of numbers, and perhaps the most insidious and demoralizing in its effects upon mankind, is the use of numbers in games of chance or gambling. It is said that every confirmed gambler has a more or less well developed system which he believes is bound to win. The so-called element of chance as applied to numbers has been demonstrated to be subject to certain laws which bring success for a time, and it is this mysterious property of numbers, which the gambler senses and tries to control, that lures him on to his inevitable ruin. For the law of numbers does not belong to the realm of chance. Numbers are potent factors in the working out of Divine Law, hence no system devised by man for his own aggrandizement or advantage at the expense of others, can ultimately succeed. It may seemingly do so up to a certain point or until the cycle of that particular combination of numbers reverts back to its true rate of vibration or the key-note which belongs to that particular expression of the Divine Law, and fulfills its real mission. The Law of Numbers, being the law of the progressive manifestation of the Christos or the Divine Light penetrating Chaos and evolving all manifested things back to ultimate unity, in certain stages may seemingly lend itself to the furtherance of evil, but in the end this will be shown to be but the gathering together of the forces of Chaos (chance) that they may be swept aside, swallowed up and ultimately transmuted into unity.

> "Number is, as the great writer (Balzac) thought, an Entity, and, at the same time, a Breath emanating from what he called God and what we call the ALL, the Breath which alone could organize the physical Cosmos, 'where naught obtains its form but through Diety,' which is an effect of Number."[11]

Numbers may be compared to the bones of the body in that they are the framework upon which the superstructure of manifestation is erected. Therefore, even if the study of occult mathematics may seem to some but a study of dry bones, it is as necessary to the occult student as a study of osteology to the medical student. Its study was considered so important by the Greeks, that it, together with physical culture, comprised the entire educational curriculum. Their system of mathematics, however, embraced 4 categories, arithmetic or the laws of numbers; geometry or the laws of plane and solid figures; astronomy, which included astrology, or the laws of both planetary motions and their spiritual and magnetic influences; and, finally, music, under which heading they included harmony, rhythm and poetry, their poetry in turn embracing the history of the world.

In the *Bible,* from the days of creation to the *Apocalypse,* great stress is laid upon numbers, especially 3, 4, 7, and 12. In the Hindu scriptures, the *Vedas, Upanishads,* etc., numbers underlie every hymn, and stress is laid upon 1, 3 and 7; the same system upon which *Vach* or the sacred speech of Zoroaster was built. Hence it is impossible to become an Adept and fully grasp the deep problems of either the Brahmanical, Buddhistic, Zoroastrian or Christian sacred books with-

---

[11] *S. D.,* I, 95-6.

out a knowledge of the significance of numbers. The power of a mantram or hymn, or a reading from 1 of the sacred books, varies with the numbers and syllables of the words, the rhythm of the meter and the vibrations of the tones used, in addition to the meaning of the words themselves. This is recognized more or less clearly in all religions, from the chanting of the sacred sentence *Om mani padme hum* of the Hindu and Thibetan monks, the rhythmic reading from *Granth Sahib* and the repetition of the sacred name *Wahguru* of the Sikhs, to the intoning of the service in many branches of the Christian church. If these various forms of mantra are intoned slowly and with a rhythmic cadence a certain effect is produced; if quickly and sharply quite a different effect results. These effects, being founded upon the laws of vibration, are not imaginary nor merely the result of suggestion upon especially sensitive persons. The nerves are like the strings of a musical instrument and try to respond and adjust themselves to the vibrations playing upon them, and the effects are plainly apparent both upon the mind and the emotions. This is the secret of the soothing and healing power of music, as well as the stimulating effect of martial airs.

Since all things manifest according to the laws of numbers and vibration, everything can be made to respond to these laws. Hence, 1 who has gained the mastery over his voice, or as the occultist would say, can command the "Army of the Voice," is master over all. This is the only true magic, "Know thyself." Know the key-note of that which you desire, harmonize yourself with it and then sound it.

"God geometrizes" is an ancient occult axiom which cryptically expresses the fact that all manifestations of God, life, nature, as they come into objectivity from subjectivity, flow along geometrical lines and follow geometrical laws. "It is an interesting fact that the superior metals crystallize at the angle or complemental angle of a regular polygon. If they sometimes followed one form and sometimes another we should not recognize them for what they are. We depend for the fidelity of our perceptions upon the integrity of the Great Geometer. * * * If we steadily regard the geometry of Nature in the same patient and sincere manner as did Hipparchus, Ptolemy, Kepler, Tycho, Newton, Kelvin, and others we shall probably come to the conclusion that number, as expressed in geometrical relations, is the most intimate expression of the Soul of things."[12] Each such expression has its number, rate of vibration or wave-length, its sound, color and form, and its own place in the Grand Plan or scheme of the universe. This is as true of the forces which create a world as of those which create a snow crystal. As we have said elsewhere: "All Nature-shapes can be traced back to and analyzed into simple geometrical figures: • |△□○ just as all musical notes produce characteristic designs when made to pass through sand or other suitable material."[13]

> "Thus the evolution and correlation of the mysteries of Kosmos, of its growth and development—spiritual and physical, abstract and concrete—were first recorded in geometrical changes of shape."[14]

In view of the above facts, some understanding of the origin and significance of numbers and geometrical forms is necessary to the larger conception of divine manifestation, whether in man, nature or the universe. For numbers are not arbitrary symbols, but constitute a sacred science, its symbols being generated by the manifestation of all nature and the Cosmos itself, as we shall endeavor to show herein.

---

[12] *The Kabala of Numbers,* Sepharial, II, 23-7.
[13] *V. of I.*, 357.
[14] *S. D.*, I, 341.

CHAPTER 2

THE SYMBOL OF THE ○ AND THE SERPENT

> "God is a circle, the center of which is everywhere and the circumference nowhere."—*Pascal.*

> "Alone, the One Form of Existence stretched boundless, infinite, causeless, in Dreamless Sleep; and Life pulsated unconscious in Universal Space, throughout that All-Presence, which is sensed by the Open Eye of Dangma."—*Stanzas of Dzyan,* I, 8.

In numerical systems the ○ is the 1st symbol to be considered, as it is the 1 from which all others proceed. It is a symbol of Unmanifested Deity; in the *Bible,* the darkness of Chaos from which the Cosmos emerges. It is the Night of Brahm in which all is latent, "a boundless darkness on the ground of which appears the first central point in white." It may sound paradoxical to call the Deity, whom we are wont to think of as Universal Life and Omnipotent Being, a circle of darkness, yet right here the student must begin to adjust his point of view to the occult and mystical conceptions. A fundamental axiom is that "extremes meet," also that vibrations of light and life may be so intense that they cannot be perceived by man's physical senses—the solar spectrum above violet, for instance—hence are apparently darkness and non-existence. Such a boundless circle of pulsating, vibrant yet undifferentiated life-force proceeding from the Center of All Life, forms the "waters of the Great Deep," deep in that they are unfathomable and incomprehensible to undeveloped man. Only when the Spirit of God moves upon these waters and the Word—the

Son of God—is sent down into manifestation, are the waves of this Great Deep stilled, *i. e.*, the vibrations are slowed down so that that which we understand as life begins to manifest.

Having neither beginning nor end, as we have said elsewhere: "The circle represents Boundless Space and limitless Time in Eternity. It marks off the space in which creation takes place, or the Circle formed by the down-pouring of the Great Creative Force. * * * It is much like the circle of light projected by a magic lantern, within which the pictures are to appear. In one sense it is the circle of the unmanifested zodiac (the pathway of our solar system)."[1] In other words it is the Boundless Sphere of Space within which our entire Cosmos is manifesting. Our earth is but 1 point or digit in this mighty circle or cipher.

The ○ is called naught or no-thing because no thing has been differentiated or manifested. It is the Silence of Non-Being. It is "the secret habitation of the ever invisible Deity."

> "In the minds of the ancient Philosophers something of the Divine and mysterious has ever been ascribed to the shape of the circle. The old world, consistent in its symbolism and with its Pantheistic intuitions, uniting the visible and the invisible Infinitudes into one, represented Deity and its outward Veil alike—by a circle."[2]

"In the beginning was a great Abyss (Chaos), neither Day nor Night existed; the Abyss was Ginnungagop, the yawning gulf, without beginning, without end. All-Father, the Uncreated, the Unseen, dwelt in the Depth of the Abyss (Space), and *willed*, and what was willed came into being."[3] Ireneus in writing of the number symbolism of the Marcosians says: "Before all universes there is a source (or beginning) before the primal source, prior even to that state which

[1] *V. of I.*, 414.
[2] *S. D.*, II, 575.
[3] *Asgard and the Gods*, 22.

is inconceivable, ineffable, unnameable, which I number as Naughtness."[4]

It may be easier to form a conception of the beginnings of a mighty universe if we apply the same laws and processes to the individual, for in our small way we are all centers which send out invisible radiations of life-force in a circle, the size of the circle being limited by the forcefulness of the life within the center. Until its forces are made concrete and directed toward definite ends this circle is an invisible and unknown ○ of darkness, a Chaos, yet vibrant with potencies—our vague and unformed desires, longings and ideals. This circle is our sea, corresponding to the Great Deep. On it we are rocking in the little boat of our personality. The Christ within is asleep and spiritual darkness is upon the face of the waters. We sail over the sea of life wholly engrossed in the things pertaining to our personality until a tempestuous and inharmonious condition arises and threatens to overwhelm us. When the personality sees no way of escape, in desperation it cries out: "Lord save us: we perish." It appeals to The Christ within: "Master, carest thou not that we perish?" Then the Son of Man, the same omnipotent Word sent forth in the beginning, arises and rebukes the tempestuous forces (winds) of adversity which manifesting normally in man's creative ○ should steadily advance his evolution without overwhelming him. The wind symbolizes the Breath of the Spirit moving upon the waters of life. While it should quicken the vibrations of the sea of life, it should not be permitted to create a storm capable of wrecking the little boat of personality. But when the Master within is awakened He is able to rebuke the tempestuous winds and say to the sea: "Peace, be still."

---

[4] *Fragments of a Faith Forgotten,* Mead, 373.

> "The Zeroâna Akerne is also the 'Boundless Circle of Unknown Time,' from which Circle issues the radiant Light—the Universal Sun, or Ormazd [the Logos or the "First Born"]—and the latter is identical with Cronus, in his Æolian form, that of a Circle. For the Circle is Sar and Saros, or Cycle. It was the Babylonian God whose circular horizon was the visible symbol of the invisible, while the Sun was the One Circle from which proceeded the cosmic orbs, of which he was considered the leader. Zeroâna, is the Chakra, or Circle, of Vishnu, the mysterious emblem which is, according to the definition of a Mystic, 'a curve of such a nature that as to any, the least possible, part thereof, if the curve be projected in either way, it will proceed and finally re-enter upon itself, and form one and the same curve—or that which we call the circle.' No better definition could thus be given of the *natural symbol* and the evident nature of Deity, which having its circumference everywhere (the boundless) has, therefore, its central point also everywhere; in other words, is in every point of the Universe."[5]

The circle also represents the Garden of Eden which contained everything that would be needed for the growth and unfoldment of the as yet unmanifested man or Adam, the number 1. It was into this great encompassing ○ or Garden that "the Lord God" (the 7 Elohim) put the 1st man, made in their 7 fold image, "to dress it and keep it." In the midst of this Garden was placed the Tree of Life which, astronomically and astrologically, is the sun with all its life-giving powers in the center of the zodiac, or the Dot in the circle. As applied to man, the Tree of Life in the midst of his "Eden" (body) refers to a deep mystery which, when understood in its fullness, will, as the gods said, make him "become as one of us" (the Elohim) a perfect ○, knowing the good as well as the evil or both halves of the ○. Man upon the physical plane stands

[5] *S. D.*, I, 139.

in the center of his circle, which reaches up to the realms of the gods and also sweeps downward into the nether worlds. Hence, ere he can manifest in and master his complete ◯ he must, like all Saviors, descend into the hell of matter and become the savior of all the lower kingdoms, ere he can ascend into the higher realms or reënter Eden. This will be elaborated in the chapter on number 17 in Volume II.

A circle formed by a serpent—symbol of life and wisdom—swallowing its tail, symbolizes unending life or immortality. But this symbol means far more than a cycle of time, for it also symbolizes the Source of all creation, the Womb of Nature from which the Universe comes forth and also the womb from which the future man proceeds, even the fetus in the womb being curved upon itself in a circular fashion. This is the esoteric meaning of the so-called temptation to create, as allegorized in the 3rd chapter of *Genesis,* when the ◯ or the serpent began its numerical evolutions within the cycle of manifestation, *i. e.,* the Garden of Eden. The serpent therefore represents the cosmic Great Creative Force[6] which manifests as sex-force only when focused in the sex organs. The Great Creative Force is The Christ-force or that fructifying and vivifying power through whose action all things are brought into manifestation, not out of nothing but out of the ◯ or great storehouse of potential energy which awaits only the creative activity of "the Lord God" (the Law of Good) to bring forth. In the biblical allegory we have the Godhead manifesting in its positive (man) and negative (woman) aspects with the magnetic attraction of the Creative Force (serpent-power) uniting them and forming His likeness or the expression of the Trinity on earth.

The manifestation of the Great Creative Force in its aspect as sex is a most potent factor in man's evolu-

---

[6] See *V. of I.,* 173, 244-6, 366.

tion—spiritual as well as physical. In fact upon its right understanding rests the destiny of mankind on this planet. For only through generation, and the lessons learned through the manifestation of the Great Creative Force in its most dense and material aspect of sex, can mankind reach regeneration. Only by the power of The Christ can man meet and conquer all that comes to him in this day of manifestation, and out of the seemingly blind forces of its chaotic night create a new day.

"Now the serpent was more subtil than any beast of the field."

In this connection many students do not observe the proper distinction between the words *subtil* which is used to describe the serpent, and *subtle* which has quite a different meaning. According to the *Standard Dictionary subtil* means "having fine structure, not gross or dense; rarified; refined; attenuated; ethereal, hence penetrating as a subtil perfume," while "*subtle* is used as an attribute of mind in the derogatory sense of crafty." We therefore see that the serpent is not represented as crafty and enticing, but as an *ethereal* creative force which unites the positive and negative and enables them to bring forth. "In the Egyptian mythology, Kneph the Eternal *unrevealed* God is represented by a snake-emblem of eternity encircling a water-urn, with his head hovering over the waters, which he incubates with his breath. In this case the serpent is Agathodaimon, the good spirit; in its opposite aspect it is the Kakothodaimon—the bad one."[7]

> "It is owing to the serpent being oviparous, that it became a symbol of Wisdom and an emblem of the Logoi, or the Self-Born. * * * The Creative God emerges from the Egg that issues from the mouth of Kneph, as a winged

[7] *Isis Unveiled,* Blavatsky, I, 133.

Serpent, for the Serpent is the symbol of the All-Wisdom. With the Hebrews the same Deity is glyphed by the Flying or 'Fiery Serpents' of Moses in the Wilderness; and with the Alexandrian Mystic she becomes the Orphio-Christos, the Logos of the Gnostics. The Protestants try to show that the allegory of the Brazen Serpent and the Fiery Serpents has a direct reference to the mystery of the Christ and the Crucifixion, whereas, in truth, it has a far nearer relation to the *Mystery of generation,* when dissociated from the Egg with the Central Germ, or the *Circle with its Central Point.* Without the Egg it was purely a phallic symbol, but when associated therewith, it related to cosmic creation."[8]

"So little have the first Christians * * * understood the first four chapters of *Genesis* in their esoteric meaning, that they have never perceived that not only was no sin intended * * * but that the 'Serpent' was actually the 'Lord God' himself, who, as Ophis, the Logos, or the bearer of the divine creative wisdom, taught mankind to become creators in their turn. They never realized that the Cross was an evolution from the Tree and the Serpent, and thus became the *salvation of mankind.* By this it would become the very first fundamental symbol of Creative Cause, applying to geometry, to numbers, to astronomy, to measure and to animal reproduction."[9]

What can be plainer? The Divine Creative Force degraded by man has become through man's evil thoughts, the Tempter and Devil! Yet it must manifest in matter (number 4) as the cross, following the sequence of the ○, 1, 2 and 3. Hence only when mere animal desire and the wrong use and abuse of this mighty *spiritual force* of creativeness, has been crucified and balanced upon the cross of matter can the scriptures be fulfilled: "For since by man came death; by man came also the resurrection from the dead."

"The divinity of the serpent is proved by the occurrence of a horned serpent with twelve Roman gods on

[8] *S. D.,* I, 389-90. [9] *S. D.,* II, 226.

a Gallo-Roman altar. In other cases a horned or ram's-headed serpent appears as an attribute of a god. * * * M. Reinach claims that the primitive elements of the Orphic myth of the Thracian Dionysos-Zagrens—the divine serpents producing an egg whence came the horned snake Zagrens, occur in dislocated form in Gaul. There enlacing serpents were believed to produce a magic egg,[10] and there a horned serpent was worshipped * * * and horned serpents are known in other mythologies—the horn being perhaps a symbol of divinity."[11] The horned serpent referred to above was not worshipped, any more than is the cross of the Christian world today, but was a symbol of Divine Wisdom. Stinson Jarvis explains it thus: "Out of the great female Egg parent, the M-O O N (Mother E G G), comes the Druid sign of Wisdom, the Serpent. Thus every tail-sign, C U, growing out of the head, or Egg (as shown in the Q), tells of the Wisdom that comes from the Head, and the carved Moon-priest at Palenke has a great C U hanging down from the back of his head, because this wisdom serpent called C U comes out of the Egg, or Head, namely, out of the M I N-D or Moon Deity, who is our word M I N D, and is also the Cat goddess pictured in my fourth Chapter. * * * Our 'Ophi-d-i-a-n' or Snake, is the Time-sign alphabetic Serpent named in the Greek word for snake as O-PH-I-S, which says C I R C-E L, 'The Island Sign,' because it named the Circle Church. * * * In the same kind of naming the Ophites, a [so-called] heretic branch of the early Christians, had a Snake god named by them as the father of sciences; and their name Ophi-Te-s records their 'Snake God,'

---

[10] "A curious amulet, connected with the Druids, became famous in Roman times and is described by Pliny. This was the 'serpent's egg'; formed from the foam produced by serpents twining themselves together. * * * Pliny has seen this egg! It was about the size of an apple, with a cartilaginous skin covered with discs. Probably it was an echinus, such as has been found in Gaulish tombs." (*S. D.*, I, 328.) Mrs. Curtiss has had 1 of these "serpent's eggs" since childhood, it having been found by her father upon the Giants' Causeway in Ireland. It is a fossil echinus.

[11] *The Religion of the Ancient Celts,* Macculoch, 211-12.

and themselves as 'Snake [Wisdom] People,' in the regular way."[12]

It is therefore a mistake, due to ignorance of its symbology, to identify the serpent with evil or the devil. It was *only by man's perversion* of his god-like power to create, and his misuse of it for mere animal gratification and to further his own selfish ends, that *he has created all the evil* from which he and all the kingdoms below him have suffered from the time of its 1st misuse. Each stage of unfoldment and each passing phase of evolution has its needs and its highest point of expression, like the crest of each in-rushing wave of the sea. The sacred function of Creation, of which sex is but 1 expression, must not be confined merely to its animal function of procreation, for procreation is but 1 breaker on the shore of time. That which is called sex when operating through the sex organs of the body, becomes Divine Creative Christ-force when operating through nature; Creative Ideation when functioning through the mind, and the out-going of the Divine Breath, or the Urge to Manifest of the God-creativeness when functioning through the Cosmos, all being expressions of the Eternal Motion or the 1 Life of the Divine ○. While the creative function must have its expression through our animal body, as must *all* our functions, and while it has its animal aspect, it is by no means limited to that animal aspect, but has its higher and spiritual uses as well.

"As to the importance of ardent love between parents, the irony would seem to be that many women, owing to early lack of hygiene and attention to perfect physical development, are incapable of reaching any depth of such feelings, while a few take actual pride in such insensitiveness due to distorted ideas of sex and chastity. Under such conditions, union for whatever purpose must be far from ideal. What it all

[12] *The Jarvis Letters,* Chapter x.

comes to is that with some temperaments, a sacramental union for the deepening of unity and the blending of the two natures should be fully recognized apart from the careful consideration due to the creation of children." [13]

When nature intends that the sex function in humanity shall be limited to procreation only, there will be but 1 season in the year when the human female can be impregnated. Until that time, the very fact that this is not the case shows that there must be other* and higher uses for that function.[14]

Among the highly cultured Druid Priests who brought with them to Britain and Gaul much of the wisdom of their Hyperborean ancestors, every letter was a word and a symbol which pictured that which it chiefly represented. Later on these single-letter-words were combined into syllables and longer words, but always carrying with them something of the original meaning of the individual letters of which they were composed. As Stinson Jarvis shows: "As on many other carvings, the Ears of the High Priest who was deity, are shown by two forms of the letter 'O'. The alphabet word 'O' is the full Celtic name of the Ear, and its naming of this god-man's Ears is of itself a complete identification of his image with the Celtic Church. * * * The Church named herself by the 'O'; and because she was the Ear, Eye and Mouth of the world, the 'O' names all three, as in Os, the mouth, Oculus and Ophthalmos, the Eye, and 'O', Og and Ous, the Ear. Consequently the winged 'O' was the regular record carving of the Church.* * * Our 'O' named the Eye, Ear and Mouth, because this was the E Y E of the Circle Church, named in the Celtic as A I N, meaning both Eye and Circle, and was carved in America and everywhere as the Winged Eye or Circle. Thus the vision-forms of Ezekiel are described as 'cov-

[13] *Modern Astrology,* Sept., 1915, letter on page 376.
[14] See *Letters from the Teacher,* Curtiss, Chapter ix.
* For a fuller explanation see page 376.

ered with eyes,' as the Los Angeles king-tablets from Teotihuacan are also covered with Eyes, picturing the all-seeing eye of the deity Church."[15] Thus the ○, as the symbol of the Boundless Deity from whence all things come into manifestation, became the symbol of their church, because the church represented that Deity among men, and because their Priests, being the descendants of the Missionary-Initiates from the original sacred college of the ancient Hyperboreans, set forth the principles and worship of the one ○ Deity to the peoples of Britain and Gaul, just as did brother Initiates sent to India, Chaldee, Egypt, North America, Mexico and Peru. The world wide travels of these ancient Missionary-Initiates and their descendants account for the finding of the same symbols and legends in all countries to express the same ideas. Their places of worship were therefore built in circular form, our modern word for a place of worship, church, being the same as the "Anglian CYRC and CIRC and KIRK are all the same in naming the 'Church,' which in Britain was formed as a CIRCLE and named it."[16] The circle was also their sign for Time, Turn and Cycle.

"Under any of its names, the Belt or Gird had the same reference to the circling of the sun which named the Church, and thus the Hawk which flies in a circle and describes this holy form in the air was chosen as a picture-name of the priesthood and named in Greek as 'KIRKos' (Church or Circle). This is the Hawk which, as Job says, was made to fly southward, and in Egypt was the head of the local priesthood—his name, 'KIRKos' recording him as the Circle and the Church."[16]

To indicate their spiritual authority derived from the one ○ or including Deity, the priests, and often the rulers of various nations, wore as a head-dress a

[15] *The Jarvis Letters,* xi, viii.
[16] *The Jarvis Letters,* Chapter ii, xi.

circlet of feathers, as do the American Indian Chiefs, the Kings of Hawaii and others. This head-dress "has the CIRC-LE-T of Feathers, because the light feather, under any of its names, always names the parent church identified with the Air; and the Anglian word for feather, as F-AE-DER, also means Father,"[16] again the parent ○ or source of all. Since the ○ is the plane in which the Deity—that which contains the potencies of all spiritual powers—is to manifest, in its perfect expression the Church on earth should be the plane of all embracing ○ which holds the potencies of all that humanity can require for the manifestation of its spiritual life, the true Priesthood being the Dot in the center of the circle.

The Round Towers of Ireland, of which only 18 or 20 out of more than 120 exist today, were connected with the Druid sacred colleges and hence were circular in shape. According to Jarvis: "The Round Towers of Ireland have never had their uses explained, but as the towers of Peru and Babylon were admittedly for astronomical purposes, so Ireland always had her observatories; and as these were her chief structures and landmarks, their names were used to identify her with the secretive stories, and also to name her Time-gods, her astronomical priests, and even her colonies—such as the Tyrians, whose name TUR-I, means 'Tower Islanders.' * * * That some of these observatories existed before the pyramids were built is shown in the fact that the picture of a Tower is built inside the Great Pyramid to name our TUR of Jupiter." [17]

In the book of *Daniel* (iii) we are told that Nebuchadnezzar set up his wonderful golden image in the Plain of Dura, the meaning of Dura being a "round or circular enclosure." And the round Tower of Belus or Bel in the center of the circular Temple of the Sun in Babylon is familiar to all classical students and anti-

---

[16] *Ibid.*, Chapter ii, xi. [17] *Ibid.*, Chapter x.

quarians. The steeple or tower connected with the temple or place of worship in Christian and other countries today is but a survival of this once sacred symbology.

We here wish to call especial attention to a remarkable series of articles by Mr. Stinson Jarvis which appeared in the Los Angeles *Sunday Times* during 1912-13. Mr. Jarvis has performed a most important service for all students of comparative religion and mythology by tracing—through the original meanings of the individual symbol-letters—the common origin of all great religions, myths, allegories, heroes, symbols and ceremonies. As we shall take pleasure in quoting frequently from these "Letters" we wish here to express our appreciation of the great work he has done in placing this vast amount of facts, together with his wonderfully consistent scheme of interpretation, at the disposal of his fellow students of religion and mythology. There is one fundamental deduction, however, with which we must take issue with Mr. Jarvis. At the time these articles were written he had evidently not looked up the ancient esoteric teachings as to the origin of the Races of mankind, hence is led to identify the Druid Priests of the historical period with the ancient Hyperboreans of the Second Great Race of mankind, and as a result credits these Priests with the origin of all religions, languages, symbols, sciences, etc. As a matter of fact the Druid Priests were merely the remote descendants of the original Missionary-Initiates, Masters of Wisdom or God-men of the Golden or Hyperborean Age, who were sent out to all lands to teach the nations of the Third (Lemurian) and Fourth (Atlantean) Races the one true, universal and all-including spiritual Sun Worship now called the Wisdom Religion. Students who are especially interested in this subject should look up the references to the Hyperboreans in Mme. Blavatsky's *Secret Doctrine* which, with the above exception, largely corroborates Mr. Jarvis' deductions.

We do not present these and subsequent quotations from the "Jarvis Letters" as having our full endorsement, but as being suggestive and in a measure corroborative of the esoteric philosophy expounded herein.

CHAPTER 3

THE ○ AS THE EGG AND THE CAT.

Brahma, the self-existing, "desiring to produce various creatures from his own body, first, with a thought, created the waters, and deposited in them a seed. This seed became a golden egg, resplendent as the sun, in which he himself was born as Brahma, the progenitor of all worlds."—*Sanskrit Texts,* Muir, 27.

"Thus when the Orphic poet desired to go further back than the point to which the Hesiodic theogony traces the generation of the Kosmos, he traced the Universe to the great mundane egg produced by Chronos, time, out of Chaos and Aithêr—a symbol answering to the mighty mixing-bowl of the Platonic demiourgos, and akin to all the circular, oval or boat-shaped emblems of fertility."—*The Mythology of the Aryan Nations,* Cox, 437.

The ○ is the "golden egg" or the "serpent's egg," the Womb of Nature from which the universe is hatched; an universal symbol.

"The mystery of the apparent self-generation and evolution through its own creative power, repeating in miniature, in the egg, the process of cosmic evolution—both due to heat and moisture under the efflux of the unseen creative spirit—fully justified the selection of this graphic symbol. The 'Virgin-Egg' is the microcosmic symbol of the macrocosmic prototype, the 'Virgin Mother'—Chaos or the Primeval Deep. * * * Kosmos, as receptive Nature, is an egg fructified —yet left immaculate; for once regarded as boundless, it could have no other representation than a spheroid."[1]

[1] *S. D.,* I, 95.

While the egg is a true symbol of all physical generation, it is also a symbol of The Christ Seed within each heart. For within the spheroidal aura surrounding each Soul like the shell of an egg, there is a germinal center, The Christ Seed, common to all his bodies—physical, astral, mental, etc.—which, like the germ center within the egg, gradually grows and unfolds until The Christ Man emerges. He is then just as much a new and altogether different expression of the Soul as is the chicken different from the egg when it emerges from its shell.

> "The Chinese believe that their First Man was born from an Egg, which Tien dropped down from Heaven to Earth into the Waters. This egg-symbol is still regarded by some as representing the idea of the origin of life, which is a scientific truth, though the human *ovum* is invisible to the naked eye. * * * The Christians—especially the Greek and Latin Churches—have fully adopted the symbol, and see in it a commemoration of life eternal, of salvation and of resurrection. This is found in, and corroborated by, the time-honored custom of exchanging 'Easter-Eggs'. From the Anguinum, the 'Egg' of the Pagan Druid, whose name alone made Rome tremble with fear, to the red Easter Egg of the Slavonian peasant, a cycle has passed. And yet, whether in civilized Europe, or among the abject savages of Central America, we find the same archaic, primitive thought."[2]

Among the Greeks, Eros (Love) is poetically described as having issued from the Egg of Night as it floated on the waters of Chaos. Since Divine Love is the outbreathing whose vibrations quicken the Chaos of unmanifested life held within the mighty circle of the Great Deep, Eros, as the symbol of Love manifesting on the physical plane, can indeed be said to issue from the Egg of Night. The goddess Venus, his

---

[2] *S. D., I,* 391-2-4.

mother, is the Ruler of the planet Venus, the sister planet of our earth.

> "According to the Occult Doctrine, this Planet is our Earth's *primary* and its Spiritual prototype."[3]

The planet Venus is so closely affinitized with our earth and so closely connected with its evolution, as with its birth, that it is said that every sin committed on earth is felt by its Guardian Spirit, also that every great regenerating or spiritual movement on earth, like a great wave of Love and helpfulness, is 1st communicated to the Ruler of Earth by the Spirit of Venus. The sea-foam from which she is represented to have arisen was the result of the churning of the Great Deep as Chaos responded to the life-giving vibrations of Creative Love when the Word was spoken: "Let there be Light."

It will be remembered, however, that Venus complained to Themis that her son Eros remained ever a child; in other words, human love remained undeveloped. Themis assured Venus that this was because he was solitary, so soon afterward another son was born to Venus, whom she called Anteros. He is represented both as the Avenger of slighted love and as symbolic of reciprocal affection. Themis, who in the myth is called Divine Justice, was the wife of Zeus and mother of the Fates, hence represents Karma, while Anteros is that aspect of Love which brings dire results when Love is degraded or unrequited. He is that aspect of Love which enables the serpent to swallow its tail or the circle to be completed, that human love may once more be swallowed up in the ocean of Divine Love from whence it emerged.

> "Ra is shown like Brahmâ gestating in the Egg of the Universe * * *Among the Greeks the

[3] *S. D.*, II, 34.

> Orphic Egg is described by Aristophanes, and was a part of the Dionysiac and other Mysteries, during which the Mundane Egg was consecrated and its significance explained; Porphry also shows it to be a representation of the world."[4]

The myth of Leda is another symbol of the feminine aspect of Divine Love, *i. e.,* Libra, the Sheath of Venus, for she was visited by Zeus in the guise of a Swan (the Bird of Life) and is then said to have produced 2 eggs, from 1 of which Castor and Pollux—immortalized in the heavens as the sign Gemini, the Twins—were born, and from the other Helen, she for whose blandishments the Trojan War was waged. Thus does life bring forth from the great Mundane Egg, 1st, duality—Castor and Pollux symbolizing the intellectual faculties brought forth from an earthly mother and a Divine father, hence always vacillating and unbalanced—and 2nd, Helen, the symbol of purely human love, beautiful, seductive and the stirrer up of strife and bloodshed among men.

> "As Bryant shows, it [the egg] was a symbol adopted among the Greeks, the Syrians, the Persians and Egyptians. In the Egyptian *Ritual,* Seb, the God of Time and of the Earth, is spoken of as having laid an 'Egg conceived at the hour of the Great One of the Dual Force.' * * * Whence this universal symbol? The Egg was incorporated as a sacred sign in the Cosmogany of every people on the earth, and was revered both on account of its form and of its inner mystery. From the earliest mental conceptions of man, it has been known as that which represented most successfully the origin and secret of Being. The gradual development of the imperceptible germ within the closed shell; the inward working, without any apparent outward interference of force, which from a latent *nothing* produced an active *something,* needing naught save heat; and which, having gradually evolved into a

[4] *S. D.* I, 385.

concrete, living creature, broke its shell, appearing to the outward senses of all as a self-generated and self-created being; all this must have been a standing miracle from the beginning.

"The Secret Teaching explains the reason for this reverence by the symbolism of the prehistoric races. In the beginnings, the 'First Cause' had no name. Later it was pictured in the fancy of the thinkers, as an ever invisible, mysterious Bird that dropped an Egg into Chaos, which Egg became the Universe. Hence Brahmâ was called Kâla-hansa, the 'Swan in (Space and) Time'. Becoming the swan of Eternity, Brahmâ, at the beginning of each Mahâmanvantara, lays a Golden Egg which typifies the Great Circle, or ○, itself a symbol for the Universe and its spherical bodies."[5]

It was this mystery which was always presented to the candidates and explained during the Mysteries. While the myth of the Mundane Egg was used as an illustration to bring this great truth to their minds and make it a living reality in their hearts, they were taught that The Christ Seed or Egg was dropped by the Heavenly Dove—call it Bird of Life, Parahamsa, Holy Ghost, or what you will—in the nest of their hearts, which they themselves had to build, purify and prepare for its reception. Hence only as they made conditions possible for this Divine Bird to hover over them and find a nesting place in their hearts, could she lay and hatch out the Egg. After the Egg was hatched the Heavenly Dove brought daily to her nestlings the heavenly food, Mother-love, on which they could feed and flourish. Also as she made her home in the heart and soared into the heaven world, she created a spiral of magnetic life-force over which the fledgling candidate could consciously ascend and gather the experience of the higher realms. This is what is meant when we are told: "Bestride the Bird of Life."

"The engraving of a papyrus in Kircher's *Œdipus Egyptiacus,* shows an egg floating above

[5] *S. D.,* I, 384-5.

the mummy. This is the symbol of hope and the promise of a Second Birth for the Osirified Dead; his Soul, after due purification in Amenti, will gestate in this Egg of Immortality, to be reborn therefrom into a new life on earth. For this Egg, in the Esoteric Doctrine, is Devachan, the Abode of Bliss, the Winged Scarabæus also being another symbol of it. The Winged Globe is but another form of the Egg and has the same significance."[6]

"A second reason for the Egg having been chosen as the symbolical representation of the Universe, and of our Earth, was its form. It was a Circle and a Sphere; and the ovi-form shape of our Globe must have been known from the beginning of symbology, since it was so universally adopted."[7]

"The symbol of an egg also expresses the fact taught in Occultism that the primordial form of everything manifested, from atom to globe, from man to angel, is spheroidal, the sphere being with all nations the emblem of eternity and infinity—a serpent swallowing its tail."[8]

It is a scientific fact that in nature all eggs and most seeds, in which the future animal, plant or man is latent, are either circular or more or less modified spheroids in shape. This is a scientific corroboration of the occult teaching that the origins of all forms of manifested life are spheroidal, "from the birth of new Worlds out of central suns, down to the microscopic cells of which all flesh is grown. * * * Our word 'cell' is the Celtic name of 'Heaven,' Cel, and this continuous birth of cell from cell was identical with Deity, Church and priesthood—all belonging to the one system for continuous gift and parturition."[9] Even the astral manifestations in a seance room, prior to their etherealization or materialization, appear as globes of light of more or less brilliancy.

---

[6] *S. D.*, I, 391.
[7] *S. D.*, I, 384-5.
[8] *S. D.*, I, 94.
[9] *The Jarvis Letters*, xi.

THE ○ AND THE CAT.

The cat, owing to its habit of curling up in a circle with its tail around its head—to give but 1 reason—was considered as a symbol of the ○. Hence, just as the ○ contains within itself the life and power of the 9 digits, so the cat is said to have 9 lives. The term "lives" however, was originally not taken in its literal sense, but as referring to the 9 manifestations of the 1 Life-current represented in the 9 digits.

> "The Goddess Basht, or Pasht, was represented with the head of a cat. This animal was held sacred for several reasons. It was the symbol of the Moon, the 'Eye of Osiris' or the 'sun', during night. The cat was also sacred to Sokhit. One of the mystic reasons was because of its body being rolled up in a circle when asleep. The posture is prescribed for occult and magnetic purposes, * * * the circulation of the vital fluid, with which the cat is pre-eminently endowed. The 'nine lives of a cat' is a popular saying based on good physiological and occult reasons.[10]
>
> "Thus, the God Shoo, the personification of Ra, who appears as the 'Great Cat' of the Basin of Persæa in An, was often represented in Egyptian monuments seated and holding a cross * * * attached to a circle." [11]

Among the Egyptians the cat was held sacred not only because it slept in the form of a ○ or, as many suppose, because of its ability to see in the dark, but because of its association with the Goddess Basht and the moon. This relation has been explained by Professor Max Müller as due to the fact that the eyes of the cat become full orbed and grow most luminous in the dark, and also because the moon was the Seer by night in the heavens. The esoteric reason, however, is the ability of the cat to give out large quantities of animal magnetism and physical life-force, as can so easily be proved by stroking a cat in the dark. The

[10] *S. D.*, II, 583.

[11] *S. D.*, II, 576.

Egyptians knew that this magnetism was but the outer manifestation of the life-force and that under proper treatment this life-force could be given out so as to be absorbed by man. They understood the law that only through kindness and love could man make the lower kingdoms yield him their forces in such a way as to aid his own development. Hence, large numbers of cats were kept in the temples and treated with great care, that they might supply the Priests and Seers with purified and harmonized animal magnetism which certain of their duties and exercises abstracted from their bodies. This use of the cat is probably the origin of the superstition that a witch always had a "familiar spirit" in the form of a black cat, as the magnetism could of course be put to unholy as well as holy uses. Also by observing them many auguries were made, and much esoteric knowledge was deduced from their disposition and actions which would surprise the modern scholars who think of the cat only as a mouse-catcher and midnight prowler.

In the ancient ruins called Tell Basta near Zagazig a cemetery has been found devoted exclusively to mummified cats. In the tombs of Beni Hasan and elsewhere are found quantities of small images, not only of Isis, Osiris and Horus, but also of the cat sitting in watchful attitude, its eyes always prominent no matter how small or crude the image. These images are often strung on chains with mummy beads and wrapped in the folds of the mummy cloths. Such images were not used for mere decoration as many think, but because the cat was looked upon as the "Watcher of the Night," not only owing to its ability to see in the dark, but also because of its extreme sensitiveness to all astral influences and its unmistakable ability to see astral entities. Cats were made household pets and closely watched so the owner might be warned of the approach of undesirable astral forces and entities which he would then proceed to exorcise. They were placed in the tomb with the mummy for the same purpose, *i.e.*, to watch over the deceased and warn him of evil influences in the nether world.

Among the Egyptians, "The male Cat is Ra himself, and he is called 'Mau' by reason of the speech of the God Sa, (who said) covering him: 'He is like unto that which he hath made'; thus his name became 'Maau'."[12]

In Ireland and Scotland it is the common belief that a 3 colored cat (tortoise-shell) brings good fortune, hence if such a cat attaches itself to a home it is considered a sign of great good luck. The selection of this particular kind of a cat is based upon the 3 colors combined in its fur, namely, black, white and yellow, thus showing that the ancient Celts had a practical understanding of both color and number. It was also held that the 3 colored cat was an aid to the unfoldment of the astral senses or "second-sight," the black aiding clairvoyance, the yellow clairsentience and the white ability to receive spiritual inspiration and prophesy. For these reasons a 3 colored kitten was often given to a child as a constant companion and playmate, believing that it would enable the child to see in the 3 worlds. Much of the psychic ability of the "canny Scot" is attributed to this custom.

In *The Jarvis Letters* previously referred to, the Great Cat or Lion is connected with the Jews and Judah as follows: "Our big C A T lion made the whole cat family sacred as a record-name; our Celtic C A T naming the House or Family of Deity, and her picture always named the Moon goddess, she being specially identified with astronomy, being addressed on the walls of Thebes as, 'O thou great C A T, thou who canst see at night.' * * * This Lion represents the deity

[12] *Book of the Dead,* xvii.

and the priesthood, always identified with these namings. This sitting L - I O N has the same posture as the lion Sphinx whose Egyptian name is H - U-piter, or H U - father. The H U, or J U, named all the J U - peoples of Denmark, America, England and Syria, and the Lion of J U D A was the biblical sign-name of the Hebrews or J U s."[13] It will be remembered that in *Revelation*[14] it was only this Great Cat or Lion which was found worthy to open the Book of Life and loose its 7 seals, *i. e.*, only the ability to see in the darkness of earth conditions the heavenly visions; the ability to store up and give out to the Race the Divine Life-force; the ability to manifest the powers of the 9 digits latent in the ○; and the ability consciously to cope with all astral conditions, make of man the Lion of the Tribe of Judah and enable him to unloose the 7 Seals and open the Book of Life. At the opening of the 5th Seal there was a plague of locusts having lions' teeth; at the opening of the 6th Seal horses appeared having lions' heads, and when the 7 thunders uttered their voices they roared as a lion, all of which points out to the world the old esoteric doctrine that man becomes the Lion only when he has completed his ○ and reached number 10; also that it is man himself, while passing through the lower phases of animal passion, who brings to the Race the 7 plagues, judgments, cataclysms, etc. Hence only when the lion and the lamb can lie down together and submit to the leading of The Christ-child, can the Lion of the Tribe of Judah find his true place in the perfect city of the New Jerusalem, number 12.

---

[13] *The Jarvis Letters,* Chapter ii. [14] Chapter v, 5.

CHAPTER 4

THE ○ AS THE AURA AND THE RING PASS NOT.

> "Just as the Square is the symbol of the Four sacred Forces or Powers, Tetraktys, * * * so the Circle shows the boundary within Infinity that no man, even in spirit, or Deva or Dhyan Chohan can cross."
>
> —*The Secret Doctrine,* Blavatsky, I, 159.

Applied to man the ○ symbolizes the sacred Auric Egg which envelops him

> "like the yolk of an egg (the future embryo) by the albumen and shell. This to the perceptions of higher Beings from other planes, makes of each individuality an oval sphere of more or less radiancy."[1]

The esoteric teaching is that after its involution into matter, the evolution of each Soul takes place along a spiral pathway within a series of concentric spheres of differing densities, whose centers are all within the physical shell, corresponding to the concentric globes forming the Earth Chain, the finer interpenetrating all the denser. Since the law followed by the cosmic is also followed by the individual manifestation, we refer the reader to what we have said elsewhere concerning those interpenetrating spheres, as it describes the corresponding make up of man's Aura.[2]

When the Soul has manifested the most essential and characteristic possibilities of the smallest, inmost and densest sphere of the aura, it breaks through that confining shell following a spiral path, and is born into a larger sphere of consciousness, being or orbit of evolution, whose forces will aid in perfecting and com-

[1] *S. D.,* III, 440. [2] *V. of I.,* 207-8.

pleting the possibilities of the former sphere. For instance, as long as man's consciousness responds only to the sense impressions from the physical world he is confined within that sphere of matter and consciousness which vibrates to the physical plane. But as soon as his sense organs are attuned to the vibrations of the next finer and larger sphere of substance and consciousness, which surrounds and interpenetrates the lesser, he is born into the astral world or sphere of his aura, called "The Hall of Learning," and so on into the still higher spheres. Only when man is able to vibrate in unison with all the spheres which surround him, and has brought into expression the potencies of them all, has he completed his evolution of man as man.

Physical man, and the physical globe, like a seed or egg, therefore contains within him, in germ, all the forces, powers and materials necessary for him to manifest his godlike possibilities. But this physical seed of the Real Man stands in the center of 7 concentric spheres, in each of which certain of his possibilities must manifest. And to evolve into and manifest in these various spheres the shell of his physical limitations, like the shell of the egg or seed, must be opened through the growth of the germ already present within that shell. To more fully explain this point and emphasize the importance of the teaching, we quote from *The Voice of Isis*. "Undeveloped man responds chiefly to the vibrations of the physical globe, those things which he can see, hear, taste, handle, etc., and cannot comprehend or function in the globes belonging to the psychic and spiritual planes. * * * Man must ultimately function and gain experience on all seven globes at the same time, checking up, balancing and perfecting the experience of one by that gained on the other, thus rounding out his seven-fold nature into the Real Man.

Only thus can he gain Mastery over the portion of goods given him by his Father-in-heaven." [3] As it contains in potentiality all that his later evolution can unfold in any 1 cycle of manifestation, man's aura may be compared to a school-boy's trunk packed for a distant journey; for it contains all the goods given him by his father, together with the provisions necessary for the journey itself.

The aura is called the

> "'Luminous Egg' (Hiranyagarbha), or the invisible magnetic sphere in which every man is enveloped. (So are the animals, the plants, and even the minerals.) It is the direct emanation: (a) from the Atmic Ray in its triple aspect of Creator, Preserver and Destroyer (Regenerator); and (b) from Buddhi-Manas. The *seventh* aspect of this individual Aura is the faculty of assuming the form of its body and becoming the 'Radiant', the Luminous Augoeides. It is this, strictly speaking, which at times becomes the form called Mâyâvi Rûpa. It is also the material from which the Adept forms his Astral Bodies, from the Augoeides and the Mâyâvi Rûpa downwards." [4]

Just as the decimal system was formerly esoteric, so was all information concerning the nature of the aura until some time after the teachings concerning it were brought to the Western world by Mme. Blavatsky. There is always, however, a good and wise reason for thus guarding certain truths from 1 generation and revealing them to a subsequent. Since the days of the Atlanteans, when much dangerous knowledge was extant concerning the performance of magic, the aura has been known to be the storehouse of the forces called into activity in magical procedures. And because of the degrading use (black magic) made of this knowledge by those who used it unlawfully, those who faithfully follow their Divine Instructors are carefully

---

[3] *V. of I.*, 208-9. [4] *S. D.*, III, 445-6.

taught the responsibility incurred by those who publicly give out information likely to bring upon mankind a catastrophe similar to that which destroyed Atlantis. But in the present age, when there is a tendency among certain classes of scholars to decry the existence or possibility of what is called Magic and belittle the necessity of understanding the Mysteries, it is the policy of the Great Teachers to stimulate such lines of investigation by revealing certain ancient truths long hidden from the general public. The Great Law today is just as inexorable as in former ages, and no firebrand of esoteric knowledge will be given directly to man. The way to the higher knowledge may be pointed out. The Great Teachers may say, "Search here," but only the diligent and the pure in heart, the true and the faithful will be given knowledge which, in the hands of the ignorant, the ambitious or the impure, might be turned to the injury and degradation of the Race. This is why only by the general advance of the Race can the hidden things of 1 cycle, as evolution unfolds mankind, become the revealed of succeeding cycles. It is the same law by which the inner and hidden petals of a rose are revealed only as the flower as a whole advances in its unfoldment. And just as the evolving Soul steps over his Ring Pass Not only as he vibrates to the rate of the larger sphere, so with the Race.

As we have said elsewhere: "In another sense the circle is the (individual) Ring Pass Not (the limit of the auric zone) which every true disciple should put around himself, and whose Gates (corresponding to the centers of the body) he must open and close at will to admit or exclude that which he chooses."[5] This Ring is a boundary which separates each of the concentric spheres mentioned above, from the next finer, but is a Ring Pass Not to the substance and conscious-

[5] *V. of I.*, 414.

ness of the denser sphere only until the vibrations of the latter have been raised to harmonize or become 1 with the rate of the finer sphere, whereupon there is no barrier between the 2. It is because of this Ring Pass Not, like a shell around every sphere, that at every decisive step from 1 sphere of consciousness to the next higher, the student is met with the axiom "Know Thyself." For the knowledge of the Self must include a knowledge of how to raise the vibrations of the sphere in which the aspirant is manifesting until they become 1 with those of the higher sphere which he desires to enter. Each student must live his life from within and unfold his possibilities through his own efforts and through the bringing into manifestation of the powers which each has in potentiality within.

This is the basic reason why we oppose all negative forms of abnormally breaking through the Ring by the aid of alcohol, drugs or psychic forces invoked while in a negative state.[6] As we have explained elsewhere: "Another way in which the doors (of the aura or Ring) are frequently broken open is by placing yourself in a passive, non-resisting state and making the demand for psychic experiences, or sitting for development as it is called (something quite different from entering the silence for spiritual communion). In this practice you are placing yourself in such a negative state that *any entity* dwelling even on the lower astral-plane can help you break open the doors. This either destroys the doors or abnormally forces the development of the psychic centers instead of unfolding them as a natural accompaniment of spiritual growth."[7]

In 1 sense the aura is the Holy Ghost, the sin against which is the perversion of the auric forces and

---

[6] It is a reprehensible practice among some mediums to take a glass of whiskey before going into the cabinet, even though better phenomena are produced as a result. See *The Life of James (Farmer) Riley,* Vlerebone, 102-3, where his astral guide recommends the practice. This is one of the reasons why many mediums ultimately become the victims of alcoholism.

[7] This matter is fully discussed in *The Voice of Isis* in the chapter of "Narcotics, Alcohol and Psychism."

the destruction of the centers. While each individual and each globe has its Ring Pass Not, it is the Ring Pass Not of the Cosmos which is referred to in the quotation which heads this chapter, and also in the following:

> "No spirits except the 'Recorders' (Lipika) have ever crossed the forbidden line of the Ring, nor will any do so until the day of the next Pralaya, for it is the boundary that separates the Finite—however infinite in man's sight—from the truly Infinite."[8]

From all that has been said we see that the ○ as a symbol of the Source from which all manifestation proceeds, is no arbitrary or man-made symbol, but is inherent in Nature herself. Therefore let the circle remind you that you have the potency and power of the Unmanifested overshadowing you; that you are dwelling in a mighty sphere of unmanifested powers which it is your duty to understand, unfold and bring into manifestation ere you can pass through the evolution of the numerals and reach the perfection of your cycle of manifestation in number 10. Let it remind you of the source from whence you have received the portion of goods given you by your Father-in-heaven ere you took your journey into this far country of material embodiment, and that these goods are the materials out of which you must furnish your mansion in heaven or the immortal, spiritual vehicle which you must ultimately attain ere you can manifest the Real Self or the God-within on all planes.

---

[8] *S. D.*, I., 157.

CHAPTER 5

THE SYMBOL OF THE ⊙.

> "The Infinite was entirely unknown and diffused no light before the luminous point violently broke through into vision."—*Zohar.*

> "The Monad, or Point, is the original and is the Unit from which follows the entire numeral system."
>
> —*The Secret Doctrine,* Blavatsky, I, 459-60.

The point within the circle ⊙ is a symbol which must be considered both with the ○ and the 1 as it is the connecting link between the 2. The Dot within the circle is the 1st manifestation of the latent Deity or Deity in activity, the 1st Cause; Unity within Eternity, the 1st differentiation from the homogeneous state represented by the circle.

> "In the metaphysical world, the Circle with its one central Point in it has no number, and is called Anupâdaka—parentless and numberless, for it can fall under no calculation * * * It is * * * a center of energy, which I shall for the present call the Logos. * * * It is called the Verbum * * * by the Christians, and it is the divine Christos who is eternal in the bosom of his Father."[1]

"In him is an illimitable abyss of glory, and from it there goeth forth one little spark which maketh all the glory of the sun, and of the moon, and of the stars."[2]

The Dot within the circle is the Causal Soul or personal god of each individual, while the Higher Self is the Causal Soul enriched by the experiences garnered by the personalities in which it incarnates life after life, and stored up as individuality in the Higher Self.

---

[1] *S. D.,* I., 118-155.

[2] An ancient oracle quoted in *The Kabbalah Unveiled,* 19-20.

In the individual man the Dot is the manifestation of the Ray shot out in the beginning from 1 of the 7 Elohim (the 7 Flames), and becomes the Creative Dot in that individual, which remains throughout the entire Kalpa as a nucleus and overshadowing Principle. This Dot periodically sends down its 1 Ray into manifestation through a personality. For a Ray must incarnate again and again until all the experiences represented by the cycle of numbers from 1 to 9 are stored up in the Higher Self. Thus the Dot and the 1 with the ○ together make the Higher Self (10). It is the potency of this Dot in all the numbers, stimulated by the overshadowing of the Dot itself, which causes their evolution or unfoldment. In turn this Dot in the individual is overshadowed by the Causal Soul of the Universe. This is not the Absolute or Causeless Cause, the fathomless Eternal, but is that which the Christians call God, the Lord, and the Hindus Ishvara, the Lord.

If we consider the Dot as a bright flame in the center of a circle, or say the pure white light of the sun in the center of the zodiac, as the sun sends forth its rays they manifest the 7 colors of the spectrum, and as each ray touches the circumference it makes a Dot of its own color. The sun in the center will therefore represent the Higher Self or the Divine Dot, while the many lesser dots on the circumference will represent its many personalities, each manifesting but 1 shade of the central Light, and each becoming pure white light only as all are indrawn into the center. The entire circle will then become a globe of pure white radiance and take its place in turn as a dot upon the circumference of a still mightier circle whose center is God.

In the case of an Avatar it is this overshadowing Dot or Causal Soul of the Universe which sends into manifestation a 1, the Son, who united with the Father, becomes not 1 of the 7 Rays or Flames (Elohim), but the 1 Great Ray in which all the 7 Rays are united. Hence all Avatars are like pearls strung on this mighty manifestation of the 1 God, just as all the lives of an individual are strung upon the individualized Ray from 1 of the 7 Elohim, the Higher Self.

Speaking of an ancient record written on palm leaves and illustrating the symbology of primordial beginnings, Mme. Blavatsky says:

> "On the first page in an immaculate white disk within a dull black ground. On the following page, the same disk, but with a central point. The first, the student knows, represents Kosmos in Eternity, before the reäwakening of still slumbering Energy, the Emanation of the World in later systems. The point in the hitherto immaculate disk, Space and Eternity in Pralaya, denotes the dawn of differentiation. It is the Point in the Mundane Egg, the Germ within it which will become the Universe, the All, the boundless, periodical Kosmos."[3]

The ⊙ is the universal hieroglyph of the sun in the center of the zodiac, the manifestor and giver of light, life and energy to its system. It also represents Jacob in the midst of his 12 sons and Jesus in the midst of his 12 disciples. Among the Egyptians the Dot or Sun is Ra, and in the *Book of the Dead* is thus described: "I am Ra at his first appearance. I am the great god, *self-reproduced;* his Names together compose the cycle of the gods. * * * O Ra, in thine Egg, who risest up in thine orb, and shinest from thine Horizon."[4] In a later chapter Ra makes a prayer as follows: "I shine forth out of the Egg which is in the unseen (unmanifested) world. * * * Let not mine hand be repulsed by the Divine Circle of the great god. * * * I am come to do the will of my heart, out of the abode of Flame, which I extinguished when I came forth."[5]

---

[3] *S. D.*, I, 31.
[4] Chapter xvii.
[5] Chapter xxii.

This symbol also has its reflection or correspondence in Nature as the nucleus in the egg. The nucleus has the same significance as the Dot and the sun, *i. e.*, the Source of Life to its system, for without the vitalizing, creative power emanating from its nucleus no egg could be fructified or developed. The Druids taught this same mystery by their symbolic dance around what later came to be the May-pole. As we have said elsewhere: "In the later symbolism the dance was performed around the sacred oak and still later, if an oak was not available, the masculine principle of fire or the sun was symbolized by the upright May-pole, while the feminine principle was indicated by the circle drawn on the ground, the two having the same significance, as a creative symbol, as the dot within the circle or the lingam and the yoni, all of which later became degraded into objects of phallic worship. * * * Therefore, just as the Christian ceremonies of Easter bring to our mind the great cosmic fact of the resurrection of the sun or the renewal of the life-force (The Christ-force) of nature from the tomb of winter, as well as the personal significance of the resurrection of The Christ in each heart, so the bonfires and May-poles, with their attendant dances and ceremonials, had the same double significance and symbolized the same grand truths to the early inhabitants of Ireland, Britain and Gaul, *i. e.*, that the masculine Principle of Fire had again descended to fructify Mother Earth that she might bring forth her increase."[6] "The dot in the center is always a small circle in the old picture-writing, and its present name as the D O - T names the 'Gift God.' In the Indian sign-language the interior small circle names the Son of the Mother, or any 'Descendant,' which is its meaning today in the Celtic alphabet."[7]

---

[6] See *The Message of Aquaria*, Curtiss, 280. [7] *The Jarvis Letters*, xi.

> "Philosophy, however, could never have found its conception of a logical, universal and absolute Deity, if it had had no Mathematical Point within the Circle upon which to base its speculations. It is only the manifested Point, lost to our senses after its pregenetic appearance in the infinitude and incognizability of the Circle, that makes a reconciliation between Philosophy and Theology possible—on condition that the latter should abandon its crude materialistic dogmas."[8]

We may think of our aura as a circle, but we should think of our Higher Self as the Dot or God within this circle; the manifested Source from whence emanates the Light, Life and Love of our existence. And only because of that Source within have we the power to bring into manifestation and evolve the inchoate forces which we find within the circle of our Being. Hence only when we realize and manifest the power of the indwelling creative Dot to bring forth and use, to the limits of our circle of manifestation, all that is contained therein, can we become the true I. Every unit of life is the center or Dot of its own universe (circle), has its own sphere of activity and influence and rate of vibration, and is its own center of cosmic energy; a microcosm, an individualized reflection in time and space of the 1 Life of the ⊙.

The Dot may also be looked upon as the Spiritual Star of Initiation which overshadows the Candidate from the time when the spiritual Light "broke through into vision" or was born in his consciousness. But we become aware of it only when we look toward it, feel its life-giving warmth and see its Light streaming down upon us and forming the straight and narrow Path (number 1) that leadeth unto salvation (Mastery).

Looked at from above, the Dot is seen to be the end of the axis of a sphere, or an aspect of number 1. It

[8] *S. D.*, I, 672-3.

appears within the circle when the World Mother breathes upon the waters of Chaos.

Let the Dot within the circle remind you that no matter how dark and chaotic the circle of your life may seem, you have within you the Dot of pure, white, spiritual light, the Sun of your Soul whose rays can unfold and illumine every condition in your life and help you to manifest their highest possibilities, if you will but open the door of your heart and let them in. But only as you fearlessly and determinedly and from the Christ-consciousness within say, "Let there be light," understanding all that this implies[9] and all that will result, can its force start the circle of darkness or chaos in your spiritual life to revolving, and the Spirit of God—the white Dot or Dove—move on the troubled waters of your life and evolve into the 1, and then on through the rest of the decade back to oneness with the ○ in the number 10. Do not be appalled at that which the Light reveals within you, for the so-called things of evil, those which are unredeemed, will 1st be stirred up that they may come into the Light and be transmuted, spiritualized and redeemed. Remember the divine Dot or Spiritual Sun within must shine if evolution is to take place.

---

[9] See *The Symbology of the Light*, Chapter xxiv, *The Voice of Isis.*

CHAPTER 6

THE NUMBER 1.

"O descendant of Bharata! see wonders in numbers, unseen before. Within my body, O Gudakesa! See today the whole universe, including every thing movable and immovable, all in one." —*Bhagavad Gita,* XI.

"The sacredness of numbers begins with the great First—the ONE, and ends only with the nought or zero—symbol of the infinite and boundless circle which represents the universe. All the intervening figures, in whatever combination, or however multiplied, represent philosophical ideas, from vague outlines down to a definitely-established Scientific axiom, relating either to a moral or a physical fact in nature."

—*Isis Unveiled,* Blavatsky, II, 407.

As we have said elsewhere: "All even numbers are mundane and pertain to the physical plane, while all odd numbers are Divine. They contain something which cannot be measured by the two forces, positive and negative, always operative on the physical plane. Among the Pythagoreans odd numbers were connected with the major deities, while even numbers were assigned to the inferior and terrestrial gods."[1] In the *Yi-King,* an ancient Chinese book on symbolism referring to cosmogony and man and to the purposes of life, the initial symbols used are *Yang* (male) and *Yin* (female). *Yang* is associated with heaven, the sun, light and odd numbers, while *Yin* is associated with the moon, the earth, darkness and even numbers.

Odd numbers are considered sacred because when we attempt to divide them into equal parts they leave

[1] *V. of I.,* 160.

the Monad or the 1 God standing unaffected between them, thus: 3=1+1+1, 5=2+1+2, 7=3+1+3, etc. Thus they reveal the Supreme Deity in the midst of His works. Even numbers are those which can be divided into 2 equal parts without revealing the 1 God in their midst. When odd numbers are divided 1 part will always be odd—representing the Divine—and 1 even—representing the manifestation of the Divine, *i.e.*, 7=3 (the Divine) plus 4 (the mundane). The most potent odd numbers are composed of trinities, each of which is odd, thus: 3=3×1, 9=3×3, 15=3×5, 21=3×7, 27=3×9, etc. While even numbers can always be measured by the "pairs of opposites," they can also be separated (except 2 which is simply 2 unities) into 2 equal and 2 or more unequal parts, thus, 10=5+5, also 1+9, 3+7, 2+8. Even numbers whose equal divisions can be further divided into equal parts are called "evenly even." For example 2, 4, 8, 16, 32, 64, etc. Those even numbers whose equal divisions cannot be further divided into equal parts are called "evenly odd." For example 6, 10, 14, 28, 56, etc.

"We now come to the consideration of the first Sephira, or the Number One, the Monad of Pythagoras. In this number are the other nine hidden. It is indivisible, it is also incapable of multiplication; divide 1 by itself and it still remains 1, multiply 1 by itself and it is still 1 and unchanged. Thus it is a fitting representative of the great unchangeable Father of all."[2]

Number 1 is the symbol of Unity, Indivisibility, Individuality. It is that which is born from Spirit, (the Dot), and is therefore Divine. "For God is Superlative in his Unity, there is none equal unto him: what number canst thou place before 1?"[3] It is Primordial Substance undifferentiated, also Cosmic Ideation.

---

[2] *Kabbalah Unveiled*, Mathers, 22.
[3] *Sepher Yetzirah*, I, 7.

Since 1 stands by itself and is indivisible, it is considered no number, but represents perfection, harmony, order, good and God. It is the only number that does not have 1 aspect above or pertaining to the heavens and 1 lower pertaining to the earth. It symbolizes the Deity descending to earth in an undifferentiated state, the 1 God, without attributes. It also symbolizes the *descent* of the Light when, at the beginning of the cycle of manifestation of this system, the 1st Day of Creation, the gods—the 7 fold Elohim—said: "Let there be light," and the Dot within the circle sent forth its Ray to manifest in matter. It is the *descent* of the creative aspect of the 1 Life, the Christ-power, into Chaos that Chaos might become Cosmos, evolve and be redeemed.

Number 1 represents the principle of Unity which underlies all numbers. By multiplication it creates all others, but multiplied by itself to infinity it always retains its unity.

Since it is the 1st manifestation of the Unmanifested, 1 represents the unity of all forms of life in the 1 Life, or the Brotherhood of Man and Nature. This is the mathematical basis for what we have said elsewhere:[4] "All life comes from the One Life of the Absolute and normally should evolve back to God in perfect purity and harmony." "As all Souls are but differing expressions of the One Life, each must bring back into the One Life a special experience. Unity does not mean an everlasting recurrence of one experience for all, but all experiences in the One. As each different part of the body has its own function, the experience of which is subject to and is registered in the brain—the sum total of the experiences of all organs and parts being necessary to complete a Man—so are all Soul-experiences comprised in the One Life."[5] It is Unity but not uniformity.

[4] *V. of I.*, 225.

[5] *V. of I.*, 285.

The number 1 also symbolizes Adam Kadmon, the 1st man. Since man is the only erect animal, the only 1 whose spinal column is vertical instead of horizontal, 1 symbolizes man's power to stand erect, also his uprightness of both body and character. It also symbolizes the straight and narrow Path which the personality must follow to reach the Divine or Christ-consciousness. It is the line of spiritual aspiration which must ascend from the heart of man to unite the human with the Divine. It is the line whose continuation unites the personality (the little i) with the Higher Self (the Dot) to form the Real Self; the silver thread which unites us with the Master; the unity of man with God, the capital I which can stand alone. Jesus expressed this same idea when He said: "I and my Father are 1."

Script letters are symbols which have been so modified by modern ideas that they have little occult significance, yet they do express the idea of dependence one upon the other, a late development of tribal and community life. So, to merge the little i into the I we must learn to stand alone, for the i could never become the I until it had ceased to depend on others for its meaning. As the personality learns to stand alone and ascend the straight and narrow Path and merges into the overshadowing Dot, the Dot spreads out as sheltering wings above, fills out and enlarges and also makes a firm foundation below, thus I. When the little i has reached up to the Dot in the center of its orbit, has become the I and is able to stand alone in the presence of the Master, it must then "do the works of its Father in Heaven" or continue the extension of the Path in the higher realms and complete the diameter of the circle thus:  Number 1 also symbolizes the Magic Wand with which the magician performs his Great Work.

Among man's 7 principles 1 represents Atma, the Ray from the Divine, 1 with the Father, through which man becomes 1 with the All.

Like the ○, number 1 is a natural geometric figure. For, using our previous symbol of the sphere, if any line of force, either from within or from without, acts upon it, it will begin to revolve and thus generate an axis, or the vertical line which bisects the circle ⦶ forming the figure 1. Therefore *no other figure could be the 1st of the numerical system,* for 1 is the figure generated by the 1st manifestation of motion in the Cosmos. 1 is positive and masculine in its characteristics, as it is the outgoing Ray of the Divine proceeding from the negative or subjective into the positive or objective life. This symbolism of the number 1 is confirmed in nature. In animal life we find in the developing egg a straight line, called "the primitive streak," as the 1st positive sign of the character of the future form and the forerunner of the spinal column; the positive, supporting factor that enables it to stand erect. In vegetable life we find that out of the heart of the seed (its Dot within the encircling husk) the 1st manifestation of life causes a sprout to shoot upward and a tap-root downward, as the positive and negative expressions of the Dot. These burst the shell or husk and form a straight vertical line which bisects the seed and enables the plant to stand alone as an independent manifesting individual or 1.

Whenever your attention is called to the number 1, let it remind you of the 1 God, the 1 Life; the oneness of mankind or the Brotherhood of Man; the power of Selfhood; of self-reliance, dignity, rulership; the Wand of the Magician, the Rod of Power; the power to bring forth the Self from the divine Dot within, through the all-embracing power of the circle. Let it remind you of the unity of nature, man and God; the union of the human with the Divine through the following of the straight and narrow Path upward until the personality is merged into the Father-in-heaven, and you can say with Jesus, "I and my Father are 1."

CHAPTER 7

THE 1ST LETTER, *Aleph* (א).

"All Hebrew letters contain a number, a hieroglyph, a symbol, and a place. To know these in their relation to each other, and to numbers, is to hold in the hands the chart that will guide us unerringly across the ocean of ignorance into the 'Thirty-Two Paths of Wisdom'."

—*Numbers and Letters,* Peek, 79.

"From the Spirit He produced Air, and found in it twenty-two sounds * * * the letters; three are mothers, seven are double, and twelve are simple; but the Spirit is first and above these."

—*Sepher Yetzirah,* i, 10.

The Hebrew alphabet is composed of 22 letters, of which 3 are "Mother Letters," 7 are double and 12 are simple letters. The 3 "mother letters" are associated with the 3 elements, air, fire and water. These elements are manifestations of the Divine Trinity from which all things are brought forth in the 3 worlds. The 7 double letters are associated with the 7 sacred planets and the 7 fold power of the Elohim through which the Mother Trinity must conceive. They are double because each planet has its dual aspects, positive and negative, favorable and unfavorable, benefic and malific. And just as the astrological aspects of these planets are modified by the influences of other planets, so the double letters have a hard and soft sound according to the influence of the other letters in the words in which they appear. They are also connected with certain other powers described elsewhere.[1] The 12 simple letters are associated with the 12 signs of the zodiac, the 12 months in the year and the 12 parts

[1] *V. of I.,* Chapter xii.

of the human body. The zodiac being the circle of manifestation or the limit of the field of operation of our system, and its circumference having 12 points of contact through which the force of the sun is transmitted to earth, the 12 signs may be compared to a gigantic switch-board through which the creative power—corresponding to that generated by the 3 mothers and manipulated by the 7 doubles through the 12 simples—is transmitted to earth, under the guidance of the 7 Planetary Deities. According to this conception the 12 simple letters may be looked upon as a perfect distributing apparatus for transmitting the messages of the Spiritual Sun. But according as these messages are interpreted by man, the receiver, are they true, helpful and uplifting or false, misleading and depressing. But in considering the letters and their associations we must not fall into the error of thinking that the letters are either the elements, the planets or the zodiacal signs with which they are connected. The letters simply respond to the vibrations from those forces to which they are related and which they symbolize. Nevertheless, the letters, either written or spoken, awaken certain potencies and are avenues through which certain cosmic forces operate in the worlds of manifestation.

The 1st letter of the Hebrew alphabet is Aleph (א), corresponding to our letter A, and its numerical value is 1. Like number 1 it expresses the outbreathing of the Divine or as the Kabalah expresses it, "soft breathing." Aleph is the 1st of the mother letters out of which all the others are produced. Also out of soft breathing are all the sounds expressed by the 22 letters produced. "But their (the Druids) name for 'A,' which by itself names a Mountain, is AIL-M, saying Mountain Parent. The same letter is the whole name of the palm called P-AILM, or 'The A.' This one letter also names the Celtic 'Man' and makes our word FIR-S-T."[2]

Aleph symbolizes the Breath of Life as manifested in man, for God "breathed into his nostrils the breath of life, and man became a living soul." Just as the primitive streak in the embryo forms the spinal column and makes the upright man, so must the forces whose centers lie within the spinal column be awakened, developed and blended ere man can grasp his Rod of Power and become The Christ-man. The physical agent through which this development is accomplished is the breath, properly directed and controlled. According to Éliphas Lévi: "Aleph indicates the balance of universal equilibrium, the division of the day and the night, the reign of the sun and that of the moon, the approaching struggle between Cain and Abel. It is related to the angel of Mercury, represented in the Tarot by the Bateleur."[3]

The astrological symbol corresponding to Aleph is the ox, the sign Taurus in the zodiac. Some claim to find a satisfactory explanation of the origin of this letter in the head of the ox, his horns forming an inverted A, the top of his head supplying the cross-bar, thus ∀. But this reverses the symbol. It is not more fanciful however to regard the lungs, through which the Breath of Life functions, as forming a rough letter Λ, with the arching diaphragm as the cross-bar. But we will look for a deeper similarity, for the characteristic of the letter is more an inner quality than an outer appearance.

The sign Taurus is ruled by Venus and is the 1st feminine sign, as Aleph is the 1st mother letter. Taurus is the accepted symbol of terrestrial and physical generation. The full significance of the correspondence, however, is that the brightest star of the constellation, Aldebaran, situated in the eye of Taurus,

---

[2] *The Jarvis Letters,* vi.
[3] Unpublished Letters of Éliphas Lévi.

together with the constellation of the Pleiades in the neck of Taurus, in ancient Hindu chronology were the determiners used for finding the beginning of our present Iron Age or *Kali Yuga.* This is the cycle of man's most dense physical expression and greatest spiritual darkness, a period during which he is learning the bitterest lessons of terrestrial generation, brought about by his misuse of his creative powers.

The Pleiades, the constellation in the neck of Taurus, is regarded

> "in the *Kabbalah* and Eastern Esotericism, as the *sidereal septenate* born from the first manifested side of the upper triangle, the concealed A. This manifested side is Taurus, the symbol of One (the figure 1), or the first letter of the Hebrew alphabet, Aleph (א) 'bull' or 'ox', whose synthesis is Ten (10), or Yod (י), the perfect letter and number. The Pleiades (Alcyone especially), are thus considered, even in Astronomy, as the central point around which *our universe of fixed stars revolves,* the focus from which, and into which, the Divine Breath, Motion, works incessantly during the Manvantara."[4]

Since Aleph is the 1 which finds its completion in Yod, the 10, it corresponds to the Alpha of the Greek alphabet which is completed by the letter Omega. Hence, Chronus, the god Time, the terrestrial expression of the 1, who says: "I am Alpha and Omega, the beginning and the end, the first and the last" (I am 1 and 10), is but another expression of the outbreathing of the Breath of Brahm, the Absolute, apparently swallowed up in matter, yet bringing forth all things upon the terrestrial plane.

As a hieroglyph, that is, the letter considered as a sign or symbol, Aleph represents man as a collective unit, the ruler of the earth, "the sign of Power and Stability." It carries the idea of man both as the mi-

[4] *S. D., II,* 581-2.

crocosm and as the unity of the 1 Life, synthesized in man through the Breath of Life

THE 1ST COMMANDMENT.

> "I am the Lord thy God, which have brought thee out of the land of Egypt, out of the house of bondage. Thou shalt have no other gods before me."
>
> —*Exodus,* xx, 2-3.

The significance of each Commandment is revealed by its number and is emphasized by the order in which it is given. Thus, in the 1st Commandment we find that number 1, the 1 Life and the 1 God, is expressed in the words "I am the Lord thy God." As we have said elsewhere: "The I is the only symbol in the alphabet that stands for both Deity—the straight vertical line symbolizing Spirit descending into matter—and for personality."[5] It represents the Divine Light sent down into the darkness of Chaos; the straight and narrow Path by which alone the Pilgrim can emerge from the land of Egypt or the state of spiritual darkness wherein he is in bondage to King Desire. The "I AM" is also the Father-force, the quickening Ray, by whose illumination the bonds of ignorance are broken and the Soul is led into the Promised Land of spiritual consciousness. Therefore, we may read the 1st Commandment thus: I, or number 1, am the Law (Lord) of thy godhood, which hath brought thee—cosmicly, the Chaos of unredeemed substances and forces left over from a previous period of manifestation; individually, the Soul that is responding to the Divine Light and treading the straight and narrow Path—out of the darkness of inertia and resistance to the Divine. And I will ultimately lead thee out of the house of flesh and the bondage of limitation into the fulness of spiritual consciousness.

---

[5] *V. of I.*, 127.

Since 1 is the 1st of the series of numerals and the 1 God is the 1st manifestation of the Divine, we can have nothing before Him. Every god which man creates and tries to place before the 1 God must be swallowed up in the ○ of that Chaos which must be redeemed in the next great Day-period of evolution. For nothing but ○ (naught) can stand before the 1. This Commandment means then that we are to recognize this 1 God above all things and seek to become 1 with Him; that we are to make the attainment of that oneness the chief and underlying aim of our lives, placing nothing before that 1 great goal; that we are to recognize the unity of all in the 1 God and worship Him "in spirit and in truth" (unity). "It is not what your hands are doing, *but what your heart is worshiping* that determines your growth. If you make business or household cares your God, you will, of necessity, retard your more rapid spiritual advance; for as long as you are worshiping a false God before the 1 God your spiritual evolution is being retarded."[6]

[6] *V. of I.*, 33.

THE 1st TAROT CARD

THE JUGGLER

Papus

MEDIEVAL

Papus

St. Germain
EGYPTIAN

Smith
MODERN

CHAPTER 8

THE 1ST TAROT CARD, *The Juggler.*

"A hieroglyphic and numeral alphabet, expressing by characters and numbers a series of universal and absolute ideas."

—*Transcendental Magic,* Lévi, 368.

The Tarot is the most ancient of books, a collection of cards embodying the Secret Doctrine of the ages, almost every nation having its version or variation of this synthetic exposition of the Ancient Wisdom. The Egyptian version is called *The Book of Hermes,* the Hebrew *The Book of Adam,* while the version which we shall interpret is the 1 best known to the Western world, the Bohemian *Tarot,* or "Bible of the Gypsies." This Gypsy Bible is made up of a deck of cards upon which the Ancient Wisdom is expressed in symbols, but like all symbols that are true and basic, they reveal their meaning only to those who are capable of receiving it. In many respects it is the key which will unlock the mystical doctrines and philosophies of the Old World, and is called the Arcana of the Clavicles of Solomon. It is symbolized by a key whose head is a ring composed of a circle containing the 4 Cardinal Signs, the Bull, the Lion, the Eagle and the Angel; its trunk or body bearing the 22 characters, and having the 3 degrees of the triad for its wards. It is sometimes called "The Key of things kept secret from the Foundation."

The word Tarot may be written in the form of a cross

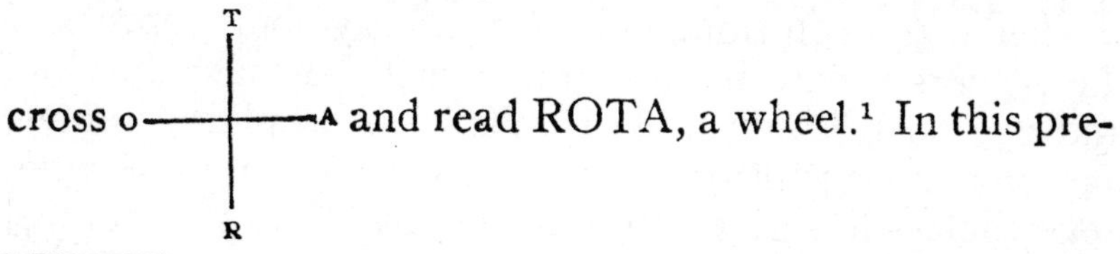

and read ROTA, a wheel.[1] In this pre-

[1] See page 361.

sentation it is the wheel of Ezekiel. It is also formed by Constantine's monogram of Christ—the Latin P or R found between the Alpha and Omega—engraved upon the cross which Constantine saw in his vision, ☧

The 1st card of the Tarot, corresponding to the letter A, is called the Juggler. Occupying the central position in the picture stands a young man with a rude wooden table in front of him upon which are placed 3 of the symbols which distinguish the 4 suits of Tarot cards, *i. e.*, Cup, Sword, Pentacles, while the 4th, the Scepter, is in his left hand. Corresponding to and derived from these symbols, the signs denoting the suits of the modern playing cards are respectively hearts, spades, diamonds and clubs. On his head is a hat which forms the Symbol of Life and evolution ∞. As a sign of his dominion over the earth and her increase he stands firmly upon the ground which is bringing forth vegetation. In his left hand, which is raised toward heaven, he carries the Scepter, the magic wand, symbolizing that only as man draws his power from on high can he become the Master over the forces within himself and nature. His right hand bent towards the earth is a symbol of his power to accomplish upon the physical plane. The position of his hands symbolizes man's position in evolution. In man, The Christ-principle, the "Breath of Life," has become more than the passive Urge of Evolution towards perfection, for man as here represented is the active principle, or the co-worker with evolution. The 4 mystic symbols represent the powers innate in man, but which he must develop and use. The rude table symbolizes the plain, unpretentious and uncultured character of physical man, who nevertheless has given to him the possibilities of future greatness. These are the portion of goods given to the prodigal Son (man) by his Father-in-heaven, by the right use and understanding of which he must accomplish his Great Work.

The powers contained in the 4 symbols—the Cup, the Sword, the Wand or Scepter and the Pentacle, are summed up by Éliphas Lévi in the following words: "To attain the *sanctum regnum,* in other words, the knowledge and power of the magi, there are four indispensable conditions—an intelligence illuminated by study, an intrepidity which nothing can check, a will which nothing can break, and a discretion which nothing can interrupt and nothing intoxicate. To Know, To Dare, To Will, To Keep Silence—such are the four words of the Magus, inscribed upon the four symbolical forms of the sphinx." [2]

These 4 words correspond to the 4 mystic symbols in our modern playing cards. 1st the Cup *(To Know),* which corresponds to Hearts. The Cup is the container into which is poured all life's experiences and from which the Soul drinks either the Wine of the Spirit, or the dregs of bitterness and sorrow. The heart suit in modern playing cards has the same symbology. This is the Cup given by The Christ to His disciples which He blessed, saying: "Drink ye all of it; for this is my blood" (life-force). But it is man himself who can make it "The cup of blessing which we bless," the drinking from which in love, is indeed the true Communion with The Christ. Or in man's hands it may become like the Cup in the hands of the Woman in Scarlet spoken of in *Revelation*:[3] "Having a golden cup in her hand full of abominations and filthiness of her fornication." Equally is it true that "whosoever shall * * * drink of this cup of the Lord (the heart or esoteric doctrine of the law), unworthily, shall be guilty of the body and blood of the Lord." The same symbology

[2] *Transcendental Magic,* Lévi, 30. [3] Chapter xvii, 4.

is expressed by the Chalice or the Cup used in the Eucharist, also by the Holy Grail, the vision of which is vouchsafed only to the pure in the heart.

This is beautifully expressed in Tennyson's poem, "Sir Galahad"; for if we would find the Holy Grail we too must be, "A maiden Knight—to me is given such hope, I know not fear." Then will we hear in all nature the voice of the angelic hosts, as did he.

> "Then move the trees, the copses nod,
> Wings flutter, voices hover clear;
> 'O just and faithful Knight of God!
> Ride on! the prize is near' * * *
> All-armed I ride, whate'er betide,
> Until I find the Holy Grail."

For the quest of the Holy Grail is man's most important task on earth.

The Sword *(To Dare)* corresponds in our modern playing cards to Spades, and symbolizes primarily the "Sword of the Spirit" penetrating matter and informing it; secondarily it symbolizes the courage which every true man must have to face himself and cut from the personality every thing that hinders his advance; to fight the foes within and without, or the power needed to "fight the good fight"; the attitude of the True Knight, who dares to face the foe because his heart is true and his sword is keen and strong. As Sir Galahad, after his vision of the Holy Grail, is made to say: "My strength is like the strength of ten, because my heart is pure." Hence he is undaunted though his way lead through ignorance, superstition, persecution and crucifixion. The Sword is also the cross on which The Christ is crucified until he has vanquished his last enemy, death. Truly the modern playing cards have turned the Swords, if not into plow shares, at least into spades.

Yet the symbology is similar, for with the spade we labor to make the earth give forth her increase; with it we overcome the inertia of matter and by the might of man's industry conquer physical conditions. But perverted, the Sword becomes the instrument which digs and undermines man's citadel.

The Wand or Scepter *(To Do)*, corresponding in modern playing cards to Clubs, is a conventionalized figure, embracing the idea of power. It is 1st the Wand of the Magician, the power placed in man's hands to accomplish through Will. It is also the Staff of Wisdom upon which man can lean as he climbs the difficult Path of Spiritual Attainment; the Staff or 1 Life given him by his Divine Self; that which he can trust and lean upon. It is also the Shepherd's Crook which not only helps him to climb the steep heights, but also by using the crook at its end he can lift and assist the lambs over the dangerous places, *i. e.*, by the use of this Staff man can help those weaker than himself and thus obey the mandate: "feed my lambs." The same idea is represented by the Bishop's Crozier or Pastoral Staff. This is an emblem of high authority, dignity and power carried upon great occasions by Bishops and Archbishops, but only after special sanction from the Pope, as it is not a Dignity belonging to the office of Bishop itself. In giving a pontifical blessing the Bishop holds the Crozier erect in his left hand, with the crook pointing toward the penitent, leaving the right hand free to touch the head of the kneeling penitent or to bless a congregation. This posture is but a variation of that assumed by the Juggler with his Wand.

The Crozier carried by the Armenian Bishops is formed by 2 intertwined serpents whose combined heads form the crook, thus connecting it with the Caduceus of Hermes, 1 of the most ancient and mystical of symbols. Among the Bishops of the Greek, Coptic and Armenian churches a veil is thrown over the Crozier and entwined in the crook, thus symbolizing the fact that in this material age the full meaning of the Crozier is veiled from the multitude. Just as in our present day playing cards the Wand has become the Club, so has this symbol of power been degraded until we find it in the shillalah of the Irishman, the walking-stick of the Englishman, and even the billy of the policeman, as well as in the baton of the musical director—always, however, the symbol of authority and power of some sort. Instead of ruling through the Staff of Divine Authority (Wisdom), it has come to mean ruling through personal will or force.

The Pentacles *(To Keep Silent)*, correspond in modern playing cards to Diamonds. In the Tarot pentacles are round discs supposed to be talismans, an idea hard to fully understand today but very common in former ages. By their shape they symbolize cycles. They represent the ○ in which all things can manifest; in other words man's field of operation; a talisman for good if rightly used, or for evil if abused. They represent man's possibilities. The meaning, however, that has crystallized around the Pentacles, as well as around the Diamond, is that of money or worldly wealth. This is quite natural in an age when the enlightened mind can conceive of no good for man higher than that represented by worldly wealth.

The Pentacles also represent in a religious sense the "Host," or the bread which is given by The Christ to His disciples when He says, "Take eat, this is my body which is given for you." Hence they represent man's field of operation in which he must build up The Christ or Spiritual Body in himself and in humanity. This growth can only take place in the silent communion within the Sanctuary of his own heart, or the Closet in which when ye have entered in and shut the door, "The Father which seeth in secret shall reward thee openly."

The Juggler symbolizes man with the 2 principles, active and passive, positive and negative. This is represented by the position of the Juggler's hands, symbolizing man's power to stand in the midst of his creations and by the power of his Will, represented by the Magic Wand, find his balance. Through man's power to accomplish, with 1 hand he reaches up to God, with the other he reaches down to earth and makes her forces subservient to him. Hence the meaning of this Card is God, man and the Universe.

CHAPTER 9

THE NUMBER 2.

"How is number 2 to be found? *By reflection of itself.* For though 0 be incapable of definition, 1 is definable. And the effect of a definition is to form an Eidolon, duplicate or image, of the thing defined. Thus, then, we obtain a duad composed of 1 and its reflection. Now also we have *the commencement of a vibration* established, for the number 1 vibrates alternately from changelessness to definition and back to changelessness again."

—*The Kabbalah Unveiled,* Mathers, 23.

"But Unity alone cannot produce anything except by opposing itself to itself thus $\frac{1}{1}$. From this proceeds duality, the principle of opposition represented by 2, the passive principle preeminent."

—*The Tarot,* Papus, 30.

The number 2 is the symbol of Duality. It is the Number of Differentiation, the "fall into matter." It is the Number of Separation, and by the Pythagorians was called *audacity* because it was the 1st to separate from the Divine Unity. It is the Number of Polarity; the Mother-principle separates from the Father and becomes mundane; the unity of the 1 is broken up into its positive and negative aspects, the upper pole being Spirit and the lower matter. From another aspect, when the Divine 1 descends into the sphere of physical manifestation it is separated into its positive and negative expressions, Spirit and Matter, male and female, etc., hence all forces show polarity* thus:

* The recent experiments of Dr. Albert Abrams have proved that not only do all forces and forms of life show polarity, but all *objects* as well. It has been demonstrated in our presence that a stick of wood, for instance, radiates positive energy at one end and negative at the other, thus confirming the above statement.

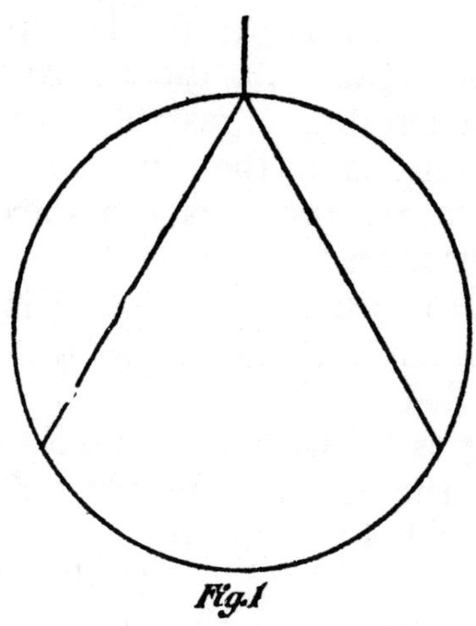

Fig. 1

Many philosophers teach a mystical relationship between numbers and marriage. In fact such teachings will be found scattered through almost every work on numbers and by such authorities as Pythagoras, Plato, Nicomachus, Aristotle, etc. For the return to oneness or Unity (God) in the higher cycle (10), through the blending of its positive and negative aspects, makes the perfect union of man and woman the ideal state. The solution of the sex-problem is therefore the great lesson for the humanity of this planet.[1] This is symbolized by the Egyptian hieroglyph for number 2, which is formed by 2 serpents encircling a globe or egg. Another symbol is a tree with a serpent twined around it or wisdom planted in the earth entwined by the Spirit, or the spiral evolution of the Soul through following the 1 God.

Number 2 is, therefore, the Number of Contrasts and the "pairs of opposites," good and evil, truth and error, day and night, heat and cold, health and sickness, pleasure and pain, joy and sorrow, male and female, etc., and because of this it is called by some "the

[1] See *V. of I.*, 257.

beginning of evil." In nature the 1st differentiation of the upright sprout (the 1), is the 2 leaves which appear simultaneously when it emerges above the ground.* In fact, all manifestations on the physical plane fall under this Law of Duality, for it is the inexorable law of physical manifestation.

"The ancient form-name of Gemini is two 'I' forms joined, as 'II,' which in the numerals means Two * * * our T-W-IN is T-UU-IN or 'Deity 2 Fire Island' and has the meaning as all words for T-UU-O."[2]

According to the *Kabalah* number 2 is the Second Sephiroth called Chokma, Wisdom, and is produced by number 1 casting its reflection into the sphere of manifestation, thus agreeing with our statement that all manifestations on the physical plane *are necessarily dual.*

As 1 symbolizes the 1st Adam, so 2 symbolizes Adam and Eve, man and woman; sex or the masculine and feminine aspects of the Great Creative Force manifesting in human form; for form can result only from the interaction of the positive and negative poles. Thus we have a mathematical basis for our statement that after the separation of the sexes each of the 2 Rays maintains its sex polarity throughout all its incarnations.[3] This is also the geometrical basis for our teaching that as long as humanity manifests in masculine and feminine bodies, the highest ideal and the nearest approach to unity which the sexes can attain is the perfect blending of the 2 in a true marriage of the Soul, not mere union of the sexes. This Soul-marriage truly is "made is heaven" or in the realms of the Spirit, and can be brought about only by pure love. But ere such a divine marriage can be consummated on all planes it must be confirmed on earth according to the legal requirements of the country in which the ones so united dwell. For marriage is far more than

* In the egg the first differentiation of the primitive layer of the germinal disc is into two, the ectoderm and the endoderm, epiblast and hypoblast.

merely a convenient and personal arrangement between the man and woman concerned. It is the foundation, not only of society and all human relations, but of the higher spiritual life as well. Hence no couple is truly married who do not in some measure recognize that in the solemnization of their physical union they are fulfilling a divine mandate, *i. e.,* the reunion of the 2 expressions of the 1 Soul. Any couple looking upon marriage in this light would naturally recognize their duty to the community as well as themselves, hence would gladly comply with the laws of the community of which they were a part. The laws of the country neither make nor mar the true Soul-marriage, yet obedience to the laws of the country which protects their marriage rights is the way to fulfill their obligations to that country. Since to "Do the duty that lies nearest" is the surest way to freedom, to deny or refuse to fulfill marital duties when brought to us by the Great Law is to close a most important avenue to higher attainment. In other words, the perfect family life is man's highest state of existence while manifesting on the physical plane in separated sexes. And he will not transcend that state until he has thoroughly learned all its lessons.

2 is the Binary, the symbol of all that is double, also all that is false, in the sense of being transitory and not eternal, or opposed to the 1 Reality. It is the Number of Matter whose inertia opposes the manifestation of the Spirit. As the vertical line represents the descent of Spirit, so the horizontal line represents matter, thus forming the cross upon which the Divine is crucified in its efforts to express in the physical world. The cross is, therefore, a cosmic symbol and should not be identified exclusively with any 1 incarnation of the Divine in human form.

Geometrically, the 2 is generated by the equator bisecting the axis of the circle midway between its poles, thus ⊕ (N, S) The square root of 2 ($\sqrt{2}$) is the ratio between the diagonal and any side of a square, but since that ratio (1.4142135-∞) is incapable of exact expression it leads to infinity ∞. This indicates that the pairs of opposites cannot be balanced upon the physical plane without calling into play an Infinite factor, a force from the higher, super-physical realms. It also indicates that *infinite progression,* through the pairs of opposites, is the divine Law of Manifestation in duality.

As 1 is considered positive and masculine, so 2 is considered as negative, receptive and feminine in its characteristics. 2 manifests in all realms of nature through the pairs of opposites. Number 2 is sacred to all female deities, such as Rhea, Isis, Vishnu, the Virgin Mary, etc., as it represents the Mother-force separated from the Father and ever seeking reunion that it may bring forth. It represents all the productive forces in nature, including nature-sounds, voice and speech; for it is through sound that creation is brought forth. "For he spake, and it was done; he commanded, and it stood fast."[4] "The words that I speak unto you, they are spirit, and they are life."[5] The sounds of nature, especially the songs of birds, are a great factor in calling forth the leaf-buds of early spring, and later the flower-buds.

Among man's Principles 2 represents Buddhi.[6]

When you contemplate the figure 2, let it remind you that while matter, through its inertia, opposes Spirit, still *it is necessary* to enable Spirit to express on all planes. By harmonizing the pairs of opposites

---

[4] *Psalms,* xxxiii, 9.
[5] *St. John,* vi, 63.
[6] See Chapter 28 herein.

as they express in matter, and by learning the lessons they can teach, you will be progressing toward the Infinite Balance of the heaven world; will be spiritualizing matter and making possible the manifestation of the Infinite and Divine on earth. Matter is, therefore, not to be either denied or despised, but purified, spiritualized and redeemed.

Let 2 also remind you of the inevitable crucifixion which must ensue when you endeavor to oppose the manifestation of the Divine within you; when you refuse to live The Christ-life. Also let it remind you that the great problem of humanity on this globe is the perfect blending and mastery of the positive and negative expressions of the Great Creative Force through its pairs of opposites, the sexes. And, lastly, let it remind you of the essential purity and sacredness of sex, the 2 expressions of the Divine in humanity.

THE KEY TO THE UNIVERSAL LAW OF SEX.

> "And the Lord said, it is not good that the man should be alone; I will make him an help meet for him."
>
> —*Genesis*, ii, 18.

The 1 great and fundamental Law back of the differentiation of the 1 Life into the 2 opposite sexes is primarily the fact that the Great Law, as we have shown, must have its 2 poles, positive and negative, within the circle. These 2 expressions are forever blended into each other, or the serpent is forever swallowing its tail, *i. e.*, the life-force goes round and round, making a great egg in which both currents are unmanifested and latent.

If we consider the egg as our symbol we see that the moment the egg is laid or expressed on the physical plane and these 2 poles begin to manifest, the result is an individualized living entity. And when we follow this symbol into the higher realms we see that within the unmanifested egg or ○, the 1 Life is both Father and Mother. Hence, since to manifest on earth the 2 poles must be separated, they are expressed below as masculine and feminine, both born of the 1 Life, both a part of the one ○, which is able to experience and manifest only when separated into masculine and feminine. We have seen that within the circle the forces from the 2 poles are forever flowing round and round, but undifferentiated, therefore unable to express on the physical plane because they are ○, naught. Yet on earth in the separated sexes they must find the same divine union, must blend and interchange the life-forces as perfectly and as harmoniously in the 2 separated sexes as they did in the circle; that is, do the will of God on earth as they did, and as they still are doing, in heaven; for every man or woman is a separated expression from 1 pole of an unmanifested Divine ○ in which the 2 forces are forever circling round and round with their opposites in perfect harmony and bliss. Each such circle makes a radiant Sun of Light—each having its own place and its own work—which circles around the Central Sun of the Universe or around the Throne of God.

Man is the masculine Ray or the expression on earth of the Divine Father-force, that aspect of the Divine which is ever fructifying, ever creating and expressing itself in forms. It is that divine potency designated in the Apostles' Creed as, "God the Father Almighty, maker of Heaven and earth, and of all things visible and invisible." Hence, since man expresses this Father-ray he is the positive pole and his function in life is creativeness. Therefore the foundation of all his love and his seeking for union with God expresses itself in the desire to fructify and create. Woman, on the other hand, is the expression of the divine Mother-force, that which is called the "Holy Ghost," the "Comforter"—in Egyptian symbology, Isis the Great Mother, and in Hindu philosophy Vishnu the preserver. Hence the foundation of all woman's love is divine Motherhood. The expression of Mother-love is woman's nearest approach to the divine state, therefore, the more a woman loves, even her husband, the more the element of mothering enters into it. Even though she have no children she will mother all she loves, for this is the fundamental well-spring of her very existence as a separated sex. For this reason we often find that a woman can live in happiness and express her love in caresses, cherishing and in motherly solicitude, but a man has his equally strong and divine love built upon the great Father-force of creativeness, hence the more true, sincere and God-like man grows, the higher, purer and more intense will be his desire to fructify and create on all planes. If these 2 great and fundamental laws of the opposite poles of sex-life were better understood there would not only be less marital unhappiness, but the Race as a whole would evolve much more quickly back to its Edenic oneness. The great lesson for each to learn is, that the functions of sex are Divine and are not a gift given to man and woman as evolved animal organisms merely for the purpose of procreation and peopling the earth, but are innate God-qualities, *the very essence of their divine oneness* which they as immortal Souls must manifest through their animal bodies. This is necessary as a means of informing, purifying and evolving those animal bodies to a state of perfection in which the complete God-consciousness can flow unimpeded from 1 to the other, and they can be as truly 1 on earth in 2 separated bodies as they were in the one ○, yet with all the experience gained from the long journey into the far country of embodiment, and the strength and power of son-hood which has made them truly "as one of us," the Elohim.

CHAPTER 10

THE 2ND LETTER, *Beth* (ב).

"He produced Beth, and referred it to Wisdom; He crowned it, combined and formed with it the Moon in the universe, the first day of the week, and the right eye of man."

—*Sepher Yetzirah*, 22.

The 2nd Hebrew letter is Beth (ב), 1 of the 7 double letters, corresponding to our letter B. Hieroglyphically it stands for the mouth of man and is referred to Wisdom, but since out of the "mouth of man" proceedeth both Wisdom and Folly this letter is called double. Its radical meaning is a "house" or "birth-place" and it is used with this meaning throughout the *Bible*. For instance, *Beth-el* is the "house of God"; *Eliza-beth* the "house of Eliza"; *Beth-lehem* the "house of bread"; *Bal-beth* the "house or temple of the sun," etc. Its symbolic meaning, derived from the house as a birth place, is both the Womb of Nature and of woman, from which all comes forth. From this meaning we deduce the idea of a sanctuary or inner shrine or that secret place where we can retire without fear of disturbance, the closet into which we can go and having shut the door pray to our Father in secret. Out of this sanctuary come forth the true characteristics which make us what we are, also from it issues the inspiration and instruction given us from the Divine in the Silence. Hence Beth expresses everything that emanates from this mysterious retreat.

"B, called BE-I-T, pictures and names the Bee or Bi and means BEing, Existence; names LIFE, BEe, Bios

* * * The colonial priests of a remote time sent a present from Delphi to England, being a miniature Temple in the form of a Hive, carved out of Beeswax. This was a primal picture, which in the double meanings, and for the wonderment of the ignorant, was always the House of the god Be, and making the Hebrew word for the original 'House of God' as BE-TH, which says 'B-Deity', and is also their alphabetic name of their letter 'B', showing that our 'B' is named in this 'BETH' * * * The universal picture-language Bow, which Egyptian deities carry to identify themselves, is made as an elongated 'B', and names the Be priesthood that was the shooter of the 'A' light or Arrow, the Celtic 'S-A-I-S'." [1]

Just as man, as the active Father-principle, is represented by Aleph, so in Beth we find the inner, passive or feminine Principle, the Mother-force, through which his characteristics are brought forth. While both man and woman express both Aleph and Beth, man is more Aleph than Beth and woman is more Beth than Aleph. The 3 primal meanings of Beth—the house, the mouth and the womb—are therefore but different expressions of the idea of bringing forth through the Mother-principle; for out of the house or inner sanctuary of the heart is brought forth man's spiritual nature; out of the womb is brought forth man's physical body, and out of the mouth man himself brings forth his ideas or thought creations. "For of the abundance of the heart his mouth speaketh." [2]

"The Beth represents hieroglyphically the heaven and the earth. It also represents unity made manifest in space and stability, and life made manifest by movement. It represents the Spirit of God born upon the waters and the fecundation of matter by Spirit." [3]

---

[1] *The Jarvis Letters*, I.
[2] *St. Luke*, vi, 45.
[3] *Unpublished Letters of Éliphas Lévi.*

THE 2ND COMMANDMENT.

> "Thou shalt not make unto thee any graven image, or any likeness of any thing that is in the heaven above, or that is in the earth beneath, or that is in the water under the earth. Thou shalt not bow down thyself to them, nor serve them."
>
> —*Exodus,* xx, 4.

Since number 2 is the symbol of Duality and marks the 1st step in the differentiation of the 1, nothing can manifest objectively upon the mundane plane without duality. That which appears upon the lower planes is but the shadow of the unseen Reality. Hence the 2nd Commandment deals with the ever present danger into which unenlightened man is only too apt to fall, namely, mistaking the shadow for the Reality. Therefore the Commandments begin with a warning against mistaking the reflection for the Substance; against making an idol out of material things and worshiping it. Note that the text says, "Thou shalt not make *unto thee.*" Others may carve statues or images for us, but no 1 but ourselves can make us create an idol out of the shadow. The Commandment is not to be taken in the literal sense that we should never carve an image or symbol of any holy ideal, principle or thing, a custom common in the Christian churches today. For when properly used such images or symbols serve to recall and impress more vividly upon the mind the unseen Reality for which they stand. They also have a mystical power in themselves. The Commandment means far more. It deals with all that number 2 expresses.

The overshadowing God-consciousness, fully comprehending the law of the descent of the Light into Chaos, and realizing all the pitfalls and mistakes into which man was likely to fall during his long pilgrimage, gave him at the outset a solemn warning against building up, through the creative power of his newly acquired self-conscious thought, earthly images of the Divine, and through the ignorance and darkness of the land in which he toiled, falling down to worship them. Even today many savage tribes have created thought-form-elementals which have become tribal gods, many of which must be propitiated by offerings of blood. Such worship of the false would lead man age after age farther and farther from the worship of the Spiritual Light, which was to lead him out of the darkness of Egypt if he would but worship the True instead of an image of his own creation. The duality of shadow and Substance is but a passing manifestation belonging to this Day-period and will cease to exist when the shadow has been indrawn into the Reality.

Since all God's creations in heaven above, in the earth beneath and in the waters under the earth, are images of divine and immutable Realities, if we hold fast to this thought and through the image seek to come into harmony with its Reality, we will find our Path of Attainment a joyous and fascinating journey through a wonderful country full of objects, each of which represents a marvelous God-mystery, instead of a wearisome climb up a rocky pathway through chilling darkness, dull misery, suffering and despair. The words, "The waters under the earth" give the key to the understanding of the Commandment. Waters, tossed by every wind that blows, symbolize the changing and unstable conditions of earthly manifestation. They are the unstable and varying conditions which, in the sense of back of, are underneath every earth condition.

> "I the Lord thy God am a jealous God, visiting the iniquity of the fathers upon the children unto the third and fourth generation of them that hate me; and shewing mercy unto thousands of them that love me, and keep my commandments."
>
> —*Exodus,* xx, 5.

The Lord thy God is a jealous God in the sense that nothing can stand between Him and man's love for the Divine. Anything which diverts man's allegiance from Him or is placed before Him must be swallowed up in the ○, naught.

The latter part of this Commandment may sound like a threat. In reality it is but a setting forth of the Law in its aspect as Karma. 1st, it is plainly stated that we are not to make images, mistake them for Realities and worship them. Then the inevitable result of so doing is set forth. Is not the world today suffering from the "iniquities of the fathers" or the disobedience to this 2nd Commandment? this 1st and primal rule of the plane of differentiation or duality? Have not our fathers mistaken the shadow for the Substance and fallen down and worshipped the Golden Calf? Have they not graven images of that which the Light revealed to them instead of the Light? Do we not today worship various man-made images of God? Do we not worship tradition—a graven image of the revelation of the Light—instead of turning our eyes to the Light ourselves and knowing that it will lead us out of the bondage of our fathers' false images and conceptions of Life, its needs and requirements, into a realization of our spiritual heritage? Esoterically this means that by his misuse of his creative powers man has impregnated the aura of the world upon the 3 planes with his mistakes and these must finally manifest upon the 4th or physical plane. Hence the children of man will suffer until his false images have had their day upon earth; have manifested their human origin; have proved their fallibility and have been replaced by the true worship of the 1 Reality, the Divine Light.

Those who "hate" the Lord are those who reverse Divine Love or who refuse to work in harmony with the Law. They suffer unto the 3rd and 4th generation, not in the sense of a punishment for something their fathers did, but because they continue to worship the graven images handed down by their fathers. They give their lives and the mighty power of their thought to preserve the images which are literally graven upon the Akashic Records by their fathers' misconceptions of the 1 God. Variation and progression are the basic principles of all evolution; an ever changing manifestation and an ever widening comprehension of unity in the manifold expressions of the 1 God.

The same divine and inexorable Law must show mercy to thousands (an indefinite term expressing a vast number) of those who love the Reality; who seek the Light; who endeavor to keep the Commandments and live in harmony with the Law as it is revealed to them, instead of worshiping the graven images of tradition. Mercy is shown us, even when we falter and fail, so long as we give our love and allegiance to the 1 God and earnestly strive to follow the Light which has brought us out of Egypt and out of the house of bondage, the senses.

THE 2ND TAROT CARD

HIGH PRIESTESS

Papus

Papus

MEDIEVAL

St. Germain
EGYPTIAN

II
B J
THE HIGH PRIESTESS

Smith
MODERN

CHAPTER 11

THE 2ND TAROT CARD, *The High Priestess.*

This card beautifully expresses the Mother idea contained in number 2. In the 1st card we see man standing in the midst of nature and surrounded by all the attributes of power or the ability to rule outwardly. In the 2nd card we find woman veiled and enthroned between the 2 columns of the Temple, in the portico or entrance to the inner shrine. She is invested with the insignia of spiritual authority, the Robe of purity; the Triple Crown showing that she must rule on the 3 planes through her Divine Motherhood. In her right hand she holds the partly opened Book of the Law, which, however, is partially hidden from the profane within the folds of her Mantle. In her left hand she holds the symbol of her authority as interpreter of the Law, possessing its positive and negative Keys. The Tiara upon her head is surmounted by the lunar crescent, symbol of her feminine functions and her power as the Bringer-forth of the Race. She rules not by might nor by force, but by the mysterious power of Mother-love, which under the influence of the invisible and periodic forces of the moon enables her to bring forth, as it also does the earth. By the unenlightened the moon is supposed to be but a satellite of the earth, altho in reality it is the mother of the earth, the giver of its life terrestrial. In a similar manner throughout many ages, among the spiritually unenlightened, woman has been looked upon as a mere chattel or satellite of man, yet from whom he has ever received his inspiration as well as his physical body, and to whose mystic power he instinctively bows. Even though ignored, degraded and denied a Soul, she has nevertheless swayed nations and kingdoms and been a powerful factor in the world, through the influence proceeding from the sacred inner shrine of Motherhood.

Woman's true place is as the High Priestess of mankind and she should fill the same position in each home. As we have said elsewhere: "True woman is positive upon the spiritual plane, where man is negative, and negative upon the physical plane, where man is positive. To her belongs the control of all those questions which deal with the higher life. She must use her intuition in the directing of all activities pertaining to the altruistic side of life, just as man uses his reason in worldly affairs. She should be man's moral and spiritual monitor and his source of inspiration and spiritual help."[1] She it is, as this Tarot card shows, who can open for him the Book of the Law and inspire him with its truths. For he can read and grasp its real meaning only as he seeks, within the sheltering porch of the Temple of Isis, for a true revelation of the mysteries of the Mother.

The 2 columns express, from this inner or feminine aspect, the same meaning as the 2 arms of the Juggler in the 1st card expressed outwardly, *i. e.*, positive and negative, or Jakin and Boas, Justice and Mercy. In much of the Moorish architecture, especially in their temples, we find at the entrance 2 columns united by an arch, with an interlacing of lattice work just beneath it. The symbology of this characteristic form of entrance, either to the home or the temple, is the same as we find in this Tarot card, namely, that the 2 columns, Justice and Mercy, man and woman, intellect and heart, must be united in the higher aspects of all their forces, and must each send out and interlace their

[1] *V. of I.*, 339.

forces over the portal by which humanity must enter the Temple of the higher life.

On her breast the Priestess bears the Solar Cross, the symbol that must ever express the crucifixion; the effort of Spirit to penetrate matter; the Light to illumine darkness, and that which is inner and sacred to express outwardly in the life. Hence this symbol upon the breast (over the heart) expresses woman, who ever bears the cross in her heart, while man bears it before the world and fights its battles in the arena of life.

The Veil represents the sacred Mystery of Motherhood not to be rudely lifted by the profane or desecrated by the impious, whether this be the motherhood that gives birth to the physical body or the far more sacred and veiled birth of The Christ-child within the heart. Isis is represented as having 7 veils[2] which shroud the mystery of birth, hence birth is the most profound and sacred of all mysteries, and has its correspondence on the 7 planes of consciousness.

The first 2 letters of the Hebrew alphabet, with their corresponding numbers, 1 and 2, as well as the 1st and 2nd cards of the symbolic Tarot, reveal the true relationship of man and woman. God is represented as taking Eve out of Adam's side during a deep sleep, because it was not good for man to be alone. In other words number 1 pierced the darkness or deep sleep of matter and when by its brightness it was able to produce its shadow, number 2 came into manifestation. Hence man is the positive or outer expression of the microcosm, and it is man who must fight the outer conditions and make a place for himself, while woman is the inner Soul or Inspirer, or shadow of God to man. That is, since number 1 produced 2 as a shadow or impression in matter, number 2 must have been an inner aspect or the real Soul of the manifesting 1. For

[2] *V. of I.*, 253.

1 stands alone until out of its Side or Heart or Inner Self it can impress the reality of the Light upon the darkness.

If we think of number 2 as radiance instead of a shadow we will get a better conception of its real meaning, for number 2 is the radiance produced by the light of the 1 piercing the darkness of Chaos. Indeed, this is the true mission of woman, *i. e.*, to be the radiance and the light of mankind, giving birth to the ideals of the Race. Hence the position held by woman in any country has always indicated its degree of true civilization and progress. Woman should always be the High Priestess, reading from the book of the Divine Law of Love in the shelter of the Temple, or home, that man in his struggle with outer conditions may catch the radiance of Love, Truth and Wisdom reflected on his Path of Attainment. This, however, in no way implies that woman should confine herself to the duties of the household and become a household drudge and mere breeder of the race, for the home or Temple is the sacred Shrine of Inspiration to be found in every walk of life. It should be the duty of every true woman not only to sit within the portal of this Shrine, be she engaged in whatsoever duty in whatsoever capacity, but she should also be the Inspirer or radiant Light leading and guiding man toward ever higher ideals, and to greater efforts toward reaching the goal of his highest attainment. Even though she be walking side by side with him, yet in a mystical sense she should ever be the Light set in the window of the home to guide him safely through the storms and darkness of outer conditions. It is also woman's place to cover with her Mantle of Love and healing the scars and wounds received by man in the battles of life which he fights for her and the home. For within those magic folds the Great Law shall bring understanding out of confusion, Wisdom out of experience and strength out of failure. In the hands of the mothers of the Race rests its salvation, no matter if they be mothers of physical children or mothers of ideals and reforms.

Like all things intended for the highest good, the perversion of woman's forces has done more to push man deeper into the mire of selfishness, sensuality and despair than all other things combined. But the Lords of Karma who ever hold a just balance, hold out to woman the opportunity for an advanced step, because of the lessons learned through suffering and degradation. Because the cross has rested heavily upon her heart, The Christ in her has been crucified and must be lifted up that He may draw all men unto Him. Woe then to the woman who lives in frivolity and idleness, as the plaything of humanity. Woe to the mothers who bring not forth children of Light, but perverted temples of iniquity full of pride, lust and all manner of unworthiness. Woe to the women who, because of pride, vanity and lust, seek not to inspire man but to entice, seduce and enslave him.

Woman today stands in the portal of the Temple of the New Humanity and only she can throw wide the Door. The day is coming when the eyes of all must be opened, and both man and woman behold the Living Christ whom they have crucified. In that day there can be no recriminations, 1 saying to the other, "thou art to blame, or thou didst tempt me and I did eat," for man and woman are 1 in the sight of God. A perfect humanity must express absolute equality, but not uniformity. The shell of the nut represents the nut to the outer world and protects the kernel, but if the kernel is bad the nut is worthless.

CHAPTER 12

THE NUMBER 3.

"The Deity is one, because It is infinite. It is triple, because It is ever manifesting."
—*The Kabbalah.*

"The King of ages, the merciful and gracious God, the exalted One, the Dweller in Eternity, most high and holy—engraved his name by the three Seraphim—Numbers, Letters, and Sounds."
—*Sepher Yetzirah,* Chapter i.

Since 1 is unity and hence no number, 3 is called the 1st odd number. 3 is the Number of the Trinity, hence Divine. In number 1 the Divine came down into manifestation, in 2 it was met by the inertia of matter, but in 3 it penetrated into matter and manifested the "only begotten Son." This process is illustrated by the equilateral triangle △ in which the positive and negative forces from the dot above bring forth a stable manifestation on the physical-plane, the base line. The triangle is the 1st geometrical figure, for "the number 2 is like two straight lines which can never enclose a space, and therefore it is powerless till the number 3 forms a triangle." Again the triangle may be considered as Spirit and Matter united by Mind.

Number 3 is sacred and Divine because it symbolizes the 3 fold Deity, the Trinity; the Father, the Mother and the Son; the Father, Son and Holy Ghost of the Christians; the Brahma, Siva and Vishnu of the Hindus; the Osiris, Isis and Horus of the Egyptians, etc. In another aspect 3 is the number of the 3 manifestations of Deity, the Logoi. The 1st Logos is Unity, the Undifferentiated; the 2nd Logos is a trinity of the

1 Life, Spirit-Matter and Cosmic Consciousness; the 3rd Logos is Mahat, Cosmic Ideation or Universal Mind. 3 is the Number of the Mystery of Life.* Stinson Jarvis in his articles on the Druids[1] states that, "The Druids described deity as being ONE and TWO and THREE; and, by itself, our T means Three, and our word 'T.R.I.', meaning Three, named this number from the Isthmus of Darien to the remote Pacific islands, showing that there was one Druid word-making for the entire world, and one priesthood to carry our words into every country. Father Smiddy says: 'Three was the Druid mystical number. With them nearly all things resolved themselves into a Trine.' This was the D-OC-TRINE, or 'Trine-Teaching,' preached in America for ages, and TRI-N-I-TE says 'Three, Heaven Island God'."

3 is the number of the trilogies used to measure the manifestations of all things to the human consciousness, such as substance, life, intelligence; matter, force, consciousness; heat, light, electricity; length, breadth, thickness; creation, preservation, dissolution; thinker, thought, thing thought of, etc. By some 3 is loosely spoken of as the number of man because of his division into body, Soul and Spirit, but as this is only a superficial and exoteric division, 3 is not properly man's symbol. As 3 includes past, present and future it is sometimes called the Number of Time. It is also called the Middle or the Analogy, because all comparisons are expressed in 3 terms, good, bad and indifferent.

The Egyptian Trinity is composed of Osiris (water, especially their sacred river Nile), Isis (earth, especially the land of Egypt over which she reigned), and Horus (air, especially the moist warm air after the overflow of the Nile in spring). Thus the Nile represented to the Egyptians the great fertilizing power of the Father, and at its annual overflow there was great

* The third stage in the manifestation of life in the plant after the two horizontal leaves are put forth is the stalk springing up from them. In the developing egg the last of the three fundamental tissues is developed between the two mentioned in the note to page 84. This third tissue is the mesoderm or mesoblast, thus completing the trinity of tissues from which the whole body is made up.

rejoicing and many religious rites were celebrated because Osiris was fecundating the Queen Mother, Isis. After the river receded the entire valley, which before the overflow was dry and brown, was covered with the tender green of the spring crops. The moist balmy air which pervades the valley at that time was considered the child of Isis and Osiris, Horus. If the rains in the interior were late and the rising of the Nile was delayed, processions were formed and prayers offered entreating Osiris to look upon his spouse with favor.

In astronomy recent discoveries[2] have revealed a trinity in the motions of the stars, each having 3 distinct motions—rotatory, orbital, linear—*i. e.,* each rotates on its axis, gyrates around the central sun of its system, and also drifts toward a point outside its zodiac. Just so does each Soul have its inner point about which it rotates; its Spiritual Sun about which it gyrates and which determines the orbit of its evolution, and also its Destiny or place in the Grand Plan of the Universe, toward which it is steadily being swept by the Great Law while evolving the qualities necessary to enable it to fulfill its Destiny.

In addition to the 2 great star-streams well known to astronomers, a 3rd but much smaller stream has recently been discovered which is independent of the other 2. Such is the mysterious law called gravitation, that the heavenly bodies are not only bound together by mutual attraction, but are also held at relatively fixed distances apart; as though gravitation brought them only so near to each other and some counter repellant force kept them from approaching nearer. In reality that which limits their nearer approach is the limits of their auras. Of these 3 star-streams 1 is going outward into manifestation—a cycle requiring some aeons of ages—and 1 stream is going inward to

---

[2] See *Stellar Movements and the Structure of the Universe,* Prof. A. S. Eddington. Also monographs by Dr. Campbell and Prof. Aitken of Lick Observatory.

its rest or pralaya, while the 3rd and smaller stream is composed of those stars and systems which have attained Mastery and become independent of the other 2 streams; in other words, have become immortal for the cycle of the mahamanvantara or great world-period. Just so are there 3 streams of humanity, 1 going out into manifestation in incarnation, 1 going inward to rest between incarnations, and a 3rd and very small stream of those who have attained Mastery and immortality for this manvantara or world-period.

Science has recently discovered that the entire visible universe is a huge spiral made up of a series of lesser spiral systems. It has long been known that the giant nebulae, or world systems in the process of formation, are spiral in shape, each having its central nucleus or Dot from which the system emanated. And since the outline of a spiral is △, we see that the △ with a dot at the apex is a cosmic symbol which correctly portrays the Law of Manifestation—of individuals, of worlds, of universes—for the life cycle of all forms of manifestation is spiral in character. "As above, so below." We may think our lives are on a dead level, because our physical, mental and spiritual lives may seem to be but a succession of days and nights in which we experience similar conditions, but by a study of the Law we find that all evolution is in spirals, each life having its personal, racial and universal motions. Hence we find that as we evolve we pass over, again and again, the decisive points in our lives, but at each repetition we are on a little higher round of experience and attainment. Each Race as a whole, and the planet itself, also have their spirals of evolution.

The widespread manifestation of triplicities is shown in the celestial signs, each of which has a fixed, movable and common quarternion, also 3 decans. Among these signs there is a triplicity for each of the 4 elements, thus: the Fire signs are Aries, Leo, Saggitarius; the Earth signs Taurus, Virgo, Capricorn; the Air signs Gemini, Libra, Aquarius; the Water signs Cancer, Scorpio, Pisces. Astrologers also regard the 3rd day after the new moon as the most fortunate day of the month. The Hermetics had 3 symbolic animals connected with their magic: the Bull, symbol of earth or philosophic Salt; the Dog, Herm-anubis, the Mercury of the Sages or fluid, air and water; the Goat, symbol of Fire and generation. 3 is also the Number of the Akasha, the so-called Veil of Deity, the great storehouse of all events, past, present and future.

3 is the Number of Divine Love, also man, woman and the magnetic attraction between them united in the Divine. It is Divine Love overshadowing and manifesting through the "two witnesses" mentioned in *Revelation,*[3] *i. e.,* man and woman. For every true marriage in which human love reaches up to and blends with Divine Love is a witness on earth that Divine Love has been able to penetrate into and manifest through humanity. 3 is therefore the number of a perfect marriage made in heaven, or the masculine and feminine expression of human love united above the earth in Divine Love, the completion of the triangle.

The triangle is pre-eminently the symbol of the triune Godhead. But all manifestations of that Godhead must contain a reflection of the triangle—(a) the inner reality, (b) the outer manifestation, and (c) the life-force which unites the 2—else the Deity would not be represented in His works. As number 2 symbolizes the 1 Ray separated and manifested upon the physical plane in the pairs of opposites, so number 3 symbolizes the evolution of the pairs of opposites to a point of perfect balance or at-one-ment with their source; the Divine merging into them that it may uplift and redeem them. In other words, in 3 there is the

[3] Chapter xi, 3.

Dot which overshadows each pair of opposites $\dot{\Delta}$, the goal toward which they are evolving; the state of perfection which will manifest when the experience of both extremes has been garnered and indrawn to the point above the physical plane. Number 3 therefore symbolizes the balance of all manifested things in the Godhead; is a prophecy of their ultimate perfection and their unity in the Divine. Hence the sacredness with which number 3 has always been regarded in religions.

Applying this triune principle to humanity we find that man and woman, being the microcosm of the macrocosm and embodying all the pairs of opposites in nature—heat and cold, pleasure and pain, good and evil, etc.—must ultimately find their completion, balance and perfection in union in the Dot—in the divine marriage—above the physical plane. As they advance toward this perfection they will, of necessity, balance all the pairs of opposites manifesting in their microcosm.

"All Souls are pre-existent in the world of emanations, and are in their original state androgynous, but when they descend upon the earth they become separated into male and female, and inhabit different bodies; if therefore in this mortal life the male half encounters the female half, a strong attachment springs up between them, and hence it is said that in marriage the separated halves are again conjoined; and the hidden forms of the soul are akin to the kerubim."[4]

Since the great goal toward which all manifested things are evolving is the reunion of the many in the One from which they emanated, as the positive and negative poles express on earth they are ever seeking to return to their unity in the Dot. Hence they attract or reach toward each other (Fig. 2). When they unite and are balanced they bring forth a 3rd line,

[4] *The Kabbalah Unveiled,* Mathers, 34-5.

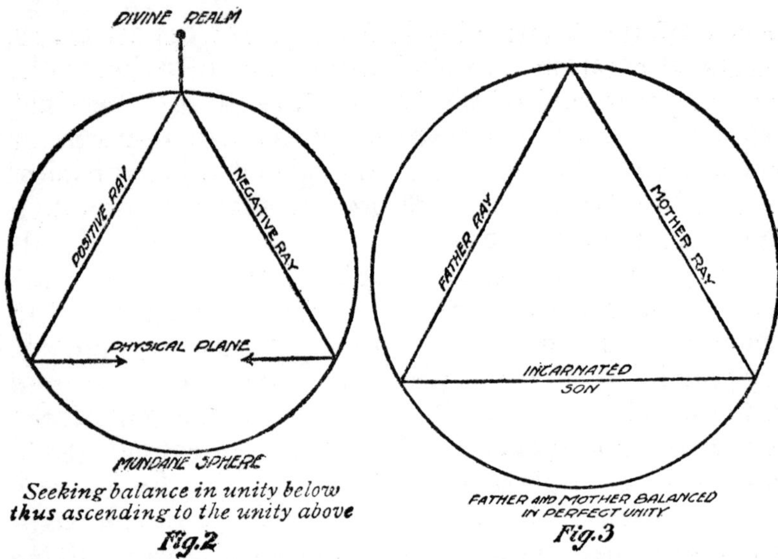

Seeking balance in unity below thus ascending to the unity above
Fig.2

FATHER AND MOTHER BALANCED IN PERFECT UNITY
Fig.3

the base of the triangle or "the only begotten son," (Fig. 3).

The triangle is therefore the symbol of Satisfaction, for the only true satisfaction is the response we feel to the force poured out through some form of union with the Divine. The only real satisfaction is experienced in the thrill of oneness that comes when a Ray from the Divine within us finds expression in manifestation on any plane, physical, mental or spiritual, from the thrill that results from an unselfish deed, a kind word or a generous forgiveness, to the ecstasy of conscious union with the Higher Self in the highest Initiation or in that most mystical sacrament "the marriage of the Lamb." Union between the positive and negative poles of dissimilar Rays may make a union on the physical plane, but it can never bring more than physical satisfaction. And as this can be but temporary, it cannot bring that true happiness which results from union on all planes.

As man and woman are the "lords of creation," so must they in turn become the redeemers (the Dot above) of the lower kingdoms, and lift up all lower aspects of creation into a higher octave of expression. Even as Jesus said of the Christ within: "If I be lifted up I will draw all men unto me," so as man and woman are united and lift up The Christ within them will they draw all the lower pairs of opposites—the lower kingdoms—unto them.

Today there are many who, awakening to the vital ideal of true marriage, are no longer satisfied with the mere husks or outer conceptions of life so long considered satisfying. They realize that in contracting a marriage the religious aspirations of both the man and the woman should be centered in the same spiritual ideals (the same Dot above), so that as both evolve and advance toward the realization of those ideals they may grow ever closer and closer, thus ∴. We may illustrate this by the following diagram, which is intended to be merely illustrative and not literal:

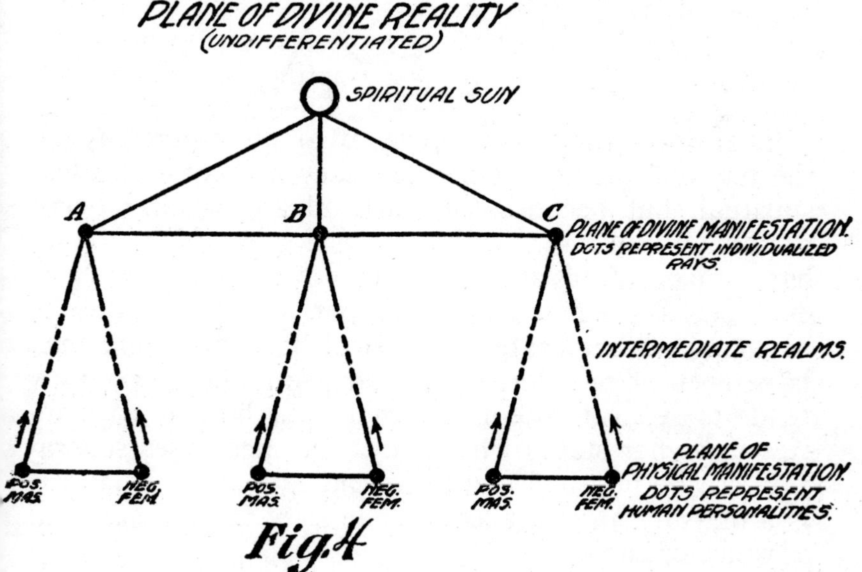

Fig. 4

If, for instance, a positive personality of the Higher Self A unites with a negative personality of the same Higher Self A—to which it could alone truly belong—as they each advance spiritually and evolve upward toward the Higher Self of each they must necessarily grow closer to each other, for they are evolving toward union with the *same* overshadowing Dot. But if a positive personality of the Higher Self A should unite with a negative personality of another Dot or Higher Self, of which it is not an emanation—say of the Higher Selves B or C—then as each personality advanced spiritually and evolved upward along its Ray toward union with its Higher Self, instead of the personalities growing closer together on all planes, they must inevitably grow farther and farther apart on the higher planes—and this must ultimately lead to separation on the physical plane—for each 1 is evolving toward union with a different Dot, thus:

Therefore, there may develop great inharmony on the physical plane, not because they are becoming less spiritual, but because they are advancing and being drawn into different currents of force which do not harmonize. And as the great Law of Divine Love ever seeks greater and more perfect expressions of harmony, when whatever physical harmony there may have been at first has expressed itself, the Great Law tends to separate them that each may be able to manifest a higher state of harmony. In such cases separation on the physical plane, instead of being a calamity, is a blessing and an absolute necessity for the spiritual advance of each.

In the marital relations of the present day these spiritual lines of force are woefully mixed and tangled, both through the Karma of similar mistakes in the past and through allowing other considerations than Divine Love to bring about union on the physical plane. No matter how eugenically perfect the animal bodies of the parents may be, perfect love is the only force that will attract advanced Souls to incarnation in the perfect bodies furnished by the parents. Without it only such Souls will be attracted as are willing to incarnate under the loveless conditions offered. But as we enter into the cycle of the new Aquarian Age there must be a great readjustment and untangling process carried out as rapidly as the working out of past Karma permits, so that each may return to his or her true spiritual allegiance and make straight the crooked paths of spiritual force ere the coming of The Christ. For The Christ—the essence of the Divine Dot—cannot manifest in perfection until its positive and negative vehicles are united and the Path made straight, thus

This is illustrated by the story of John the Baptist being clothed in skins and crying in the wilderness; for the Soul is clad in its animal nature (skin) and wanders in the wilderness of the outer life until the Path is made straight and a way for the manifestation of Divine Love through the Law of Unity is prepared.

Therefore, from a geometrical standpoint we see that a marriage can never be truly harmonious unless there is a common source of interest or aspiration outside of and above the personalities, in which the 2 can unite, or a common Dot into which the sides of the human triangle can merge. Even though both are expressions of the same Divine Self, if they are at all spiritually advanced and 1 of the 2 seeks further spiritual advance through 1 school of religious or occult teaching while the other seeks in a divergent school—for instance, if 1 be a Catholic and the other a Protestant, or 1 an Occultist and the other an orthodox literal Christian—they must at least temporarily grow apart in the higher realms, even if they remain together on the physical-plane, because they are separated in the higher realization and expression of their oneness. Of course such persons will come together ultimately through a higher understanding, but only after a period of suffering which should be unnecessary. In such cases the course of their evolution, 1st separating for a time and then returning, may be represented, not by a triangle, but by a hexagram, the figure which forms the center of the interlaced triangles, thus:

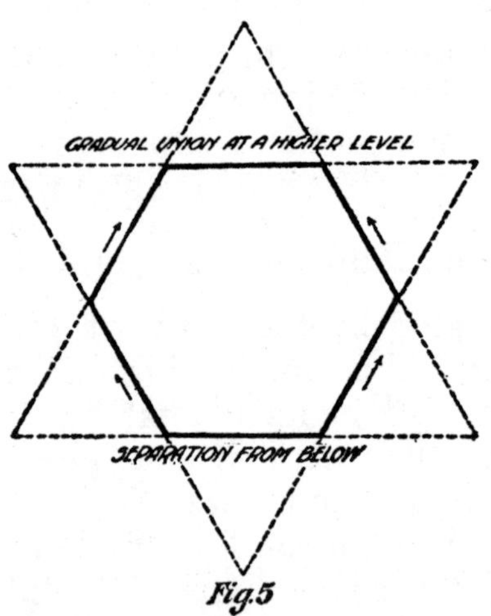

Fig. 5

This figure is the center of the Seal of Solomon or the Heart of Wisdom, hence they will reach their true union, through the suffering of spiritual loneliness etc., only after they have found the Heart of Wisdom. And if 1 subordinates his or her spiritual ideals to the other the spiritual growth of both is retarded. In other words, only as the lives of both are blended on all planes and are centered in a common ideal outside of and above their personalities, can they grow into that perfect spiritual oneness represented by the overshadowing Dot $\dot{\Delta}$.

As this spiritual oneness is attained the 2 manifestations grow closer and closer together on the base line — the physical plane — until finally, instead of reaching the Divine along the slanting, complementary lines forming the sides of the triangle, the forces from each are indrawn to the center where they blend into the vertical line—the straight and narrow Path—which reaches in oneness direct to the Divine within, thus 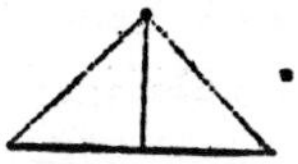 . Therefore we would say that the effective remedy for the divorce evil is to teach, firstly, the necessity for a oneness of spiritual ideals, and secondly, the necessity of both Souls following the Divine guidance of their overshadowing Dot until, through prayer and meditation, they receive the *positive assurance from within* that their lines of spiritual evolution converge toward the same spiritual Dot or that their Souls had emerged from and are evolving back to the same Divine Source, the creative Dot or Over-Soul overshadowing the 1 triangle. But before they can do this they must be sure that they have freed themselves of self-deception and a determined self-will which makes the thing they want seem to be the right thing, even though it requires excuse after excuse to make it plausible.

On the other hand do not be too hasty in deciding that each is evolving toward a different center, for it may be that in reality both are seeking the same point, but have not yet found the straight and narrow Path common to both, or even realized that their complementary lines will ultimately reach the same Dot. For even the fact that they have recognized their spiritual unity does not mean that there will be no more unpleasant lessons to learn, no friction in the adjustments necessary on the physical plane. But whatever frictions may develop and whatever inharmonies may assail them, their unity in the higher realms will enable them to recognize the true nature of these and look upon them as tests meant to prove them, while the overshadowing Divine Love will give them the strength to overcome such conditions and make them but transitory storms which clear the air. A little extra patience and toleration and a willingness to give up a preconceived idea as to what is the only or best way to reach the goal may open their eyes to the fact that each is seeking the same divine Dot, but has a different way of manifesting it for the time being. Only as we permit the divine Dot to shine into our hearts and draw our Souls into oneness with It can we attain the wisdom and love which will draw to us that which is our own and reveal to us beyond the possibility of mistake our next step.

This teaching must not be made the excuse for divorce without adequate cause;[3] for a union, even though it may not be ideal, may nevertheless be the means of teaching the most important lessons of this incarnation. And as we do not limit ourselves to the 1 life-period, there is plenty of time for adjustment in accordance with the Law.

---

[3] For our teachings on divorce see *Letters from the Teacher*, Curtiss, chapter, *The Sex Problem*.

CHAPTER 13

THE NUMBER 3—*(Continued).*

"The perfect word is the triad, because it supposes an intelligent principle, a speaking principle, and a principle spoken."

—*Transcendental Magic,* Lévi, 45.

"The heavens were produced from Fire; the earth from water; and the Air from the Spirit is as a reconciler between the Fire and the Water."

—*Sepher Yetzirah,* 19.

Number 3 is "the Word made flesh and dwelling among us," for it is the base line or the magnetic attraction which unites the positive and negative forces and completes the triangle. Similarly the sun is a manifestation of the Trinity as force, *i. e.,* heat, light and electricity, all of which are expressions of the divine Spiritual Fire or "cold flame" represented by number 1. This Spiritual Flame cannot enter the physical plane without manifesting these 3 aspects. Science tells us that if a gas—and theoretically all substances when in a gaseous state—could be reduced to a temperature called "absolute zero" (—273°), it would disappear or cease to exist; hence heat is a prime requisite for any form of manifestation. When heat is increased or its vibrations raised to a certain degree light appears, and when the note of vibration is still further increased electricity or radiant energy manifests.

Number 1 in 1 sense may be compared to man and to the heat of the sun, its active principle; number 2, to woman or the light of the sun, its passive principle, while number 3 would stand for the son or that magnetism which exists between positive and negative, heat and light, man and woman, that the 2 may manifest in oneness of being. From another standpoint the sun may also be used to symbolize the Father-in-heaven, the light of the Son sent forth to redeem the darkness, while the magnetism would be the Holy Ghost, the unseen magnetic energy which is forever with us. It is the Comforter in that it reconciles the extremes or pairs of opposites; the Revealer which shows them in their true relations. It shall bring all things to our remembrance, *i. e.*, that we may never forget the fact that no matter how lost in the darkness we may seem to be, we can always see the Light shining from our Father's home to illumine our Path, if we will but turn our faces toward it. As we realize that this spiritual magnetism pervades our body, brain and consciousness—as it pervades all nature and the universe—we find that it is a link which binds the microcosm (man) to the macrocosm. Hence, just as a paleontologist can reconstruct a prehistoric animal from 1 bone, so can we, if we find within ourselves 1 substance that is identical in man, nature and the Cosmos or 1 thread running through and connecting all, by studying that substance and correlating our consciousness with that thread, bring all things to our remembrance; for man, being a Ray from the Divine, does not so much acquire new knowledge as he gradually remembers the knowledge that was his in the realms of the Divine—his Father's home.

Heat is the result of the resistance offered by matter to the activity of the Spiritual Flame. Heat may be said to be the lowest and most physical expression or body of Fire. Light is produced by the overcoming of the resistance that a greater expression of Fire—its Soul, so to speak—may manifest. Electricity or radiant energy may be considered as the spirit of

Divine Fire, just as heat is its body and light or solar fire its soul. Hence electricity or radiant energy is the most potent of all known manifestations of force. But man has as yet touched only its outer and most gross manifestation, for he scarce knows the a-b-c of that Power of which electricity is but 1 manifestation. As he enters the new sub-race the discovery of other and greater aspects and manifestations of that Power will be the opening of a door which will admit him into a new world of force and energy. But as long as he is capable of utilizing his knowledge of the higher forms of force for selfish purposes and for the destruction of his fellow men, through engines of war, etc., the door will be kept closed against him.

All life is a manifestation of the Trinity or number 3, but since man has not yet mastered its 3 expressions he is subject to them. When he completes the creation of his spiritual or *Nirmanakaya* body[1] the heat will manifest as the glow of Immortal Youth and health, the light as Divine Illumination and the electricity as the Spirit permeating every atom of that body. Then shall man be master of all his forces.

Since the density of the physical body of unevolved man, together with his mental darkness, offers great resistance to the manifestation of the Spiritual Fire and prevents him from working in harmony with the Divine Life-forces, physical and mental suffering result. Hence the results of resistance to Divine Law are represented by a hell of blackness, intolerable heat and suffering (the Christian idea of hell), while the heaven world, in which the resistance is overcome, is represented as a realm of glorious Light and joy, the Spirit being the power which converts the hell into a heaven. Similarly, electricity corresponds to the magnetic force which forms the Path and mediates between heaven and hell, or The Christ which descends into hell

[1] See *Letters from the Teacher*, 68.

as a consuming fire, but dwells in heaven as a radiant Light.

The tripod has the same symbology as the triangle and was used in many mystic ceremonies in the ancient temples. The most famous was the Delphic Tripod or sacrificial altar upon which the Pythian Priestess sat while delivering the oracles of the gods. After chewing a sacred bay leaf and drinking from the sacred spring Cassotis (the Water of Life), the priestess took her seat upon a tripod placed in the inner shrine, and there answered the questions that had been previously submitted in writing. In other words, before receiving the revelation from the Divine the Virgin Priestess must drink of the true spiritual "Waters of Life," *i. e.*, must have received the illumination of Divine Wisdom, so that her eyes are opened and her mind illumined to comprehend the spiritual symbols given her and translate them into their corresponding terms or allegories; for only such an 1 can be a true Priestess and be used as an avenue through which the Waters of Life can flow forth for the healing of the nations. So must the Priestess of the Home have her eyes opened and her mind illumined through the consummation of the alchemical sacrifice in which the spiritual power of perfect love turns the Waters of Life into the Wine of the Spirit.

As the true office of the Priestess became overlaid with misconceptions, priestcraft and selfishness, too often the Pythian Priestess was but a subjective medium or perhaps a clairvoyant who could merely relate what she saw, without the illumination of Divine Wisdom correctly to interpret the visions seen, hence the subsequent degradation of her high office.

Another celebrated tripod was the "Plataen." This was made from a 10th part of the spoils taken from the Persian army after the battle of Plataea. It consisted of a golden basin supported by a bronze serpent with 3 heads, or 3 serpents intertwined, within the golden bowl of which the sacred fire was kept burning. The golden bowl here has the same symbology as the Holy Grail, *i. e.,* the receptacle in which the creative Christ-force is caught that it may bring forth. So frequently was the tripod used as a receptacle for dedicatory offerings to the gods that there was a street in Athens called the "Street of Tripods," from the large number of such tripods dedicated to various gods and containing live coals upon which passing pedestrians could sprinkle incense. Hence, from its true symbology, every home should have its mystic tripod. No Priest and Priestess of the Home who have lit the fire of Divine Love in the Golden Bowl need ever fear separation; for all the little differences and inharmonies will be consumed in the purifying Flame of that Love.

According to the *Sepher Yetzirah:*[2] "The Three Mothers, *Aleph, Mem* and *Shin,* are a great Mystery, very admirable and most recondite, and sealed with six rings; and from them proceed Air, Fire and Water, which divide into male and female forces. The Three Mothers, *Aleph, Mem* and *Shin,* are the Foundation, from them spring three Fathers, and from these have proceeded all things that are in the world * * * from the fire was made heat, from the waters was made cold, and from air was produced the temperate state, again a mediator between them. * * * Fire, Water and Air are found in Man: from fire was formed the head; from the water the belly; and from the air was formed the chest, again placed as a mediator between the others." In the *Bible* we again find these 3 Mothers in the 3 women at the tomb. The letter M itself means both mother and water, each name beginning with M having some connection with

[2] Chapter iii.

the idea of water or motherhood; for example, Mare or Mary is the sea or the Great Deep, the Mother of all Living, etc.

In the Kabalistic Trinity—Kether, Chokmah and Binah—the 3rd Sephira, Binah, is called Understanding. The 1st Sephira is Divine Love and the 2nd is Wisdom, but so long as they are not joined by an *understanding* of their divine qualities they are like 2 straight lines running side by side which can never unite until a 3rd line, the mediator, joins them, thus completing the manifestation of the 2, positive and negative, masculine and feminine. The 3rd Sephira is sometimes called the Great Mother who brings forth for the lower planes of manifestation. For only through an understanding of Divine Love and Wisdom can we bring them forth in our lives.

According to the Kabbalah the ideas of the learned Rabbis are as follows: "The soul is veiled in light. This light is triple: Neschamah, the pure spirit; Ruach, the soul or spirit; Nephesch, the plastic mediator. * * * The body is the veil of Nephesch, Nephesch is the veil of Ruach, Ruach is the veil of the shroud of Neschamah. * * * There are 3 habitations of souls: the Abyss of Life; the superior Eden; the inferior Eden. * * * There are 3 atmospheres for the souls. The third atmosphere finishes where the planetary attraction of other worlds commences. Souls perfected on this earth pass on to another station. After traversing the planets they come to the sun; then they ascend into another universe and recommence their planetary evolution from world to world and from sun to sun. In the sun they remember, and in the planets they forget. The solar lives are days of Eternal Life, and the planetary lives are nights with their dreams."[3]

[3] *The Kabbalah Revealed,* Mathers, 36-7.

Noah, who is a symbol of the 1 God or the Spirit of God moving on the face of the waters, had 3 sons, Shem, Ham and Japheth. This is an allegory symbolizing that the 1 must manifest on earth as the 3. Abraham, "the father of all living," entertained 3 angels who told him his wife or the feminine expression, would bring forth a son in whom all mankind would be blessed; that is, through this son the subsequent races would manifest the 3 fold Divine Fire. The 3 children of Judah cast in the fiery furnace by Nebuchadnezzar symbolize the same thing in another aspect, *i. e.,* the fiery furnace represents the resistance of physical matter (hell) and the adverse earthly conditions through which the 3 expressions of the Divine walk unharmed. Jonah spent 3 days in the belly of the great fish; the ministry of Jesus began at 30 and lasted 3 years. He said: "Destroy this temple, and in three days I will raise it up." He also lay for 3 days in the tomb.[4] All these allegories are glyphs symbolizing the fact that the Father-ray (1) after descending into the tomb of matter (2) must remain hidden in the pairs of opposites until the Trinity or triangle can manifest upon the physical plane (4), thus fulfilling the ancient occult axiom, "The Unit becomes the Three, and the Three generate the Four." Or, as the Kabalists say: "The Deity is one, because It is infinite. It is triple, because It is ever manifesting." Each of the "days" referred to symbolizes the period required for 1 aspect to complete its manifestation. And only as man's body becomes able to express in their fullness the 3 aspects of the Divine Fire —until The Christ can rise from the tomb on the 3rd day—can it be raised up to become truly the Temple of the Living God.

Let number 3 remind you of the manifestations of the Trinity, the Father, Son and Holy Ghost; of the

[4] See lesson *Three Days in the Tomb.*

mystical meaning of heat, light and electricity; of matter, force and consciousness; of the triangle with its base solidly established on earth yet ever pointing upward; of man and woman united and perfectly balanced in the physical life, yet evolving upward to oneness in the same overshadowing Dot or the Divine Marriage. Let 3 remind you of the 3 parties to the marriage tie—the man, the woman and the Divine Overshadowing—hence the beauty and sacredness of a true marriage, the ideal life as long as mankind manifests in separated sexes.

THE 3½.

The 3½, being ½ of 7, is frequently referred to with mystical significance. When the mighty angel in *Revelation* (*xi*, 1) gave the reed with which to measure the "temple of God, and the altar, and them that worship therein," the command was given not to measure the outer court, "for it is given unto the Gentiles: and the holy city shall they tread under foot forty and two months" or 3½ years. This is most significant, for the Temple is the physical body, while the altar is the inner shrine of the heart. Those who truly worship in this sacred Temple and find The Christ upon the altar will be measured, *i. e.*, will be understood, weighed and given a just balance. But those who dwell merely in the outer courts, *i. e.*, those who dwell merely in the outer sense perceptions, are the Gentiles, the unbelievers who are not measured or required to live up to the higher standards. They are given another ½ cycle of 3½ years in which to learn their lessons, even though they tread the outer courts under foot.

According to tradition Jesus remained hidden in Egypt for 3½ years. In the allegory of the woman clothed with the sun,[5] she dwelt in the wilderness "one

[5] *Revelation,* xii, 6.

thousand two hundred and three score days" or 3½ cycles of 360 each. We also read of the mystical 2 witnesses as follows: "I will give power unto my two witnesses, and they shall prophesy a thousand two hundred and three score days,"[6] again 3½ years. And all people "shall see their dead bodies three days and a half." According to Daniel *(xii, 7)*, the misfortunes of the children of Israel were to last "For a time, times, and a half."

In the life of the sincere seeker after Truth, 3½ represents a most trying and troublous period, for the manifestation of the Deity (the 3) has descended upon him; The Christ-child has been born in his heart, but must be nourished in the obscurity and darkness of Egypt—the outer life. He has consecrated his life to the Great Work and his heart is on fire to begin his ministry. Then, in some inexplicable way, life plunges him into the darkness of Egypt—poverty, sickness or some form of limitation and depression. His hands seem tied, and the Great Work which he would do he cannot do. All things seem to prevent him from giving his time, thought and strength to the upliftment of humanity. The so-called sordid duties of every day life which press upon him and demand his attention he still has to perform while he fights against the clouds of depression which surround him. He has sanctified his Holy Temple, and daily performs his worship therein. He has set up his altar within the Holy of Holies where the fires of purification burn continually, fed by the daily sacrifice of the faults, failings and limitations which he recognizes and consciously desires to transmute. Yet the outer courts are still occupied by the Gentiles. And the noise of their songs and merry-making, and of their dancing feet ruthlessly treading underfoot, in laughing indifference, the things he holds sacred, comes constantly

---

[6] *Revelation,* **xi, 1-3, 9.**

to his ears. Sometimes this merely disturbs his worship, but at other times it is disquietingly alluring and seductive; for it is hard at this step to know just how to remain in the world yet not be of it. But there is a deep significance in the experience of this step; for he is but following the universal law; is but passing through the transitional experiences of 3½ preparatory to completing his Foundation Stone in number 4.

CHAPTER 14

THE 3RD LETTER, *Gimel* (ג)

> "He produced Gimel, and referred it to Health; He crowned it, combined and joined with it Mars in the Universe, the second day of the week, and the right ear of man."
>
> —*Sepher Yetzirah*, 22.

The 3rd letter is Gimel, the 2nd of the 7 double letters, corresponding to our letter G. It is related to health and its opposite, disease, and also to the planet Mars. The force of Mars is the bright red blood or life-force of the Cosmos, hence Mars rules the blood which preserves the life and health in man, but if the blood be impure it produces fevers, humors and divers manners of diseases. Because of this connection the blood shed in battle is looked upon as a sacrifice to Mars, the god of life-force, of struggle, battle and overcoming. The force of Mars also brings courage, enthusiasm and the unrelenting effort which ever pushes on and overcomes all obstacles and difficulties. In its lower aspects this force manifests in an unfavorable and disintegrating manner through anger, passion, war and bloodshed. Mars represents that force referred to in the *Bible* as the blood of "the Lamb slain from the foundation of the world," [1] or the spiritual life-force which shall cleanse us from sin and by the sacrifice of whose shedding we must be redeemed. For just as the physical body is cleansed from disease and saved from death by being bathed in the purified blood which must wash each organ and tissue, so must the spiritual life-force bathe and purify every phase of our 7 fold being ere we can enter into eternal life.

---

[1] *Revelation*, xiii, 8.

The literal meaning of Gimel is a camel. Altho the Hebrew name for camel is *gamal,* it may require some imagination to see any relation between the letter itself and a camel. Yet the camel bears a very close analogy to the true meaning of the letter, for on account of its ability to store up large quantities of water, in desert countries the camel is looked upon as the Carrier of Life. Symbolically Gimel has come to mean that which encloses, a hollow tube or that which transmits vital life-force, such as an artery, etc. Hieroglyphically Gimel means "a hand, half closed and extended (reaching out like a camel) in order to draw to its possessor that which is needed for his own sustenance; so, finally Gimel comes to mean a hollow tube or canal (like the camel's neck)," and in man is sometimes referred to the throat. The throat contains a most important center, for it is here that the ideas conceived in thought and translated into words are enunciated into intelligible sounds. Man alone of all beings has this center developed, hence man alone can translate thought into comprehensible speech. Astronomically Gimel is associated with the star Alcyone in the neck of the Bull (Taurus) around which our universe is said to revolve.

Gimel has sometimes had ascribed to it a phallic meaning. But while the phallus may in a sense represent it, since generation is but a reflection in matter of the Great Mystery by which Spirit unites itself to matter, the Divine becomes flesh and dwells among us, we can see that it has a far deeper and more sacred meaning than physical generation. In 1 sense, just as Aleph symbolizes man and the force and activity of the physical plane, and as Beth symbolizes woman, the passive and receptive Principle, so Gimel symbolizes the magnetic link between them. Only as this magnetic attraction is regarded by them as a sacred gift entrusted to them to be used to erect in humanity the symbolic Temple of Solomon—the Temple of Wisdom—can man and woman or Aleph and Beth become the 2 pillars Jakin and Boas with Gimel as the arch which unites the 2 and completes the portal, the door through which alone mankind can enter into the Holy of Holies. Here The Christ forever stands and cries: "Verily, verily, I say unto you, He that entereth not by the door into the sheepfold, but climbeth up some other way, the same is a thief and a robber." [2]

[2] *St. John,* x, 1.

THE 3RD TAROT CARD

THE EMPRESS

Papus

Papus

MEDIEVAL

St. Germain
EGYPTIAN

Smith
MODERN

THE 3RD TAROT CARD, *The Empress*

This card is called "the Empress" and also the Son, Horus, the vivifying principle of the universe. It is represented as a woman seated and seen full face. She is seated upon the Throne of the Sun and has 2 great wings. In her right hand is an escutcheon bearing an upright Eagle with outspread wings, while in her left hand she holds a Scepter surmounted by a globe and the symbol of Venus. She is crowned with either 12 stars or a Crown with 12 points.

This card as a whole symbolizes the ultimate triumph of the generative force when balanced, lifted up and purified by the Sun of Righteousness, seated on the throne of this world and crowned with the 12 signs of the zodiac. The Eagle is Scorpio, the snake of generative force lifted up into regeneration, or freed from its perverted aspects and able to soar upward to the sun. The Scepter crowned by the symbol of Venus is the power of Motherhood, through which she rules and uplifts the generative force. It also indicates that only through the feminine principles of love, intuition and obedience to the forces of the zodiac, can the Empress reign in freedom and love. Again, as the Eagle is also the symbol of the Soul and the Scepter the symbol of life, together they indicate the Holy Ghost, the magnetic force of Divine Love permeating humanity and attracting mankind back to godhood and the Divine Marriage, even as men and women are attracted by a lower manifestation of the same force in ordinary marriage.

The Crown, whose 12 points represent the 12 stars, indicates the Path and the Power by which humanity can gather up and utilize the 12 forces of the zodiac, but only as the Great Mother-force of Love is enthroned in the sun, and the Soul, like the Eagle, is free to seek its home in the radiant light of Divine Love. It also indicates that when generation is sanctified and illumined by the Spiritual Sun it will be crowned with the 12 powers of the zodiac. Then the iron rod of passion will be turned into the golden Scepter of Love Supreme. Since the Empress combines the feminine principles of love and intuition with the masculine principles of will and power, this symbol indicates that the feminine or negative force of the universe has been combined with the masculine or positive force to form the equilibrated force of the Son or collective humanity, which when it manifests these 2 forces in equilibrium shall rule the world. This card also indicates the sacred word AUM, the creator, preserver and destroyer. The destruction takes place only that out of that which was vile the mighty Venus-Urania may re-create higher and better manifestations. This card therefore symbolizes hieroglyphically, the conveyor of the life-force; kabalistically, understanding; astronomically, Venus as the spouse of Mars, the conveyor of the life-force to earth.

THE 3RD COMMANDMENT.

> "Thou shalt not take the name of the Lord (Law) thy God in vain; for the Lord (Law) will not hold him guiltless that taketh his name in vain."
>
> —*Exodus*, xx, 7.

According to P. Christian, ' "To pronounce a word is to evoke a thought, and make it present; the magnetic potency of human speech is the commencement of every manifestation in the Occult World. To utter a Name is not only to define a Being (and Entity), but to place it under, and condemn it through the emission of the Word (Verbum) to the influence of one or more Occult potencies. Things are, for every one of us, that which it (the Word) makes them while naming them. The Word (Verbum) or the speech of every man is, quite unconsciously to himself, a *blessing* or a *curse;* * * * they are, in a certain sense, either venomous or health-giving, according to the hidden influence attached by the Supreme Wisdom to their elements, that is to say, to the letters which compose them, and the *numbers* correlative to these letters. This is strictly true as an esoteric teaching accepted by all the Eastern Schools of Occultism."[8]

The Name referred to in the Commandment is not Jehovah nor the name of any 1 Divine Being, but embraces every expression of the Divine Creative Potency. It is fitting that this should be Commandment number 3, since 3 is a symbol of the Trinity or the 3 fold expression of the Law of thy Good manifesting in all things. This Name or signature of the Divine Law is always expressed as a Trinity, (a) Divine Ideation, (b) its outpouring into manifestation or embodiment and (c) the result produced.

In its largest sense, therefore, the name of the Lord thy God comprises all the expressions by which the forces back of manifestation and evolution can be invoked. This is the ineffable Name or expression which man is unable to pronounce in its fulness until he is more than man. While man is the only animal with the power of expressing his conceptions in articulate speech, nevertheless the vibrations of the Creative Word which brought all things into manifestation reach down into every kingdom of nature and compose the mighty Army of the Voice. It is through these vibrations, invoked by man through the use of words and tones, that man affects every kingdom and awakens vibrations corresponding to his words and tones. These vibrations either help to harmonize, evolve and

[8] *S. D.,* I, 121.

perfect all expressions of the Law (Lord) or they help to create inharmony and resistance to the Law, which must result in disintegration and death instead of integration and life. All words, like the sacred AUM [4] contain the Trinity or number 3 manifesting as the forces of creation, preservation and disintegration. If the forms in the lower kingdoms did not die and disintegrate as a result of their response to the unharmonized, hence antagonistic vibrations awakened and sent forth by man, this world would long since have become a vast pandemonium of discordant, hideous sounds and terrifying noises.

Since every word uttered invokes the manifestation of certain of the potencies of the 3 or the Divine Trinity, words which pervert the Reality which they should express; words which do not embody and express truth, harmony and love, as well as words which definitely invoke and express inharmony, slander and evil, carry with them the seeds of disintegration and death, and therefore take the Name of the Lord thy God (Law of Divine Love and Harmony) in vain. It is a most important task for the aspirant who would be more than man, as well as for the man who would be master of himself and his environment, both to speak words that are true and have back of them the potent and constructive forces of Good, also to make the tones of his voice express the truth and sincerity of his heart. "But I say unto you, That every idle word that men shall speak, they shall give account thereof in the day of judgment. For by thy words thou shalt be justified, and by thy words shalt thou be condemned." [5]

Since every letter of every word we speak has a numerical value, and since numerals are symbols of the cosmic expression of Divine Realities, whose manifestation normally should and ultimately must obey

[4] Often written *OM*, although a 3 fold word. Its pronunciation involves 3 centers, for the Sanskrit *O* has the value of *AU*.

[5] *St. Matthew*, xii, 36-7.

the divine Law of Harmony under the guidance of 1 of the 10 Sephiroth, all misused words will inevitably set up inharmony. And in the process of bringing harmony out of such perversions the Great Law of Karma will not hold him, *i. e.*, the 1 speaking the false or inharmonious words, guiltless. Therefore, while cursing and blaspheming may be called the extreme of taking the Name of the Lord in vain, nevertheless we take that Name in vain in the many lesser degrees indicated above. While none of us are guiltless, yet the karmic Law metes out exact justice to all. The great mass of humanity who thoughtlessly and ignorantly take the Name in vain suffer from the results in a general way, through the inharmonies expressed through nature, *i. e.*, climatic conditions, storms, earthquakes, disease germs, the antagonism of the lower kingdoms, etc., and all the various disintegrating manifestations of the Army of the Voice. Still those who wilfully and with malice in their hearts slander, lie, curse, blaspheme and defy the Lord their God, either as a Supreme Being or as their fellow men made in His image, literally defy the Law of their Good and hence will reap a personal Karma of inharmony, suffering, disease, disintegration and death commensurate with the forces they, as creators, have thus invoked to manifest through them.

While the Law cannot hold us guiltless, until by a full understanding and determined effort we have fully grasped its mighty Truth and become 1 with it; until we have lived it and expressed the Name in all its aspects in our flesh, nevertheless the Law rewards in exact justice every effort toward manifesting its Harmony and Love through the right use of speech; through speech that is true, kind and loving. Every false or inharmonious expression that is conquered and replaced by a true and harmonious 1 is like a radiant star in the firmament of our lives, which will never be extinguished but will go on shedding upon us its light, life and power until the Sun of Righteousness shall rise and flood all our world with the Light of the New Day.

CHAPTER 15

THE NUMBER 4.

> "This number (4) * * * comprehends all powers, both of productive and produced numbers * * * Two multiplied into itself produces 4; and retorted into itself makes the first cube. This cube is the *fertile number,* the ground of multitude and variety * * * Thus the two principles of temporal things, the pyramid and cube, form and matter, flow from one fountain, the tetragon (on earth, the monad in heaven)."
> —*Reuchlin é Cabola,* Oliver, I, ii, 104.

When the Trinity descends and manifests upon the physical plane creation is said to be completed, *i. e.,* when the upper triangle is reflected in the lower, with the diameter common to them both. This descent into the lower half of the circle generates the square thus ⊖. Hence 4 is the Number of the Physical Plane, the most perfect of mundane numbers, for according to occult mathematics it contains the potency of 10, the entire cycle of manifestation.

There are 2 important laws used in occult mathematics, namely, occult *Addition* and occult *Reduction.* Occult *addition* is used to ascertain the occult value or potency of any single figure. This is obtained by adding together all the numbers from 1 up to and including the 1 indicated. Thus 4 contains the potency of 10 because 1+2+3+4=10. Following this law, 7 also equals 10, for 1+2+3+4+5+6+7=28 =10.

By occult *reduction* we ascertain the ultimate value of any number containing more than 1 figure, expressed in terms of 1 of the first 9 digits. This is accomplished by adding together horizontally the figures composing the number and repeating this process until the sum is expressed in 1 figure. All numbers may thus be reduced to 1 of the first 9 digits, thus: 11=2, 12=3, 19=10=1, 144=9, 999=27=9, 777=21=3, 1915=16=7, etc.

Continuing this process, if we arrange the figures from 1 to 19 in groups of 3, forming 7 trinities, we see that every *4th* number is an expression or further elaboration of 1 or unity, as the following tables will show:

TABLE 1.		TABLE 2.
1.	1—2—3	1=1
2.	4—5—6	4=10=1
3.	7—8—9	7=28=10=1
4.	10—11—12	10=1
5.	13—14—15	13=4=10=1
6.	16—17—18	16=7=28=10=1
7.	19	19=10=1

These tables show that the trinity manifests through 6 periods or "days of creation" and rests or is synthesized or summed up in the 7th, 19, which completes the cycle of manifestation, or 10, bringing all back again to unity 1, but in a higher cycle. This shows that 4 completes the 1st series or group of numbers, from which all others are derived, just as there are 4 fundamental geometrical figures ○ | △ □ from which all others are derived. The line in motion generates the ○, the △ and □. And applied to solid figures the ○ generates the sphere and cylinder, the △ generates the pyramid and the cone, while the □ generates the cube and the pillar.

Geometrically the figure 4 is formed by joining the right arm of the cross with the apex, thus ⊕, which symbolizes man standing upright and holding in his right hand the △ of Divinity. The geometrical figure corresponding to 4 is the square, the base of the pyramid, the most stable of all geometrical forms. Hence, both 4 and the □ are symbols of all that is stable, enduring and perfect upon the earth plane. In astrology the □ aspect is considered an evil one, symbolizing the inertia and limitations of matter, yet it can be rendered most fortunate if made into a Foundation Stone upon which to build the life; the cubic stone with which to measure and test all conditions.

The square is generated not only by the reflection  of the Trinity (Triangle) in matter, but also by uniting the 4 ends of the cosmic cross. The ancients represented the Divine Man crucified within a circle, hence the cosmic cross represents the crucifixion which must take place that the Deity may manifest in his creations. The figure of the cross is not an artificial symbol arbitrarily chosen, for it is not only formed naturally by the line containing all the neutral points between the positive and negative poles of every circle (the equator), and crossing the axis at right angles, thus  N S, but it is also naturally formed in the heavens by the 4 bright stars of the 1st magnitude which mark the cardinal points in the heavens, *i. e., Aldebaran* (North), the Eye of Taurus the Bull; *Antares* (East), the Heart of Scorpio the Eagle; *Regulus* (West), the Heart of Leo the Lion, and *Fomalhaut* (South), the Eye of the Southern Fish, or the constellation Aquarius the Man.

As we have said elsewhere: "It is a great mistake to think that the cross was first brought into notice in history during the Christian era. It was already an ancient and sacred symbol long before any of the Races now on earth began. In fact, it is almost impossible to go far enough back in the earth's history to find a period in which this symbol was not known.[1] Indeed we are told that the cross was not identified with the crucifixion of the man Jesus during the early centuries of the Christian era; for "*no figure of a man appears upon the Cross during the first six or seven centuries.* * * * The earliest known form of the human figure on the cross is the crucifix presented by Pope Gregory the Great to Queen Theodolinde of Lombardy, now in the Church of St. John at Monza, whilst no image of the Crucified is found in the catacombs at Rome earlier than that of San Giulio, belonging to the seventh or eighth century."[2]

The cross is universally used to symbolize the outpouring of the divine, creative Life-essence—the Cosmic Christos—that it may manifest within the world of creation as the creative Christ-force or that Power which is the Urge back of and the Cause of all evolution, whether or not the blood (life-force poured out) of a crucified man is the picture used to emphasize the more esoteric symbology. The Egyptian cross or Tau (┬) had this same significance, in fact it was worn not as a symbol of death or of human sacrifice, but as a protecting talisman which focused a power which would help the wearer to unfold his godlike possibilities through the crucifixion of the human and the balancing of the pairs of opposites. It was laid upon the breast of the Neophyte when, during his Initiation he was placed in a mystic sleep and laid in a crypt or tomb for 3 days. It was also placed upon the breast of the dead after embalmment. The Swastika 卐

[1] See lesson on *The Meaning of the Cross.*
[2] *The Natural Genesis,* Massy, I, 433.

or Thor's Hammer, another form of the balanced cross, is commonly worn as a talisman. In the life of the Neophyte it is supposed to bring about purification, adjustment and balance by blows from its whirling ends or by the hard knocks of Karma, hence its name "Hammer of Thor." All these various forms of the cross symbolize number 4, because Spirit cannot penetrate matter or manifest in creation without forming the cross. And man cannot become spiritualized and enter the realm of the Divine without passing his Initiation by balancing his positive and negative forces through the upliftment of the lower segment of the cross, as it rests in the mire of earth, until the upright equals and balances the horizontal arm.

> "The four arms of the X or decussated cross, and of the Hermetic cross, pointing to the four cardinal points * * * were well understood by the mystical minds of the Hindus, Brahmans and Buddhists, hundreds of years before it was heard of in Europe, for that symbol was and is found all over the world. They bent the ends of the cross and made of it their Swastika 卐, now the Wand of the Mongolian Buddhist. * * * The ⊤ and the astronomical cross of Egypt, ⊕, are conspicuous in several apertures of the remains of Palenque [State of Chiapas, Mexico, where the ruins extend over 25 acres]. In one of the *baso relievos* of the Palace of Palenque, on the West Side, sculptured as a hieroglyphic right under the seated figure, is a Tau. * * * The position is precisely that of a Christian bishop giving his blessing, or the one in which Jesus is often represented while at the Last Supper. * * * The claim that the cross is a purely Christian symbol introduced after our era, is strange indeed, when we find Ezekiel stamping the foreheads of the men of Judah who feared the Lord, with the *signum Thau,* as it is translated in the Vulgate."[8]

[8] *S. D.,* II, 586-8.

There are several forms of the cross, each having a special significance, but all contained in and representing number 4. The form of the cross best known to the Western world is the Latin or Christian cross, the cross of suffering †, but ere this can become the balanced cross +, the Greek cross or the Cross of Mastery—the sign that the Initiation is over and Mastery won—its lower aspect must be purified from misconceptions and lifted up into a perfect balance with its higher aspects.

While in 2 the Divine 1 is met by matter and is crucified upon the cross thus formed, in 4 matter or the physical plane has yielded up its experiences, and upon them as a solid foundation man (5) stands and reaches up into the higher realms. The expression of the □ in matter is the cube, but the cube unfolded forms the cross of crucifixion, thus

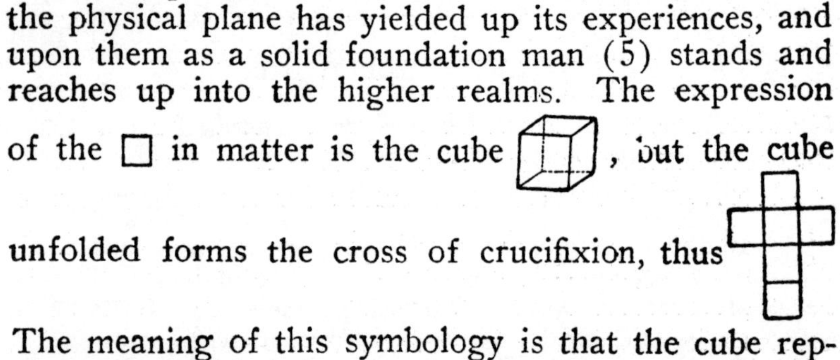

The meaning of this symbology is that the cube represents undeveloped man, the mere human personality who emanated from the 1 and contains within him the potentialities of that Divine 1. But to manifest these potentialities The Christ must be born in his heart, or the spiritual consciousness must be awakened and unfold the cross upon which the lower man must hang until spiritualized and redeemed in number 7. This is demonstrated mathematically by the fact that 4 is the arithmetical mean between 1 and 7, and 4 unfolded becomes the 7, both the 4 and the 7 containing the 10.

Since the physical plane is imperfect and there is always something to be sacrificed and redeemed, the cube is called the Stone of Sacrifice, the Altar upon which the lower personality is sacrificed until the pairs of opposites are balanced by the descent of the Divine Fire which consumes their sacrifice. Therefore if we sacrifice knowingly and willingly, the redemption is accomplished without the suffering which the crucifixion brings about for those who resist and refuse to work with the Law. By thus working with the Law, (the Law of Jesus, the Law of Redemption through Sacrifice), the cross is rolled up into the cube and the Stone of Sacrifice becomes the pure White Stone given "to him that overcometh"; the Foundation Stone to a newer and higher manifestation; that upon which all must be founded; the Stone which the builders rejected, but which is destined to become chief Stone of the corner;[4] the Rock of Ages cleft during its manifestation through man and woman, but reunited when they are united in the Divine.

"Living the higher life and laying the Foundation Stone must be a Soul choice, a response to the urge of the Divine within you; not as a matter of policy, because your friends so choose or because you thereby hope to free yourself from hampering and inharmonious conditions, but a response to the urge of the Soul for union with the Divine; because the Soul speaks. It is the stone upon which you must build your life, both the inner and the outer; for if one of the corners is lacking or imperfectly laid, the superstructure—your life in all the worlds—must totter and fall in ruins about you (to be laboriously rebuilt later on). It is that quality of stability upon which may be focused all that the Great Law shall bring into manifestation. This stability must be established upon the physical plane and remain unshaken through all the cataclysms of life ere the Temple of the Heavenly Man, your Divine Self, can be erected upon it. Nothing can endure that is not founded on this rock."[5]

---

[4] See *St. Matthew*, xxi, 44, and I *Peter*, ii, 6.
[5] See lesson *The Mental Foundation*.

After the Foundation Stone has been laid in the physical world it must also be laid in the mental world, as described under number 14 in Volume II of this work.

Regarding the circle as the limits of the cycle of manifestation, the square circumscribed *about* the circle represents the New Jerusalem of the higher realms which becomes reflected in the square inscribed *within* the circle, or the plane of its physical manifestation. 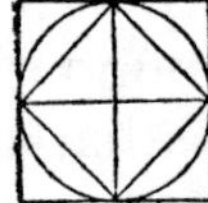

4 is the symbol of the New Jerusalem which cometh down from heaven 4 square, 1st in the hearts and lives of the followers of The Christ and later for humanity and the world. It descends as the result of the pairs of opposites, which rule the physical plane, being transmuted, balanced and squared. In other words 4 is all that is mundane and opposed to the Divine, made square with it or permeated and filled with the Divine; earth's lessons learned and the fullness of experience garnered. The New Jerusalem is described as "coming down from God out of heaven, prepared as a bride adorned for her husband." A bride is not only arrayed in gorgeous apparel, but she is also prepared to leave her old life in her father's house and through this sacrifice blend her life with that of her husband to make a foundation upon which their 1 united life can be built.

4 is used in many ways in the *Bible* and in all other sacred scriptures, as well as in occult literature. The Holy City must be laid 4 square, the mystical "white stone" is square, and there are the 4 cardinal points, North, South, East, and West, presided over by the 4 great Angels or Regents, symbolized by the 4 sacred

animals of *Ezekiel, Daniel* and the *Apocalypse,* namely, the Bull, the Lion, the Eagle and the Man.[6] In the Orient these Regents are called the 4 Great Kings or Maharajas and are related to the 4 Lords of Karma or the 4 great Powers which make square, balance and adjust the workings of the Great Law that love, justice, equilibrium and harmony may ultimately prevail. They are connected with Karma because the Law needs physical and material agents to carry out and execute its decrees; the 4 kinds of winds, for instance, admitted to have their respective evil and beneficent influences upon the health of mankind and every living thing.

> "They are the Regents, or Angels who rule over the Cosmical Forces of North, South, East and West, Forces having each a distinct Occult property. There is Occult philosophy in the Roman Catholic doctrine which traces the various public calamities, such as epidemics of disease and wars, and so on, to the invisible 'Messengers' from the North and West. 'The glory of God comes from the way of the East', says Ezekiel; while Jeremiah, Isaiah, and the Psalmist assure their readers that all the evil under the Sun comes from the North and West."[7]

This, however, must be understood in its esoteric interpretation, each point of the compass having its own occult significance and potencies. According to the *Book of Enoch:* "I then surveyed the receptacle of all the winds, perceiving that they contributed to adorn the whole creation, and preserve the foundation of the earth. * * * The first wind is called eastern, because it is the first. The second is called the south, because the Most High there descends, and frequently there descends *he who* is blessed forever. The western wind has the name of diminution, because there all the luminaries of heaven are diminished, and

[6] These zodiacal signs—*Taurus, Leo, Scorpio* and *Aquarius*—are no longer the cardinal signs, because through the precession of the equinoxes they have retrograded 1 sign, making the signs which precede each, *i. e., Aries, Cancer, Libra* and *Capricorn* the cardinal signs for the present age.

[7] *S. D.,* I, 147-8.

descend. The fourth wind, which is named north, is divided into three parts: one of which is for the habitation of man; another for seas of water, with valleys, woods, rivers, shady places, and snow; and the third part contains paradise."[8]

"Who are those whom I have seen on the four sides * * *? The first is the merciful, the patient, the holy Michael. The second is he who presides over every suffering and every affliction of the sons of men, the holy Raphael. The third, who presides over all that is powerful, is Gabriel. And the fourth, who will inherit eternal life, is Phannel. These are the four angels of the most high God, and their four voices which I heard. * * * I also beheld the four winds which bear up the earth, and the firmament of heaven."[9]

"The powers and forces thus symbolized are not mere abstractions, but are the intelligent, entitized forces so often referred to in the writings of the Christian Fathers as the "Messengers," "Angelic Virtues," "Spirits" or "Angels." Thus do the Regents of the 4 Winds, with their hosts or armies of living powers, bring to the earth and to mankind their particular forces, without which evolution could not be completed. From this we learn the great lesson of unity in diversity: that each Soul must work in its own way, just as the winds accomplish their own work even though apparently adverse."[10]

"The 4 beasts also symbolize the 4 corners of the earth and the 4 Winds of Heaven. The wind, like the breath of the physical body, is a manifestation of the Spirit, which comes from we know not whence and goeth we know not whither. It is said that from the North and West come all diseases and all afflictions, while from the East and South come all benefits. The winds, like the breath of the physical body, are but

---

[8] *Book of Enoch,* xviii, 1,—lxxvi.
[9] *Ibid,* chap. xl-xviii.
[10] See *The Message of Aquaria,* Curtiss, 128.

vehicles of spiritual powers operating on earth, through which the Lords of Karma bring about Their decrees, even that which seems to be evil ultimately resulting for the benefit of the world and its inhabitants. Just as the signs of the zodiac have their Rulers, so do the 4 quarters of the earth. The powers which operate in the creations of earth are focused in these 4 cardinal points, or rather their Rulers manipulate certain creative forces, both in the evolution of the globe and in the individual. These forces being both cause and effect are the Law of Karma. In the spiritual life these beasts, or Lords, symbolize the power *to Know,* the power *to Dare,* the power *to Do* and the power *to Keep Silent.* Without these four powers the Soul cannot reach mastery." [11]

Éliphas Lévi, in referring to these same spiritual powers, taught that there were 4 qualities of Soul without which true wisdom could not be attained, namely, "an Intelligence illuminated by study *(to Know),* an Intrepidity which nothing can check *(to Dare),* a Will that nothing can break *(to Do),* and last but most important of all, a Discretion *(Keep Silent),* which nothing can corrupt." [12]

The ancient philosophers have been much derided in modern times for teaching that the earth was square. But in speaking of "the four corners of the earth" the original teaching was not that the earth was literally square, although later on this became the belief of the uneducated masses. The ancients used this symbolic expression to indicate the balancing and squaring of earth conditions which is brought about by the 4 Regents of the 4 Winds. For only as earthly conditions are squared can this earth become the cube or "the footstool of God."

The 4 winds are said to usher in the 4 seasons, namely, the East Wind brings Spring, the South Wind

---

[11] See lesson on *The Great White Throne,* for a description of the 4 Beasts.

[12] *Transcendental Magic,* Lévi.

Summer, the West Wind Fall and the North Wind the Winter, which completes the cycle of the year. There are also 4 phases or quarters to the cycle of the moon: the new moon, 1st quarter, full moon and last quarter. Hence these are 2 more instances in which 4 equals the complete cycle 10.

The 4 winds are connected with the Lords of Karma because it is these winds, or the forces which they embody, which are continually bringing about the changes and adjustments upon the physical plane which permit the sacrifice, *i. e.,* through the sunshine and "winds" of spring and summer the matter of the earth sacrifices its gross form and is lifted up into flower, fruit and grain, there to be more perfectly impregnated with the life-force of the sun and the higher kingdoms, while by the "winds" of autumn and winter old forms and limitations are sacrificed and broken up that new and higher forms may manifest in the next cycle. Likewise the Soul in passing through the changing winds of Karma gathers up the spiritual forces and the experiences from them which place its feet (understanding) upon the square Foundation Stone of Truth. Truth is said to be square because only that which can be proved on all planes can endure, *i. e.,* only as the length, breadth and height of it can be measured by unity, the rod of power or 10.

In the *New Testament* the powers of the 4 Beasts and the 4 Winds are represented by the 4 Apostles and the 4 Gospels, Matthew, Mark, Luke and John. These are also the 4 Saints, Angels or Regents of the earth, the 4 Lords of Karma who adjust the conditions symbolized by the negative or evil aspects of the 4 Beasts. *St. Matthew,* "the Man from the East" (Aquarius, the power to Know), is the adjuster of all conditions brought about by man's ignorance. He is called the Publican or Tax-gatherer, the Angel who levies upon mankind tribute to knowledge, the knowledge which shall support the rule of the Divine King. *St. Mark* is the Lion (Leo), the power to Dare. By *Bible* students he is called "the Interpreter of Peter," the Rock. He adjusts the conditions in humanity which arise from the lack, perversion or fickleness of love, which should be the Foundation Stone of the spiritual life, the Rock of Intuition. *St. Luke,* the Bull (Taurus) is called the Physician. As the Bull symbolizes the masses of mankind who toil and labor, *St. Luke* adjusts the conditions brought about by the improper use or enslavement of labor. This he accomplishes or heals through the power of attainment through patient perseverance, the power to Do. *St. John,* the Eagle (Scorpio, the power to Keep Silent), is called "the Beloved Disciple." He adjusts the ills resulting from the stinging power of the scorpion (sexual desire) by lifting it up above the earth to soar in the higher realms. In other words, when the stings of the scorpion are healed, or the lessons resulting from the perversion of sex are learned, the Creative Force which it symbolizes rises upward "on eagle's wings" toward the sun and becomes Divine Love, the beloved of The Christ.

CHAPTER 16

THE NUMBER 4—*(Continued)*.

> "He who aspires to be a sage and to know the great enigma of nature must be the heir and despoiler of the sphinx; his the human head in order to possess speech; his the eagle's wings in order to scale the heights; his the bull's flanks in order to furrow the depths; his the lion's talons to make a way on the right and the left, before and behind."
>
> —*Transcendental Magic,* Lévi, 31.

The Pythagoreans called number 4 "the great miracle; a God after another manner, a manifold; the foundation of nature; the Key-Bearer or Key-Keeper of Nature; the Door of the East," etc. As it was held by them to be the Foundation of Truth 4 was the number upon which they took their oaths. This was to them the same as swearing upon the Foundation Stone of the Truth.

Many ancient and modern languages have a name for the Deity composed of 4 letters, thus the Assyrian *Adad;* Egyptian *Amun, Teut* or *Taut;* Persian *Syre* or *Sire;* Turkish *Esar;* Tartar *Itga;* Arabian *Allh* (or *Allah);* Samaritan *Jabe;* Greek *Theo;* Latin *Deus;* French *Dieu;* German *Gott,* etc. In all these cases the 4 letters indicate God manifesting in His Works, while the addition of another letter to the name, such as changing Allh to Allah, Taut to Thoth, Jesu to Jesus, etc., signifies a personal and human incarnation or embodiment of that God, number 5 being the number of human manifestation.

An ancient legend relates that when God created the 4 Cardinal Points, He left the North unfinished, saying: "If any be equal let him finish it." The esoteric truth back of this allegory is that the North, through the Pole Star, leads into a new and higher octave of world systems, hence cannot be "finished" until all that manifests on this planet has evolved to the point where it can enter the new system.

Éliphas Lévi connects the 4 symbolic Beasts with the 4 magic elements and elementary spirits as follows: "The magical elements are: in alchemy, salt, sulfur, mercury and azoth; in Kabbalah, the macroprosopus, and the two mothers; in hieroglyphics, the man, eagle, lion and bull; in old physics, according to vulgar names and notions, air, water, earth and fire. But in magical science we know that water is not ordinary water, fire not simply fire, etc. These expressions conceal a more recondite meaning. Modern science has decomposed the four elements of the ancients, and reduced them to a number of so-called simple bodies. That which is simple, however, is the primitive substance properly so-called; there is therefore only one material element, which always manifests by the tetrad in its forms. We shall therefore preserve the wise distinctions of elementary appearances admitted by the ancients, and shall recognize air, fire, earth and water as the four positive and visible elements[1] of magic."[2]

In *Genesis*[3] we find 4 mystical rivers represented as watering the Garden of Eden, *Pison, Gihon, Hiddekel* and *Euphrates.* Taking Eden as a symbolic reference to the body of man, these 4 rivers correspond to the 4 great arteries proceeding from the heart which carry the purified blood to the 4 regions of the body indicated. The 1st river *Pison*—whose meaning is "joined together as one"—which "compasseth the whole land of Havilah," refers to the innominate artery which is formed by the right subclavian and the right common

---

[1] For the mystic meaning of the elements see our lessons, *The Elements,* also *Rivers of Life and Death.*

[2] *Transcendental Magic,* 58-9.

[3] ii, 10-14.

carotid arteries "joined as one." The meaning of the word Havilah is "to bring forth; to form, create; to supply strength," all of which vividly portrays the offices of the brain and right arm and head which are supplied by this river of blood. The river *Gihon*—signifying "to run out; to burst forth into thought"—refers to the left common carotid artery which supplies the left side of the brain and head. The 3rd river, *Hiddekel*—meaning "freely flowing"—refers to the left subclavian artery which supplies the left arm. The 4th river, *Euphrates*—meaning to "increase; the creative power; the fruitful river," etc.—symbolizes the descending aorta, the great river of blood that supplies the lungs and the entire body below the diaphragm, including the creative centers. Thus the 4 rivers "water" the whole land of Eden.[4] Among the Greeks there were also 4 symbolic rivers, but these were represented as being in the nether world or the plane of physical embodiment, namely, the *Phlegethon, Cocytus, Styx* and *Acheron,* whose symbology we have described elsewhere.[5]

The number 4 also appears in the 4 "hours" of the day and the watches of the night; in the 4 Cherubim; in the 4 wheels of Ezekiel; in the 4 ages of man, infancy, youth, maturity, old age; in the 4 horses of Neptune and in divers other places too numerous to mention, but always carrying out the basic meaning of a physical foundation.[6]

In many places in the *Bible* we read that if anything is taken unjustly it must be repaid 4 fold. This is not to be taken literally, for it simply symbolizes that the injustice must be squared or that the 4 Lords of Karma must each be satisfied, or the adjustment made on the 4 planes—the earth, the psychic, the mental and

---

[4] See our lesson *The Sixth Angel.*

[5] *Realms of the Living Dead,* Curtiss, 29-32.

[6] For those interested in the problem of squaring the circle through the use of the ratio of 6561 for the diameter, to 20612 for the circumference, discovered by John A. Parker of New York, and proved to be the ratio upon which the pyramids were built, etc., see *S. D.,* I, 332, also *The Mystic Thesaurus,* Whitehead, 50.

the spiritual—by the synthesizing power of the Spirit. This is the key to the workings of the Law of Karma.

The Children of Israel are represented as wandering 40 years in the wilderness. A wilderness is not a desert, for it may embrace beautiful mountains, forests and streams. It is simply a region that has been left to nature and is uncultivated. If we regard the story of the wanderings of Israel as historically true there are many facts hard to reconcile. The *Encyclopedia Britannica* says: "As regards the Mountain of the Law in particular, if the record of *Exodus* 19 is strictly historical, we must seek a locality where 600,000 fighting men, or some two million souls in all, could encamp and remain for some time, finding pasture and drink for their cattle, and where there was a mountain (with a wilderness at its foot) rising so sharply that its base could be fenced in, while yet it was easily ascended, and its summit could be seen by a great multitude below. Where, then, was this mountain?" [7] It is therefore plain that the whole story is an allegory. The Wilderness is the natural or unregenerate world. The Children of Israel are those of God's people who are led out of the darkness of ignorance and the slavery of the senses by an inspired prophet or lawgiver, and who are following the Great Law through the Wilderness into the Promised Land. All the adventures described will be found to express experiences in the unfolding spiritual life.

The 40 years are composed of 4 complete cycles of 10, in this allegory called "years," but called "days" when referring to the 4 periods of fasting which Jesus is .represented as passing in the Wilderness. Those who are seeking the Promised Land and to climb the Holy Mount must wander during these 4 cycles until they learn 4 fundamental lessons concerning the Law of Divine Love. In the 1st, they must learn that all

[7] Article on *Sinai*.

their unhappy experiences, be they sickness, poverty or inharmony, are not punishments inflicted by some arbitrary God or Being, but are the results of their own disobedience to the Law either in the present or past lives. In the 2nd, they must learn that the Law of Love can so order their physical bodies that in their flesh they shall see God; that all sickness is the ultimate result of rebellion against the Law, both personally and through the race-thought. In the 3rd, they must know something of the interpenetration of the various planes of existence, how to protect themselves from undesirable influences from the astral plane, and also realize their duty to themselves, their fellow men, the lower kingdoms and elemental forces—in fact, to all things over which man was given dominion. In the 4th period they must pass a cycle of testing and proving, during which all they have learned in the 3 periods is put to the test and proved.

When this same symbol is used in connection with the 40 days of fasting in the Wilderness it deals with a different phase. Here we find the Christ-man, who has dedicated his life to the uplift of humanity, driven by the Spirit into the Wilderness. Thus are advanced Souls driven into the wilderness of the outer life by the Spirit, through their love of humanity and their desire to help. Once having incarnated in this Wilderness, to a certain extent they forget their high mission and find themselves fasting and alone, seemingly forsaken. They must fast until they learn that even though they have the power to turn the stones into bread, still they do not live by bread alone "but by every word that proceedeth out of the mouth of God." For the dense physical stage of human evolution symbolized by the stones cannot nourish the Christ-man until instead of being a stone it has become the Word made flesh.

Thus they pass 4 cycles of fasting, 1st trying to feed their spiritual hunger with the joys of the material world, but finding that the mere possession of *things* can never satisfy the Soul-hunger. Then they enter upon a new day in which they realize the greatness of mind and perhaps are swept away to the extreme of declaring that "mind is all and all is mind." They now seek in the intellectual conceptions of the mental realm, in subtle philosophies and metaphysical speculations to appease the hunger of their Souls. But sooner or later their Souls find that they are still feeding on the husks and still fasting from that true spiritual food which alone can satisfy. Then they seek satisfaction in the psychic phenomena which their intellectual search has brought to their attention. At 1st perhaps their hunger is appeased by the phenomena of séances, in messages and platitudes from their departed friends, in anything that will lift their consciousness above the material and mechanistic concept of life. Later this proves to be but a mental diversion, altho it is a training which enables them to appreciate the real spiritual Bread of Life which must come from The Christ within and not from without, not even from the disembodied. Thus they pass the 4th day or cycle in proving that none of these things bring Soul satisfaction. By this time they are "an hungered," and only then do the angels (messengers of God, not disembodied mortals) come and minister unto them.

Many sincere students are to be found in each of these cycles. But if they are all earnestly seeking spiritual food they are not to be condemned or even looked down upon by those who have taken a step higher. Perhaps no 1, except the Soul who has reached the 4th day, will pass through all phases of fasting in 1 life, but every Soul will pass through either longer or shorter expressions of these periods. The day-periods are those in which enthusiasm fills the Soul and the things it feeds on seem all-satisfying for the time being; the night-periods are those in which the former food no longer satisfies and the Soul is truly hungry and unsatisfied.

There are 4 natural classes of humanity, corresponding to the 4 main divisions of the Grand Man, in 1 of which all mankind finds expression. These great divisions or castes are not arbitrary classifications, but are expressions of the 4 characteristic forms of human activity. Among the Hindus the Grand Man is called Brahma and the 4 classes are said to have sprung from his body as follows: from his head sprang the natural teachers, philosophers, scientists and priests (Brahmans); from his arms sprang the natural warriors, soldiers, rulers and executives (Kshatriyas); from his body sprang the natural husbandmen, perveyors and merchants (Vaishyas), and from his feet those whose attainments fit them only for mechanical and manual labor (Sudras). While this is a natural classification of human activities and social life, which is as easily discernible in the Western world as in the Eastern, in the East it has been greatly over emphasized, greatly abused and degraded by hard and fast lines of cleavage which in their practical workings do not permit the entering of a higher caste from a lower through demonstrated ability and merit, altho such opportunities were always open in the earlier ages, and still are theoretically in India today.

It is unphilosophical to talk about the equality of all men, if the term is used in the usual sense of uniformity; for there is no such thing as equality or uniformity in the manifested universe. Every single expression of life is an expression of an individuality that is different from every other expression. Only in the realms of the undifferentiated is there uniformity. As soon as differentiation begins uniformity is destroyed and individuality reigns. It is true that in their Divine *Essence* and as equally precious expressions of the 1 Life, also in their divine *possibilities*, all men are equal and hence should have equal opportunities to express their Divine Essence and achieve their possibilities. But they are not equal in the degree of their expression of their divinity, nor in the degree of their attainments. The Law is "Unity in diversity," but never uniformity.

There are 4 chief stages in the civilization of man. The most primitive form is the *Nomadic*. In this stage man wanders from place to place in search of food and without any settled place of abode. His food is only that which nature produces without any effort on his part, and which she offers him for the taking, *i. e.*, fruits, nuts, game, etc. This is the stage of irresponsibility. Each day satisfies its own needs, hence no thought is taken or provision made for the future. The welfare of the self reigns supreme. In this rudimentary stage of intellectual and spiritual unfoldment man's highest conception of the Divine is as a mighty and ever-successful Hunter.

The 2nd stage is the *Pastoral*. In this stage man has grasped the idea that he can secure his food more easily by taming animals and raising them in flocks and herds than by having to hunt an individual animal every time he needs food. While he is still more or less of a wanderer, changing his abode with the needs of his flocks and herds, yet he is more settled than in the Nomadic stage; for his wanderings are only within a limited area. Altho little provision is made for the future, except to prepare for and take advantage of the seasons, still responsibility, forethought and the beginnings of unselfishness are being developed. In this stage man's highest ideal of the Divine is as a tender and loving Shepherd.

As the pastoral wanderings or migrations become more restricted man establishes a corral for his herds, founds a more permanent home and begins to cultivate the soil. Thus he passes into the *Agricultural* stage, founds a permanent home, accumulates possessions not easily kept under tents or transported in caravans, and begins to cultivate the arts. In this stage responsibility must be assumed, forethought taken and preparation made for the next year's crops. Also since provision must be made for his family and domestic animals during the winter season, man is forced to develop more unselfishness by providing for others. In this stage his ideal of the Divine is that of an Husbandman or loving head of the household or Father, and his idea of heaven is a mansion in the skies, a home in a blissful realm of perpetual summer, with singing, dancing, etc.

Overgrowth of population in a fixed position necessitates a division of labor, hence there next ensues the industrial period which evolves into the *Scientific* stage. Man now realizes that no individual can live his life to himself alone or without considering and affecting others. He therefore begins to develop co-operative efforts for the best good to all, altho still giving full scope for the expression of individuality within the unity of the whole. As such co-operation requires greater individual responsibility and still greater unselfishness on the part of the individual, in this stage unselfishness reaches its highest expression. "Greater love hath no man than this, that a man lay down his life for his friends."[8] In this stage man's highly developed intellect and spiritual unfoldment shows him that the physical world is but an imperfect materialization of that which is immaterial, hence his

---

[8] *St. John,* xv, 13.

ideal of the Divine is as an all-pervading and life-giving Spirit whose Urge to Manifest the Ideal is the cause of all manifestation and all evolution, that the manifestation and the ideal may become 1 or complete its cycle by returning to its Source.

Let number 4 remind you always to be honest and "square," with your fellow men, *with yourself* and with God. Determine that you will give others and yourself a "square deal"; that you will face and "square up" all mistakes, faults and failings, and thus lay your Foundation Stone that your future life may be founded on the Rock of Truth and be stable; that even though you find this world but a wilderness, and so-called religious teachings but stones, and the voice of the tempter ever in your ear, nevertheless, being firmly established upon your Foundation Stone of Truth, you know that you have within you the power of The Christ to conquer and make square all conditions.

CHAPTER 17

THE 4TH LETTER, *Daleth* (ד)

> "He produced Daleth, and referred it to Fertility; He crowned it, combined and formed with it the Sun in the Universe, the third day of the week, and the right nostril of man."
>
> —*Sepher Yetzirah,* 22.

The 4th letter is Daleth (D), the 3rd of the 7 double letters. It is combined with the sun and referred to fertility. The sun has a double aspect in that while in its positive aspect it is the fructifying power which stimulates fertility, in its negative aspect it scorches, kills, produces putrifaction and causes the opposite of fertility or sterility.

Daleth is called the "womb," for it is the feminine 1st Cause, just as Aleph or number 1 was the masculine 1st Cause. In Aleph the Divine is incorporated in man as Adam; in Beth it finds its home or rest in the feminine Principle, Eve; and in Gimel we have the son or offspring. In another sense Aleph represents man, Beth the home of his Soul and Daleth the offspring. Hence in the 4th letter we return again to the 1st creation, for 4 = 10 = 1.[1] Therefore Daleth is both the womb and a door which was opened only after the 1st creation, for during the 1st, 2nd and up to the middle of the 3rd Race the sexes were not separated. Conditions of physical life were so hard and strenuous that it was only the positive, forceful, masculine aspect of humanity that could fight its way into manifestation and maintain itself. By the time

[1] See page 136, Table 2.

the 4th Race was reached conditions had so evolved and modified that woman was able to maintain herself as a separate being and become the foundation (womb) for the succeeding Races.[2] The Greek form of Daleth is Delta △, a triangle resembling a tent door.

---

[2] For the details of this change see *V. of I.*, chapters xv and xvii.

THE 4TH TAROT CARD

THE EMPEROR

Papus

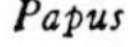

MEDIEVAL

Papus

St. Germain
EGYPTIAN

Smith
MODERN

THE 4TH TAROT CARD, *The Emperor.*

The 4th Tarot Card is called "The Emperor." It agrees with the letter Daleth, which as we have seen is both the womb of nature or the rejuvenated earth fructified by the sun that it may bring forth, and is also the offspring or that which is brought forth. This 4th card expresses the same symbology in that here we find the active aspect of all that the 3rd card expressed in passivity.

Here we see a man seated upon a cubic stone, on 1 side of which is carved an eagle with outstretched wings. The stone is the square Foundation Stone which must be established both in the individual and humanity ere the Emperor can take his seat and rule his domain. The fact that he is seated indicates that he is established, at rest and ruling in the midst of the 4 winds, the position of his legs forming the figure 4 or the completion of the foundation, the establishment of man on the earth plane. The eagle is the power of sex uplifted or Scorpio transformed. The eagle as a symbol of 1 of the 4 cardinal signs indicates freedom and aspiration, the true freedom which has risen out of the limitations of sex and drawn its creative force from the sun. That it is engraved on the cubic stone indicates that only where man and nature are squared can the Spiritual Sun become the creator; only when the New Jerusalem comes down from heaven 4 square will we find no night there, for the Law of thy Good shall be the light thereof.

The Scepter bearing the sign of Venus ♀, which the Emperor holds in his right hand, symbolizes his ability to rule both the force within himself and within his empire (the world) through the Venus-power of Love. Being held in his right hand shows that it is the active, vivifying principle that is being used. In his left hand he holds a globe surmounted by a balanced cross, symbolizing that it is through the power of the balanced cross that he rules. Also, being held in his left hand shows that only through the feminine power of Love can he balance Spirit and matter and gain the power to rule the globe. The Emperor is bearded, and upon his head is a helmet containing 12 points. This is man's Crown of Life, subject however at this 4th step to the forces operating through the 12 signs of the zodiac.

THE 4TH COMMANDMENT.

> "And on the seventh day God ended his work which he had made; and he rested on the seventh day from all his work which he had made. And God blessed the seventh day and sanctified it: because that in it he had rested from all his work which God created and made."
>
> —*Genesis,* ii, 2-3.

Since the study of numbers reveals the fact that 4 is the Number of the Physical Plane; of Stability; of the Foundation Stone upon which our spiritual structure must be reared, we are not surprised to find the 4th Commandment dealing with the 7th day, whose ruling planet, Saturn, is the planet which expresses the characteristics of number 4.

> "Remember the sabbath day to keep it holy. Six days shalt thou labor, and do all thy work; but the seventh day is the sabbath of the LORD thy God."
>
> —*Exodus,* xx, 8.

We might well expect the 4th Commandment to apply solely to man's physical well-being. Yet while its literal interpretation is valuable as an hygienic measure, its meaning cannot be relegated entirely to the physical plane, for it has correspondences on all planes. The 7th or Sabbath day, the day of rest after the 6 days of labor, should not be confused with the 1st day of the week's activities, Sunday, the Lord's Day. It is a misunderstanding of terms and a desire to exalt the day appointed for worship in the new dispensation that has led the Christians to combine the day of rest with the 1st day, their day of worship, while the Jews adhered to the 7th day.

The term Sabbath is derived from the Hebrew word for rest, *Shabbath,* a day that was observed in commemoration of the day on which God rested after the 6 days of creation, *i. e.,* the 7th day. In the Gospels the term Sabbath always indicates the 7th or day of rest, the Lord's day remaining quite distinct until the 3rd century. The dictionary tells us that: "In the middle ages Sabbath always meant Saturday. According to the elder Disraeli, it was first used in England for Sunday in 1554." And since we know that the 6 days of creation are symbols for 6 vast evolutionary periods, so must we look for a symbolic meaning for the 6 days of labor.

Each day of the week has its characteristic powers, forces and significances which should be observed. These are quite as distinct as the forces manifesting during the various seasons, and vary according to the characteristics of the Planetary Deity ruling the day. In the 4th Commandment we are dealing with the day of rest after the 6 days of activity, Saturday or Saturn's day. In 1 aspect Saturn is the same as Cronus or Time, and is represented by a ○, or a serpent swallowing its tail. Saturn is also the Ruler who represents stability, repose, rest, and also form. If we remember that Saturn is spoken of as "Alpha and Omega, the beginning and the end, the first and the last," we will see at once that the 1st and 7th days represent the 2 extremes of the same force, or the head and tail of the serpent, which must meet to close the cycle or circle. Time ultimately brings about a literal, altho often perverted, manifestation of every symbol and esoteric truth. And as we draw toward the close of this present cycle we find in the Western world the meaning of the 7th day literally swallowed up in that of the 1st. But both are necessary if we would progress. The serpent needs a tail as well as a head if we are to lift it up into a Rod of Power. If the head is allowed to swallow the tail it indicates lack of progress, for it forms a closed circuit around and around which we will circle perpetually. But if both head and tail have their proper places we can lift up the serpent's head and form a spiral, along which we can enter a higher plane and a new day of experience and expression.

The Sun's day or the Lord's day is the day in which the Lord or Law sends forth the Divine Light of the 1 God into manifestation. This must be preceded by Saturn's day, both because the ○ must precede the 1, and because the quality of poise, rest and stability must have manifested in the ○ ere the Creative Dot could appear and attract around itself the materials from which the 1 was to manifest and evolve the universe. Being the Sun's day, the 1st day of the week should be sacred to letting the Light shine; to active effort to correlate or establish our oneness with the Divine Ray of the 1 God which has shed its Light into the darkness of our life's orbit or ○. We should be as active, positive and potent in this as was the Dot in manifesting the 1. In other words, the 1st day of the week should not be a day of rest like the 7th, but should be filled with such spiritual and other activities as shall help the Light of the 1 God within us to shine forth; as shall aid the more perfect manifestation of the Law of our Good. This is our 1st duty in beginning the 6 days of labor.

Saturn is described as the 1st Planetary Deity to go forth from the bosom of the Infinite, that he might establish the boundaries of the ○ within which the universe was to manifest, and create the stability upon which the subsequent manifestation might rest and upon which the forces of the other Planetary Deities might focus to bring about the subsequent evolution.[8] Hence Saturn is called both the Initiator and the Tester who determines the degree of stability of our foundation before each advance is attempted. His force will necessarily be the last to return because the laws of stability must be maintained until the Dot has evolved through the gamut of all the numbers and has expanded to the limits of the ○ and fulfilled its cycle of manifestation. The command to rest and acquire stability is therefore an imperative and fundamental law of every form of manifestation, for it represents the completion of a certain phase or cycle of activity. Just as God rested on the 7th day and contemplated all that He had created and saw that it was very good, so must we in a corresponding way—for there is but the 1 Law back of all creation—have a period of rest, silence and meditation at the close of each cycle of activity. This rest must not be merely a change of occupation, but must be a period of cessation from all outward activity; a holy calm, a sacred meditation, during which we contemplate all that we have created during our 6 days of activity. This period of rest and self-examination should be observed not only at the close of each week, but at the close of each day and at the close of each year. It should not be filled with sighs and regrets over our failures and shortcomings, but should be filled with a high resolve and an earnest determination to create more perfect

---

[8] See *V. of I.*, 332.

manifestations during the ensuing period of activity. And this rest, meditation, recuperation and earnest determination will prepare us for the activities of the Lord's day, *i. e.*, positive, spiritual creation.

> "In it thou shalt not do any work, thou, nor thy son, nor thy daughter, thy manservant, nor thy maidservant, nor thy cattle, nor thy stranger that is within thy gates. For in six days the Lord made heaven and earth, the sea, and all that in them is, and rested on the seventh day: wherefore the Lord blessed the sabbath day and hallowed it."

On the Sabbath day not only should we rest from outer activity, gather up the experiences, ratify all that is good in them and build their force into Soul-growth, but we are commanded not to allow any of our creations to work. Our sons and daughters here symbolize the creations of our positive and negative aspects of thought. The manservant and maidservant symbolize the positive and negative acts or work of our hands which serve or accomplish for us. The cattle refer to the lower animal self with all its attendant animal desires. All these are good, useful, even necessary, and should be fed, cared for, trained and used in their proper field of activity for the general well-being of the household. But upon the 7th day or period of completion upon which the Soul enters, all these animal desires, as well as our sons, daughters and servants, must rest or cease their activities.

"Thy stranger within thy gates" refers to all those outside influences which sway or influence us. They are the thought-forces and opinions of the community, for instance, which to a certain extent we must admit within the gates of our consciousness during the 6 days of labor. If we are to be a positive influence for good in our community and be centers of love, peace and harmony in our environment we must pay a certain amount of attention to the conventionalities, and entertain as guests or strangers, according to the rules of our household—our standards of life and conduct—the ideals and thought-forces which we must admit within our gates. In other words we must practice tolerance without subservience. The strangers within our gates do not receive the same treatment as the sons and daughters or the servants and cattle, nor are we responsible for them to the same extent; only for the way we entertain them. On this 7th or Saturn's day, therefore, we must see to it that all these activities of our household shall cease. In other words, by the time we have reached our Sabbath, or the 7th great cycle of our manifestation, and in a lesser degree at the close of each 6 days of activity, we should have been able to so correlate with the force of Saturn that we have established a Place of Peace, of stability and rest, a firm foundation upon which to stand and meet Saturn in his aspect of the Tester; so that we can stand still, poised, undismayed and at rest while the creations of our 6 periods of activity are being scanned, weighed and judged. When we have attained this point in our development Saturn is no longer the grim Tester and Reaper, but is the Initiator who shall admit us into a higher world of consciousness. The 1st step is to follow the 4th Commandment and observe the Sabbath day and keep it *wholly,* in our outer as well as in our inner lives, and prepare for active worship on the Lord's day.

Man has 5 physical senses and has 5 corresponding days in which to exercise, labor with, develop and satisfy them and thus gather all their lessons for the Real Self. But there are 2 higher senses which man as yet has not developed, which correspond to the days which precede and succeed the 5 days of activity. Man can reach his Great Sabbath or period of perfect rest and stability only when he has developed these 2 senses. But to develop them he must follow the rules laid down and arrange for definite periods of rest, relaxation, silence and meditation.

All growth and development proceeds in rhythmic ebb and flow or cyclic periods of activity and inactivity, day and night, summer and winter, etc. Saturn's day is the period of rest at the turn of the tide. Like the boundaries of the ○ it sets limits to the periods of activity. It is like the arm of God reached out to force all things to observe periods of rest, as the night forces us to cease from physical labor, for without it all would soon become exhausted. The positive aspect of the life-force cannot be absorbed, whether from our food or in other ways, while the organism is tense in active work. All is then expression, giving out, it even being injurious to work directly after a hearty meal. Therefore, to renew our forces for another period of activity, a period of relaxation and rest is a vital necessity. At some time during our cycles of manifestation, even in the minor cycle of day and night, we must enter the Silence and renew our forces. If we refuse to do so voluntarily, say by remaining awake and active during night periods, we will soon lose our life-forces, and ultimately great Saturn will compel us to enter upon a period of inactivity that is so long that the organism from which we have withdrawn cannot maintain itself, and we, therefore, call this period of enforced rest and silence physical death.

On the contrary, when we have mastered the Silence and acquired its power, when we are able to keep the Sabbath day *wholly,* we can renew our life-forces, revivify and re-create our bodies periodically little by little and not be obliged to take the longer period of rest, and to re-create an entire new body in another incarnation. Through voluntarily entering the Silence and properly applying its forces, we can gradually change the outer personality so that it will continually express our stage of spiritual unfoldment. At a corresponding period the personality would therefore be quite as different and express quite as great spiritual advance as though we had been forced to leave it and take our rest in the grave and then built up a new body. In other words, if we properly correlate with Saturn through the Silence, and conquer him as the grim Reaper, we can remain incarnate cycle after cycle by re-creating the organism in accordance with the necessities of each new period. In fact this is actually done by those who have entered the higher stages of Mastery and developed the 2 higher faculties, yet who still desire to retain a physical vehicle. But of course to one who has attained such control of the life-forces, the mere possession of a physical body does not confine him to the physical plane, nor does it make the flesh an earthly prison house. This is the great truth back of the doctrine of Regeneration and Immortality in the Flesh.

The Sabbath day, therefore, means a period in which we are to rest, meditate and enter into oneness with all creation; to vibrate in unison with all planes of manifestation; to commune with the 1 God, the union with whom is the object of our evolution. Therefore, the Law blesses this period and hallows it or makes it holy, for it enables us to enter into oneness with the whole.

CHAPTER 18

THE NUMBER 5.

> "Let us note one more thing in relation to the mysterious number Five. It symbolizes at one and the same time the Spirit of Life Eternal and the spirit of life and love terrestrial * * * in the human compound; and, it includes divine and infernal magic, and the universal and the individual quintessence of being."
>
> —*The Secret Doctrine,* Blavatsky, II, 612.

> "There is but one temple in the Universe, and that is the body of Man. Nothing is holier than that high form. * * * *We* are the miracle of miracles—the great inscrutable Mystery."
>
> —*Lectures on Heroes,* Carlyle.

After the Foundation Stone has been laid 4 square, the number 5 must next be considered. This is the most deeply occult of all the digits, and few grasp its full significance and what it stands for in their evolution and accomplishment. 5 is the Number of Humanity and symbolizes man in a 2 fold aspect, for man stands at the apex of physical evolution, the crowning point of all the lower kingdoms, and the forerunner and image of God, or stands midway between 1 and 10. "Man is the universally structured type. In one aspect all lower types rise toward man and are completed in him. * * * Moreover, man is the only species that stands erect, with cerebrum poised at right angles to the spine;—the only species with a spoken language, an alphabet, a recorded history, and a prospective future."[1] Being composed of the 2 and the 3, number 5 shows that in humanity the terrestrial and the Divine meet and blend.

---

[1] *The Romance of Revelation Through Natural History,* Edward Whipple.

By occult addition 5 equals 1+2+3+4+5=15. Number 15 is sometimes called the devil, but by occult reduction 15=1+5=6, the Number of The Christ-force, the antithesis of the devil. Therefore, as number 5 man stands midway between The Christ and the devil.[2] Also number 5 is composed of 2 equal parts with 1 in the middle, thus: 2-1-2 or man and woman co-equal, with the Divine 1 life as the balance or equalizer of both.

Number 5 is composed of 4 and 1 or the foundation of nature and the divine 1 Life manifesting through it. This points to man's true constitution, for he contains within him, even in his physical body, all the principles and forces to be found in manifested nature, and during his intra-uterine life passes through stages analogous to the various kingdoms of nature—vegetable, fish, reptile, animal, up to the human. Hence man is a synthesis of the macrocosm, the squaring of all the forces or 4. But he is also the direct intelligent agent of the 1, or God's representative on earth.

Thus number 5 means man, but man standing upon and dominating the lower, the physical, the human, and reaching up into the higher realms, the Divine. For the number 5, like man's 5th Principle, mind, is dual. It belongs both to the lower square and to the higher triad. It is man with his 2 feet planted firmly upon the Foundation Stone on earth, but with his head in the heavens. His feet have 5 toes each because without the dual aspect of his 5 senses—his understanding of the physical plane—the foundation upon which he stands would be imperfect.

His 2 hands symbolize his dual power of accomplishing through the higher joined to and dominating the lower. The 5 fingers on each hand symbolize the fact that to be complete or balanced man must manifest 2 fives and become 10. For only by using both his

---

[2] See *The Key of Destiny*, Curtiss, Chapters xxiv to xxviii.

hands can he accomplish his perfect work. He has 2 hands because he must accomplish on the physical plane, by dealing with and using the pairs of opposites according to the Law of Duality, and by their use be about his Father's business, in workshop, field, office or home, even as Jesus is said to have worked in his father's carpenter shop. But at the same time he must work out and accomplish his higher mission in helping on the evolution of all the kingdoms, and hence the planet itself.

With 1 hand he can reach up and take the hand of his Father-in-heaven and accomplish in the higher realms, and at the same time he can reach down with the other and help on the evolution of the lower kingdoms, thus uniting Spirit and matter in humanity and becoming the Universal Mediator.

5 is the number of the planet Mercury, ruler of the Intelligent Principle in man. This is symbolized by the winged Messenger of the Gods, representing the power (thought) which enables man to stand in the center of the universe and either send his thought down into the depths or soar into the highest realms cognizable by man. So does number 5 stand in the center of the numerical system—1, 2, 3, 4, **5**, 6, 7, 8, 9—being the only number which is not paired to produce 10, thus: 1+9=10, 2+8, 3+7 and 4+6 all equal 10, leaving 5 unpaired, it forming 10 only when joined to another and complementary 5. As 10 is the number of a complete cycle, this proves mathematically that man or 5 can never complete his cycle of evolution and spiritual attainment until his number has been doubled or until he has found his true counterpart or complement. The same truth is revealed in the *Bible* allegory in which the pairs of birds and animals were brought to Adam to be named, "but for Adam there was not found an help meet for him,"[3] until he was

[3] *Genesis*, ii, 20.

doubled or until he had found his equal. This again shows that man stands at the middle point of evolution, overshadowing and influencing the kingdoms beneath him, as he is overshadowed and influenced by the kingdoms above him. Therefore, just as each of the other digits can be paired to make 10, while 5 remains alone, so Adam had to remain alone until his equal was evolved. This is a mathematical proof of the equality of the sexes. The true man, like number 5, is composed of the masculine and feminine principles, for 5 is made up of the masculine 3 and the feminine 2. On this account the Pythagoreans taught that number 5 rules marriage. Number 5 is called the Number of the Heart because it stands unpaired in the center of the decade (10) as the heart stands an unpaired organ in the center of the body.

5 is also called the Beam or Balance since, like the heart, it stands at the center of the cross formed by the upright body and the outstretched arms. This indicates that 1 important object of man's evolution is to attain balance upon the cross of matter, for The Christ in him must be crucified upon this cross until balance is attained. Again man is the Beam through which the Scales of the Universe, Spirit and Matter, must be balanced. "The ancients had a maxim, 'Pass not above the beam of the balance,' that is—be not cause of injury; for they said, let the members in a series form a Balance Beam. Thus when a weight depresses the Beam, an obtuse angle is formed by the Depressed side and the Tongue verticle, and an acute angle on the other. Hence it is worse to do than to suffer injury, and the authors of injury sink down to the infernal regions, but the injured rise to the gods. Since, however, injustice pertains to inequality, equalization is necessary, which is effected by addition and subtraction."[4] But reference to number 5 as the

[4] *Numbers,* Westcott, 60.

Balance Beam has a far greater significance than appears on the surface, for it again refers to man's place at the mid-point in the scale of evolution, where he must not only gain balance within himself, but must become the Beam by which the lower kingdoms shall be lifted up, weighed and matter redeemed by the power of The Christ working through him. The same idea is expressed frequently in the *Bible,* much importance being given to a just balance, "Just balances, just weights, a just ephah, and a just hin, shall ye have."[5] The book of *Job* being but an allegory of Initiation, Job is made to say: "Let me be weighed in an even balance, that God may know mine integrity."[6] Indeed this is what Initiation does. Hence to obtain the higher Initiations we must seek balance and not be tossed hither and thither by the pairs of opposites (the 2) but balance them through the power of the Divine (the 3) within. "A false balance is abomination to the Lord (the Law); but a just weight is his delight."[7] When king Belshazzar, the last king of Babylon, was judged, the 5 "fingers of a man's hand wrote over against the candlestick upon the plaister of the wall of the king's palace; and the king saw the part of the hand that wrote. * * * And this is the writing that was written * * * MENE; God hath numbered thy kingdom, and finished it. TEKEL; Thou art weighed in the balances, and art found wanting. PERES; Thy kingdom is divided."[8] Thus the division of man's kingdom is ever the final result of an unjust balance; for through an unjust balance the pairs of opposites sweep man away from the △ of the Divine; the 3 and the 2 are separated and his kingdom is divided; the earthly (4) is separated from the Divine (1).

Among the Greeks the number 5 was held so sacred that on the lintels of their temples where the numerals

---

[5] *Leviticus,* xix, 36.
[6] *Job,* xxxi, 6.
[7] *Proverbs,* xi, 1.
[8] *Daniel,* v, 5, 26-7-8.

were carved, the number 5 was inlaid in pure gold. This numeral was also carved on an amulet and worn around the neck by the Greeks and Romans as a protection against evil spirits.

5 refers to the 5 sacred words—corresponding to the 5 sacred words of Brahma—said to have been written upon the shining garment of Jesus at his glorification, namely, *"Zama Zama Ozza Rachama Ozai,"* which is translated "The robe, the glorious robe of my strength." The reality back of this symbol is that number 5 represents the 5 mystic powers which must be attained and manifested through the robe of flesh by every resurrected Initiate after he has passed his 3 days in the tomb, ere he can attain the Great Initiation symbolized by the resurrection of Jesus. These 5 mystic powers are the result of the unfoldment and use of man's 5 senses upon the inner planes of consciousness. Today the true use of man's senses is as it were covered with a veil, so that only in exceptional cases is 1 here and there able to extend the functioning of his senses to the inner worlds. Clairvoyance, while often called a 6th sense, is but the extension of the sense of sight to include the astral world, clairaudience, the extension of hearing, psychometry, the sense of touch, etc., taste and smell being generally overlooked. But this is only drawing aside 1 corner of the veil, for when man dons "the glorious robe of his strength" he will find the functioning of his senses extended as far beyond the astral as the range of a color is extended by the multiplication of its shadings. And out of the synthesis of all these extended senses there will be evolved a new or 6th sense which will be incomprehensible to the man who is confined to a more limited use of his senses, and from the perfection of the 6th sense a 7th will be evolved. It is to the experiences of these higher worlds, reached momentarily during

periods of meditation and contemplation, which St. Paul alluded when he said they were "unlawful (*i. e.*, impossible) to utter" or express in words.

The body thus glorified through the 5 powers is called the Robe of Initiation. Unless the Neophyte has donned this Robe, and manifested its powers in the flesh, the Great Initiation has not been passed. These powers become 7 only after the robe of physical existence has been laid aside and the Soul has donned the glorious, immortal Body of the Resurrection, the Seamless Robe of Jesus, called the Nirmanakaya Robe, or the Body of the Fire-breath. In other words, man is the Lord of Creation when he has woven the 5 mystic powers into his body and donned "the glorious robe of his strength." But when he has donned the Nirmanakaya body he has become more than man. This should give the student a glimpse of what ultimate Mastery means, yet it should not discourage him; for we see the miracle being foreshadowed every day in momentary glimpses and visions of the higher worlds, and we have the prophecy given us in symbolic dreams.

Man or humanity has 3 divine offices or functions, Prophet, Priest and King, and 2 physical expressions, male and female, through which the divine functions must be manifested on earth ere perfection is attained. As he transmits the Will of the Divine to earth he becomes the Prophet in the true meaning of the word, *i. e.*, "one who speaks as the inspired representative of a divine Being or interprets the divine will." As he mediates between the lower and the higher and holds out his hands in blessing he becomes the Priest; and as he rules himself and all the lower kingdoms he becomes the King who is Lord over all. As long as man instills enmity, cruelty and antagonism into the lower kingdoms by his ruthless slaughter of birds and animals for sport, etc., and slays his fellowmen in war, the lower kingdoms will retaliate. The curse which God is represented as placing on the lower kingdoms when man was turned out of Eden was in reality a prophecy of the Karma which man must continue to reap from the lower kingdoms because of the forces he places upon them, his resulting suffering and death slowly bringing about an awakening to his true heritage, *i. e.,* his power as Priest to bless all kingdoms. And verily just as the curse has operated and still operates today, so shall the blessing, until some day man shall find himself King and Ruler over all the kingdoms of earth.

CHAPTER 19

THE NUMBER 5—*(Continued).*

> "The Fifth Group of Celestial Beings is supposed to contain in itself the dual attributes of both the spiritual and physical aspects of the Universe; the two poles, so to say, of Mahat, the Universal Intelligence, and the dual nature of man, the spiritual and the physical. Hence its number Five, doubled and made into Ten, connecting it with Makara, the tenth sign of the Zodiac."
>
> —*The Secret Doctrine,* Blavatsky, I, 241.

The celestial sign Capricorn, which is today the 10th sign of the zodiac, is composed of 28 stars (28=2+8=10), grouped in the form called the goat, and symbolizes this number 5 in its dual aspect. This is the most mystical, yet the most illuminating sign of the zodiac when we learn to correlate with its forces, for it shows man how to become the Lord of Creation.

> "The *Fifth Order* [of Celestial Beings] is a very mysterious one, as it is connected with the microcosmic pentagon, the five-pointed star, representing man. In India and Egypt, these Dhyanis were connected with the Crocodile, and their abode is Capricornus. * * * It becomes the task of the Fifth Heirarchy—the mysterious Beings that preside over the constellation Capricornus, Makara, or 'Croceodile', * * * to inform the empty and ethereal animal form, and make it the Rational Man. * * * The Crocodiles in the celestial Nile are 5, and the God Toom * * * calls forth these Crocodiles in his *fifth* creation."[1]

In olden times Capricorn was called Makara, the fishman or the crocodile. Even today its symbol is a goat with the body of a fish, another glyph for man's

[1] *S. D.,* I, 254; II, 613.

power to swim in the depths, yet climb the loftiest peaks. It is the leviathan mentioned in *Job* (xli), which emerges from the depths at the beginning of every cycle, climbs to the highest point of attainment and returns to the depths at the close of the cycle. *Ma* means 5 or man and *kara* means a hand, hence *Makara* means the hand of man, his power to reach up and accomplish that unto which he puts his hand. The hand of man distinguishes him from all other animals, it being far more developed than that of the apes. It is not only the organ by which he accomplishes today, but it contains the record of all that he has accomplished in the past and a prophecy of that which he can accomplish in any 1 incarnation. "I will write my law upon their hands."

What is true of the individual is correspondingly true of the Races. We are passing through the 5th Great Race and are still within the shadow of the 5th sub-race. Bearing in mind the possibility of everything symbolized by number 5 becoming the overshadowing power and dominating that which is physical, also its dual nature by which it can reach up into the Divine, we can grasp the significance of evolution, and especially of this cycle through which mankind is passing today. A glance at history will show us how man or humanity has dominated the lower kingdoms; how he has mastered the elements as they work in and through himself and nature. He has delved into the earth and brought forth her treasures. He has harnessed the lightning and with it girdled the earth. He has made the flame his servant, and has traveled through the air. He has accomplished all this because he is man, the 5th creation; because he can reach up above the things of earth and enter the higher realms. Just as the half terrestrial and half aquatic animal Makara is supposed to dwell in the sea or climb to the mountain tops, so can man sink himself beneath the sea of illusion—the material world—or climb to the heights of spiritual attainment.

"The great warrior race of India, the Sikhs, wear 5 articles whose names begin with K. *Kes,* long hair; *Kaugha,* a comb; *Kripan,* a sword; *Kachh,* short drawers, and *Kara,* a steel bracelet." [2] They have 5 *Essentials* in their religion, namely, (1) *Simplicity* of belief, worship, life; (2) *Salvation for All;* (3) *Unworldliness*—to be in the world but not of it is their glory; (4) *The Name,* the repetition of the sacred name *Wahguru,* and (5) *Meditation,* "They who meditate on God are emancipated." Their 5 virtues are contentment, compassion, piety, patience, and morality. The 5 deadly sins are lust, anger, covetousness, worldly love, and pride.

The mystic wand—said to have been used by Moses and Aaron and all Initiates—is described as a rod with a 5-pointed star at its end (Fig. 6) with which it is

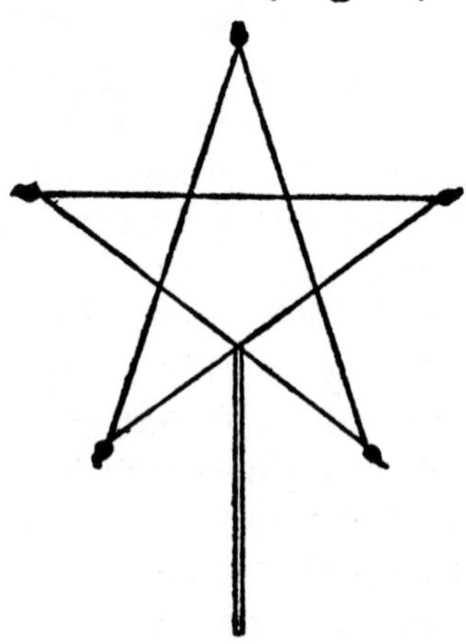

Fig. 6

said all magical rites—both white and black—are performed. Before this magic symbol of the pentacle

[2] *The Religion of the Sikhs,* Field, 26.

every elemental force must bow. According to Éliphas Lévi: "The empire of the will over the astral light, which is the physical soul of the four elements, is represented in magic by the pentagram. * * * The pentagram signifies the domination of the mind over the elements, and by this sign are enchained the demons of the air, the spirits of fire, the phantoms of the water, and ghosts of earth. Equipped with this sign, and suitably disposed, you may behold the infinite through the medium of that faculty which is like the Soul's eye, and you will be ministered unto by legions of angels and hosts of fiends."[8] But this must not be taken to mean that by the mere possession of this mystic symbol all these things can be brought to pass. For while the symbol is indeed potent, still only as man recognizes his divinity and unfolds the cube within and is crucified upon its cross, can he become both magician and the true talisman. Man himself is this pentacle, for with his hands out-stretched, his feet spread and his head erect, he forms the 5-pointed star 

Standing upon the Foundation Stone of Truth, with his hands upraised in praise or outspread in blessing, and with his head to interpret the reports of his 5 senses, he must perfect his manhood and dominate all the kingdoms. But he must begin by dominating himself, instead of oppressing and dominating his fellow man and the lower kingdoms.

The flames, which are said to issue from the 5 points of the pentacle on the end of the wand, are the powers inherent in the perfected body, the glorious robe of man's strength. For when the 5 senses of man are illumined by Divine Fire, they will radiate the spiritual powers by which he can perform all the miracles of

[8] *Transcendental Magic*, 61.

Moses the Lawgiver and Emancipator. The mystic significance of this symbol is that as man, through his spiritual development, lifts up the fiery force of the Kundalini power which functions through the spinal column (the rod), and with it flaming forth from his 5 extremities and illuminating his 5 senses (the pentacle) on all planes, he becomes indeed a magician, capable of performing either white or black magic. The flaming pentacle also represents man's uplifted hand with his magnetic force streaming from his 5 fingers. The flaming pentacle is but another version of the truth symbolized by the parable of the 5 wise virgins who kept their lamps trimmed and burning, while the pentacle reversed refers to the 5 foolish virgins who could not enter in.

The Roman general, Antigonus, who was beheaded by Mark Antony after the former's raid into Syria with the Parthians in A. D. 40, is said to have encouraged his troops on 1 occasion by telling them that he had been shown a pentacle—regarded as a symbol of power, success and safety—in a dream. In the worship of Dionysos or Bacchus, the leaves of ivy and the vine were used in symbolic decorations, both leaves being shaped like a somewhat flattened pentacle.

Since the pentacle represents man, its reversal—the 1 point down and the 2 points up—is a symbol of black magic, for this would place man's head and hands on the earth and his feet in the air. This would symbolize man focusing his 5 God-powers downward on the lower planes; on himself instead of on the Divine, and proceeding downward instead of evolving upward; using his head to scheme and his hands to pull down that which is uplifting and helpful, as he grasps for self at the expense of others, instead of blessing and uplifting all. His feet in the air would indicate man trampling God under foot and making his own intellect (feet—understanding) his God. In thus turning his powers downward he perverts both life (3) and love (2). In other words, the pentacle reversed symbolizes man immersed in self and aspiring toward self-aggrandizement instead of toward selfless union with nature, his fellow men and with the Divine. Therefore never reverse this symbol, especially when worn upon the person as an ornament.

While by reversing this magical symbol—as is intentionally done by black magicians—certain results of a diabolical character may be attained, no black magician seeking merely for phenomena or personal power has ever or can ever truly enter into man's heritage of power. Éliphas Lévi, although assuring us of the potency of this symbol and at the same time stating that the position of the points is of no consequence, nevertheless, as a result of such reversal, according to his own descriptions, passed through such experiences as the ordinary student could not endure and retain his sanity and which even Lévi could not think of without a shudder. Such diabolical experiences, while possible as a result of the perverted use of magic, are no more a necessary part of man's higher development than the ferocity and antagonism of beast, the deadliness of reptile, the poison of herb or the devastation of storms and cataclysms, are a necessary part of the phases of his physical development. Once created and brought into manifestation, however, they are utilized by the Great Law to awaken man to the necessity of seeking for a higher and more Divine power than that of his mere human intellect. All such things ultimately work for good in that even through suffering they teach man that he creates and evokes ill through his misuse or perversion of his God-powers. All the sin, suffering, disease, antagonism and unbrotherliness manifesting in the world today are the result of man's reversal or perversion of the sacred pentacle, *i. e.,* himself and his powers.

In *The Voice of the Silence* we read of the 7 portals which lead the aspirant across the waters "on to the other shore," and the mystic keys which open them. The key which opens the 5th portal is "the dauntless energy that fights its way to the supernal Truth, out of the mire of lies terrestrial."[4] Without this energy which knows no defeat, all his powers would remain dormant. In other words, it takes dauntless energy and clear seeing for man to balance in himself the extremes of the pairs of opposites, called here "lies terrestrial"; for it means being absolutely true to his Real Self, fixing his gaze upon the Divine △ whose light alone can illumine the lower self and show him how to attain a just balance. This energy is quite as necessary in his spiritual unfoldment as it is in the accomplishments of his physical life.

Let number 5 and its symbol, the pentacle, remind you 1st that man is both human and Divine; that he stands to the lower kingdoms as a God, to bless or curse in proportion to the degree to which he finds a just balance and metes out just weight to all things. Hence at the entrance to the Path of Attainment stands the injunction, "Man, know Thyself," for only as man knows his divine powers and his mundane pairs of opposites, and has earnestly gathered up all that he finds in the lower self, and has resolutely cast it into the crucible, that it may be purified and harmonized by the Divine and brought to perfect balance in him, can he truly know himself. Let it also remind you that as man you stand in the center of your universe and are responsible for your use of the powers which enable you to rise to the heights of spiritual attainment or sink lower than the beasts.

With this necessary prelude, try to realize that

---

[4] *Fragment,* III.

within you there is this divine, magical power of accomplishing; of ruling yourself, the earth and the lower kingdoms, and of knowing the secrets of Nature. But, beloved students, remember that this can be accomplished only by laying 4 square the mystic Foundation Stone in your hearts and lives, and upon it focusing the forces which you would use; for without this foundation the forces you seek to use will tear you in pieces and the structure of your lives will fall in ruins about your heads, like the man in the Gospel who built his house upon the sand instead of upon the Rock of Truth. Your magic wand, with its pentacle, must 1st be pointed inward upon the Stone and made to dominate yourself ere you can stand upon your Foundation Stone and dominate in the higher realms.

Begin then today to realize your magical possibilities. Realize that your power is commensurate with the use you make of it. While you use it to oppress, degrade or dominate your fellow men, or for selfish purposes, it is mercifully limited, but when lifted up upon the wand of spiritual aspiration, and filled with the flame of love, ardor and fervor to accomplish the mission of The Christ, there is no limit to its possibilities. Realize that while there is 1 dark corner in your personality which you refuse to make obey your magic wand, by just so much is your power curtailed. You are glued to that spot, whatever it may be, until you have become its ruler. How can you look for spiritual power or expect to penetrate into the 6th realm when you have not dominated the 4th? when you have not laid your Foundation Stone 4 square and cannot dominate yourself? Again we say: "Man, know thyself!"

CHAPTER 20

THE 5TH LETTER, *Hé* (ה).

> "God produced Hé, predominant in speech, crowned it, combined it and formed with it Aries in the Universe, Nisan (April) in the Year, and the right foot of Man."
>
> —*Sepher Yetzirah,* 24.

The 5th Hebrew letter is Hé, 1 of the 12 simple letters. It corresponds to the zodiacal sign Aries and with the function of the breath in its relation to speech. As we have learned that number 5 wherever found refers to man or humanity in some aspect, so the 5th letter represents man as distinguished from all other animals. For while Hé is the Breath of Life which is shared by all animals, yet only man has the principle of Intelligence (Aries, the head) so well developed that he can use the breath to formulate and express his ideas in intelligent speech. While all animals have some form of intelligent communication, still only man has the power of speech.

Hé, however, expresses more than the breath which forms speech. Its greatest and most important meaning, and the 1 which was generally used by the Hebrews, is in its relation to the renewal of life. Physical breath alone cannot accomplish this. It can prolong physical life somewhat, but is incapable of renewing it until it is consciously combined with the psychic breath, in which case it at once becomes the mediating principle between God and man, and between man and nature, also the link which attaches body to Spirit. Hence Hé is not only breath, but vitalized and spiritualized breath.

The sign Aries, which is here referred to the 5th letter, is the crown-sign of man, ruling the head. While we are told that "out of the abundance of the heart, the mouth speaketh," yet if man did not manifest his supremacy in his position at the head of the animal kingdom through the use of his head and the power of speech, he could not maintain that position. In the letter Hé, as in number 5, we find man or the microcosm considered as a vehicle for the expression of the forces of the macrocosm; again the link between God and Nature.

Hé is also called a Window in that he who has mastered the mysteries of the breath can look with clear eyes—which are the windows of the Soul—through the prison house of flesh and the limitations of matter and behold the glories of the heaven world. It was this letter Hé, corresponding to our letter H, that was added to the names of both Sarai and Abram to make them Sarah and Abraham. And by the bringing forth of their son Isaac—meaning laughter—the life of both was renewed and prolonged. Later on Abraham was commanded by the Lord (the Law) to offer up as a burnt offering his renewed life, joy and laughter (Isaac). Indeed, many of us think we are called upon to make the same sacrifice when life seems to demand that we give up that which is most dear to us. But after submitting to the decree and passing his test Abraham found a ram (Aries) caught by its horns (powers of the head) in the thicket to take the place of his child of promise as a sacrifice. Thus will we always find that when we are willing to make the sacrifice which the Law seems to demand, after we have passed the test interiorly we will not have to make the sacrifice outwardly, for we will find a substitute at our right hand.

The ram symbolizes the head and its powers which

are caught in the tangle of intellectual misconceptions which have resulted because man has been misled by the speech of those who have misinterpreted the Law (Lord), so that the physical mind or rational, human consciousness cannot see the Angel of Truth standing before the altar upon which we must place our sacrifice. Yet as a result of the cry which bursts from our hearts as we bind our Isaac upon the altar a new vision is vouchsafed to us. We open our eyes and see the ram and realize that it is the misconceptions of the head and the perversions of our powers which we must lay upon the altar that they may be purified by the Fire of the Law. We will then understand that it is this ram that must be the real sacrifice that it may become the lamb which was slain from the foundation of the world, that its mystical "blood"—symbolizing the spiritual life-force—might be given freely for the renewal and regeneration of all. This interpretation may seem vague and mystical to some, but to those who are real students of mysticism, *i. e.*, who have been able to correlate to some extent with the ever hidden springs of Being, there will be no difficulty.

Another interpretation is that the ram represents the powers of man's head caught in the thickets of worldly conditions where life itself makes him the victim of his use of speech.

Just as Aries leads the signs of the zodiac, so does the letter Hé become a leader, and so in turn must the masculine force of intellect be the power which shall lead the flocks of masculine thoughts and feminine intuitions into the green pastures and beside the still waters. Just as the ram tears down the underbrush with his strong horns and makes a path through which the sheep and lambs may reach the tender, succulent grass which grows under the brush, so should the intellect tear aside all hampering conceptions, overcome mental difficulties and lead the thoughts where they can feed upon the tender manifestations of Divine Love and Compassion which are growing unseen about the roots of the outward conditions. Yet the intellect should always be ready to sacrifice itself at the dictates of the Law as revealed through the illumined heart.

THE 5TH TAROT CARD

THE POPE

Papus

MEDIEVAL

Papus

St. Germain
EGYPTIAN

Smith
MODERN

THE 5TH TAROT CARD, *The Pope.*

The 5th card is called the Pope or High Priest. It represents an Initiate into the Mysteries seated between the 2 pillars of the sanctuary. This symbolizes that to become an Initiate man must find a perfect balance and rule his spiritual life while sitting at rest between the 2 pillars Jakin and Boas, Justice and Mercy, or the masculine and feminine aspects of sex.

Another meaning of Jakin and Boas is that the right hand pillar represents the Law, the left hand pillar Liberty to obey or disobey. Both are necessary to uphold the Temple of Humanity and to sound the sacred word, for obedience through compulsion can never bring freedom. Man must deliberately choose to obey. Hence, only as man finds this seat and chooses to sit in it and rule, can he understand and fulfill his office of Priest.

In his left hand he holds erect the triple cross. This is the Rod of Power by which he can penetrate into and rule the 3 worlds, and with poise, equilibrium and a calm understanding utilize the powers entrusted to him to bring forth on the 3 planes—physical, mental and spiritual. As ruler of the 3 worlds he wears the triple crown. His right hand forms the sign of Esotericism and is raised in blessing over the heads of 2 kneeling figures, symbolizing that when the spiritual man has taken his seat as priest and ruler of the life he will bless both the masculine and feminine expressions of humanity which bow in reverence before him.

THE 5TH COMMANDMENT.

> "Honor thy father and thy mother: that thy days may be long upon the land which the Lord thy God giveth thee."
>
> —*Exodus,* xx, 12.

To take this Commandment literally is to play sad havoc with all occult teaching; for are we not taught that the aim of evolution is to rise above the bondage of physical existence, *i. e.*, to accomplish our work in the Grand Plan, help our fellow men and spiritualize our bodies and the planet on which we dwell, in as short a time as possible? Why, then, should we be enticed into paying filial respect by what, from an occult standpoint, is an empty promise, namely, that our days of pilgrimage and travail here on earth should be lengthened?

While exoterically filial respect, honor and obedience to parents is a positive virtue which should early be inculcated, for it is sadly lacking in present-day children, still by the illumination of the Inner Light we see that to take this merely as a literal command to simply honor the man and woman who supplied us with a physical vehicle in which to incarnate, would not give us its true meaning. For in the case of bodies conceived in lust and sin and brought into the world sick, deformed, mentally deficient and physically cursed from birth, little honor is due the parents, except for affording us an opportunity to work out the past Karma which drew us to them for incarnation.

Since 5 is the Number of Humanity, while we can personalize this Commandment we must also consider it in its universal aspect. The Father of humanity, the Father of all, is the active or Positive Principle of the Godhead; that active Principle which ever cleaves the darkness of Chaos when the gods say: "Let there be light." The Mother of humanity is that mighty Passive Principle which gathers up the Light as it penetrates Chaos and cherishes it in her bosom. It is forever the tender, brooding Mother-force which works on the germs of good in all things that they may ultimately bring forth that good. It is that unseen Mother-love of the Godhead, hovering like a dove over its nestlings, which feeds with "food convenient for us" every hungry heart, even if that food be seemingly bitter to the taste; the unseen agency which, when the fury of the tempest has spent itself and the sun shines forth, brings out the purifying effects. It is that mysterious force of healing which makes every wound, be it of the physical body, the mind or the heart, tend to heal, unless infected by man's interference, through his wrong thoughts, impure emanations or evil creations. It is that love which makes Time the great healer of all woes, the soother of all sorrows, the adjuster of all inharmonies; that brings sunshine after rain, laughter after tears, and joy, deep and abiding, after sin, sorrow and repentance. In fact, it is the Illumination produced by the Light, the effect of its shining. Therefore, to honor the divine and living Father-Mother forces is to recognize that humanity is not mere

> "Dumb driven cattle * * *
> Whose hearts like muffled drums are beating
> Funeral marches to the grave,"

but children of the Divine Father-Mother, who must correlate with and obey their divine parents.

The "land" which the Law of thy Good hath given thee is an abiding place in the field of manifestation, and a work to do in the Grand Plan of Redemption. Therefore, in so far as you make your life an honor to God and The Christ—the Divine Incarnation in the flesh of the Son of the Father-Mother—by giving honor and obedience to the divinc laws, so shall you, in your immortal Divine Self, be long with or continue to work consciously with the positive and negative forces back of humanity and evolution, until the Light of The Christ has been able to shine forth in and spiritualize all things—or the 5 of humanity is swallowed up in the 6 of The Christ—and the great Redemption of Manifestation is accomplished in number 7.

CHAPTER 21

THE NUMBER 6.

Magical equilibrium is expressed in the Kabalah by the senery. "Considered in its first cause, this equilibrium is the will of God; it is liberty in man, and mathematical equilibrium in matter. Equilibrium produces stability and duration. Liberty generates the immortality of man, and the will of God gives effect to the laws of eternal reason."

—*Transcendental Magic,* Lévi, 75-6.

Number 6 is primarily the Number of The Christ-force in nature, the force back of evolution. It is the Number of Unrest and Incompleteness in that it represents the unrest of nature incomplete and ever becoming, ever striving for perfection, ever changing form that The Christ-force may manifest more perfectly. The Christ-force is the spiritual creative power back of the universal Urge Toward Perfection which is inherent in both nature and man. As we have said elsewhere:[1] "It is a spiritual emanation from the godhead, the Son of God, or the godhead in its creative aspect; that mystic Power or Principle which fructifies and animates all manifestations of life. It is the Divine Creative Force, a great stream of life-giving, creative Essence which manifests in all things on all planes as the Animating Principle of the One Life. In Nature it is focused in and through the physical sun, for only as the sun pours out its life-giving, fructifying power—sheds its symbolic blood—can the One Life manifest in the various forms of Nature and evolve them to perfection. In the physical universe it is the same Animating Principle that

[1] See lesson *The Mystic Christ.*

flamed out from the godhead in the beginning when the Elohim said: 'Let there be light.' And it is this same mystic, creative Light which must enter the Chaos of your outer life, even as it did the Chaos of the solar system, ere your life can begin its *conscious* spiritual evolution. All the physical and mental evolution is but a preparation for this new and higher step. Witness Paul's confirmation of this view: 'For God, who commanded the light to shine out of darkness, hath shined in our hearts, to give the light of the knowledge of the glory of God in the face of Jesus Christ.' "[2]

Number 6 therefore shows that the cause of all evolution is the Urge to Perfection *inherent* in every living thing. This urge results in the conscious adaptation of the organism to its environment, in contradistinction to the so-called scientific theory that evolution results from blind and mechanical reaction of the organism to its environment. This inherent Urge Toward Perfection is symbolized by the geometrical formation of the figure 6 itself. In the vertical line | we have the 1 God, the 1 Life, etc., coming down to manifest within the ○ of the microcosm, man, thus: 6, that it may inform, fructify and evolve all the germs of life within it. The ○ of the 6 may also be considered as the microcosm which contains all man's unmanifested God-powers, while the line running upward symbolizes the unrest and aspiration of the Soul which is determinedly reaching up and endeavoring to manifest ever greater degrees of Divinity. It is also the Ladder of God, the *Antaskarana* along which the angels are continually descending and ascending.

The 6th Principle in man is Buddhi or the Soul-principle which cannot rest until it finds its spiritual home and reaches the perfection of manifestation in

[2] II *Corinthians*, iv, 6.

number 7. Great as is number 5, it is but the preparation of man for number 6, for in number 6 we have a higher principle (Soul) added to the merely human (5)—just as the human was added to the merely animal—the "breath of life" which makes him "a living Soul" and Divine, instead of allowing him to remain merely a human animal. It is the inner urge of this Soul-principle toward perfection of unfoldment and expression that causes the 6 sided cube of the purely animal man to unfold into the cross 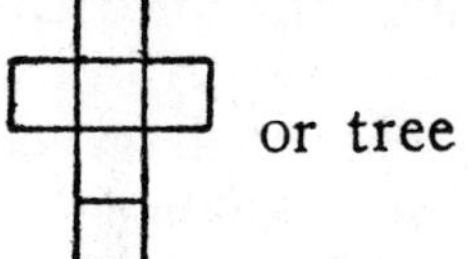 or tree upon which the spiritual man must be crucified in matter until the lower square of the unfolded cube has been lifted up or indrawn and the cross has been balanced. Man cannot be at rest until he has become 1 with the Animating Principle of nature, and recognizes that the same creative Principle works in him to bring forth perfection as it does in Nature.

That 6 is the Number of The Christ-force is confirmed by the number symbolism of the Gnostics as set forth by Marcus. "After 'six days,' that is to say, in the seventh stage since the disciple first set his feet upon the path, he ascended into the 'mountain'—a graphic symbol for the higher states of consciousness. * * * The six (the *arahat*) being thus of the same essence as the World-mother (Wisdom) contains essentially in himself the whole number of all the elements or powers. * * * Again, it was on the 'sixth day,' the 'preparation,' that the divine economy or order of things, manifested the 'last man,' the 'man from heaven,' for the new birth or regeneration of the 'first man' or 'man of earth'; and further the passion began in the sixth hour and ended in the sixth hour, when the initiate was nailed to the cross. All of which was designated to indicate *the power of creation* (inception) *and regeneration* or rebirth (consummation), typified in the number 6. * * * Again, the spoken or effable name of the Savior, Jesus, consists of 6 letters, while His ineffable name consists of 24. * * * Again, at the baptism there descended upon Jesus * * * the dove, which soars again to heaven, its upward course completing the Jesus (or 6) and making him into the Christ (or 12), the enformation according to knowledge, or perfect illumination."[3]

Much has been said about the coming 6th sub-race into which we are now entering and in which the seed of the 6th Great Race shall be sown, and we look forward with great expectation to its accomplishments, but to comprehend that which shall be we must consider the significance of the various Races. In the 5th Race man reaches the point where he is above the mere physical, animal man (4), and is the human (5), with the power to dominate. But at this point in his evolution he has also the power to reach out to number 6 and begin to contact 6th Race powers. During the 4th Race man struggled through the astral world, and by his psychic powers and the lower aspects of mind dominated and enslaved the lower kingdoms. During the 5th Race man has been learning to dominate the lower kingdoms through the use of his magic pentacle and is reaching up into the 6th or Christ-power. During the 6th Race he will evolve and ultimately dominate through spiritual power. Even today man is grasping the ideal of dominating as a Soul rather than as a king of the physical world. Ultimately there must come the Super-man, who shall dominate the physical and reach up into the higher realms and find his fulfillment in the 7th Race. Number 5 is the sign of accomplishment, number 6 the struggle toward

---

[3] *Fragments of a Faith Forgotten*, Mead, 370-1-5.

a higher accomplishment, and number 7 the Crown of Attainment.

6 is the Number of Toil and Labor, also the Great Work which each Soul must accomplish. "Six days shalt thou labor, and do all thy work," says the Commandment. The Children of Israel gathered their manna during 6 days of the week, but none on the 7th. "In 6 days the Lord (Elohim) made heaven and earth, the sea, and all that in them is, and rested on the seventh day."[4]

Remembering that the word *Lord* refers to the great *Law* governing the manifestations of The Christ-force, we at once grasp the significance of these 6 days of creation. Their symbolism is given by Éliphas Lévi as follows:

1st day of creation. "The light splendid and radiant, Unity (No. 1)."

2nd day. "The firmament, or the necessary separation between Spirit and form, between the fixed and the volatile, between the heavens and the earth (No. 2)."

3d day. "Germination of the earth under the influence of the heavens. Germination begins with the revelation of the ternary (No. 3)."

4th day. "The Sun and the Moon rule over the day and the night. Division of the seasons by the quarternary. Primitive quadrature of the circle (No. 4)."

5th day. "Life manifests itself in the bosom of the elements; constitution of the kingdom of man in the number five (No. 5)."

6th day. "The earth and the fire respond to the air and the water and give their living animals; the triangle which is the reflection of that of Jehovah forms itself in the soul of man and God says to him: 'facimus

[4] *Exodus*, xx, 11.

hominem,' for man must share in his own creation (No. 6)."

7th day. "On the Seventh day God rests; that is, the Septenary, being the perfect number, there remains nothing to be done after it (No. 7)."

He also gives the symbolism of the first 6 chapters of *Genesis* as follows:

1st Chapter. "The unity of God manifests and sums itself up in the unity of man (No. 1)."

2nd Chapter. "God completes man by woman, and intelligence by the law (No. 2)."

3rd Chapter. "The serpent interposes as a third between innocent man and woman. God interposes as a third between guilty man and woman (No. 3)."

4th Chapter. "Adam and Eve begot Cain and Abel and from two they became four (No. 4)."

5th Chapter. "Humanity sums itself up in the person of Seth, who is the heir of Adam and Eve in the place of Cain and Abel: one becomes the synthesis of four; It is the five in its whole power (No. 5)."

6th Chapter. "Creation of political and religious humanity; beginning of the antagonism between the Sons of God and the children of men (No. 6)."

7th Chapter. Noah and all his household rested in the ark for 40 days and 40 nights ere the raven was sent forth. "And the ark rested in the seventh month, on the seventeenth day of the month, upon the mountains of Ararat." (No. 7).

"Can you believe that all this is found thus arranged by chance? and do you imagine one can understand a single word of the *Bible* without the key of the sacred numbers?" [5]

Not only did the Great Law create the earth, the sea, the heavens and the material universe, but that same Law is continually creating the same conditions both in nature and in man. Is it not the incessant

---

[5] *Unpublished Letters of Éliphas Lévi.*

working through matter of the same Christ-force that creates (evolves) out of the seed the tree? Out of the bud the flower and fruit? And in man, out of his fleshly desires spiritual aspiration? Out of a dense physical body a Spiritual Body? All as a result of the godward Urge to Perfection? And the Law will continue thus to work as long as number 6 prevails; for number 6 is Incompleteness, and the Great Law will rest only when the 7th day dawns, *i. e.*, when there is no more incompleteness, hence nothing to work through. Therefore the Lord (Law) blessed the 7th day and hallowed it. This blessing is the result of work accomplished, the blessing of rest and satisfaction. All things that are completed are hallowed by the very fact of their completion. We toil over a task and when it is done and well done—which is the meaning of completeness—what a feeling of perfect satisfaction is ours! We not only rest from our labor outwardly, but within we rest in the hallowed content that comes from a task accomplished. Hence number 7 is always a time of hallowed rest, a blessing of accomplishment, and it is the Law which brings it.

It was also on the 6th day that man was created in the image of the Elohim. The Elohim are none other than,

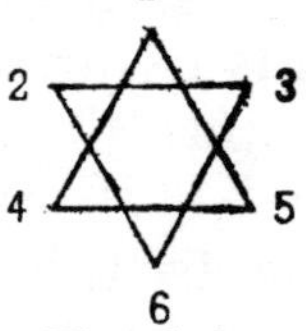

> "The 'Sephiroth of Construction'—the 6 Dhyân Chohans, or Manus, or Prajâpatis, synthesized by the seventh 'B'raisheeth,' the First Emanation, or Logos, and who are called, therefore, the Builders of the Lower or Physical Universe, all belonging Below. These Six whose essence is of the *Seventh,* are the Upadhi, the Base or Fundamental Stone, on which the ob-

> jective Universe is built, the Noumenoi of all things. Hence they are, at the same time the Forces of Nature; the Seven Angels of the Presence; the Sixth and Seventh Principles in Man; the spirito-psycho-physical Spheres of the Septenary Chain, the Root Races, etc."[6]

In the vision of Enoch he tells us that the 6th gate of heaven is at the East. "The sun *now* returns to the east, entering into the sixth gate, and rising and setting in the sixth gate thirty-one days, on account of its signs."[7] At that period the day is twice as long as the night. In other words, the 6th gate or number 6 represents the period for labor or, as Enoch called it, the 6 "hours" or the period for work. It is the long day, twice as long as the night, in which evolution struggles for perfection. And since the life-force manifests in a spiral, if we take a spiral having 6 turns we find that at the 6th turn the line representing the outgoing force is twice as long as that of the previous turn.

The idea of connecting number 6 with Labor and the working forces of nature is well illustrated in the structure of the bee and the ant, which are important factors in evolution and the most widely accepted symbols of industry and systematized labor. Bees, wasps and ants, which all belong to the same family, are recognized as being 6 structured, being made up of mandibles, 2 pairs of wings and 3 abdominal segments, the head being classed as 1 of these. They also have 6 legs. The social instincts and industrial habits of the ant have made a great impression on the minds of men in all ages. Solomon tells us: "Go to the ant, thou sluggard; consider her ways and be wise."[8] Both the bee and the ant are said to have come to this planet from Venus, and in the Greek legend of Cupid and Psyche—which is the story of the Soul (Psyche) in its struggles through matter, its

---

[6] *S. D.*, I, 402.
[7] *Book of Enoch*, 94.
[8] Remarkable that this is found in the 6th Chapter and 6th Verse of *Proverbs*.

seduction by mortal love (Cupid), and its final purification through incessant labor (6) and suffering—we again find the ant. When Venus gave Psyche seemingly impossible tasks to perform, the 6 legged ants came to her assistance and by their industry and patient perseverance ultimately performed every task, even though Psyche had to descend to the infernal regions and wrest from Proserpine the secret of her beauty. Proserpine, who spent half her time among the gods and the other in the nether world as the wife of Pluto, represents nature. Hence the secret which the Soul must wrest from nature is the secret of the ever-working, rejuvenating and active power of the 1 Life, The Christ-force or number 6.

CHAPTER 22

THE NUMBER 6—*(Continued)*.

"The Sixth Group (of the Dhyânis) remains almost inseparable from man, who draws from it all but his highest and lowest principles, or his spirit and body; the 5 middle human principles being the very essence of those Dhyânis."

—*The Secret Doctrine,* Blavatsky, I, 242.

Hence it is that the elementals of the 4 elements or nature-forces emanating from the 6th Group, each appear to man's inner sight bearing the imprint of the number 6 as the seal or signature of their Group, just as man's body bears number 5 as the signature of the Group by which it was fashioned. The figure 6 borne by the earth elementals or Gnomes is small, short, squat, very thick and black, thus: 6o′o′o′; that borne by the water elementals or Undines is larger, taller and in double outline instead of solid, thus: 6o′o′; that borne by the air elementals or Sylphs is very tall and slender with wavy double outlines, thus: 6; while that borne by the fire elementals or Salamanders, as seen in a flame, is composed of many vibrating ethereal lines having a curl or hook at the bottom thus:

It must be understood that just as Man's

body suggests the 5 pointed star and hence number 5, so do the bodies of the nature sprites suggest the number 6; for number 6 dominates them and their structure, even more completely than number 5 dominates man in his 5 extremities, 5 fingers, 5 toes, 5 senses, etc. Also, if we take the product of these 4 kingdoms of nature we still have 6, thus, $4 \times 6 = 24 = 6$.

This is another proof that 6 is the Number of Nature, for it is through the activities of the elementals of those 4 great kingdoms that The Christ-force is evolving nature toward perfection. It is this incessant activity, labor and *change of form* that connects number 6 with suffering and woe such as befell at the opening of the 6th Seal of the Book of Life,[1] also at the sounding of the 6th Angel,[2] the pouring out of the 6th Vial[3] and the 6 periods of war with the Beast.

The geometrical symbol of number 6 is the interlaced triangles or the 6 pointed star ✡, called by the Hindus the Sign of Vishnu, and by the Hebrews the Shield of David, often mis-called the Seal of Solomon. Among the Egyptians it was the symbol of generation, the union of fire and water, the male and female. Among the Pythagoreans it was called the Hexad or "the perfection of parts," and with them was also a symbol of creation. The Neo-Pythagorean philosopher Nichomachus called it "the form of forms, the only number adapted to the Soul, the distinct union of the parts of the Universe, the fabricator of the Soul, and also Harmony." The interlaced triangles symbolize the triune God reflected by His creations, or God in man and nature. "The trinity of nature is the lock, the trinity of man is the key that fits it."[4] It also symbolizes the 6 Creative Groups, the 6 powers of nature, the 6 planes of consciousness

[1] *Revelation*, vi, 12.
[2] *Revelation*, ix, 13.
[3] *Revelation*, xvi, 12.
[4] *Isis Unveiled*, Blavatsky, II, 635.

and of evolution, and the 6 Principles of man, all of which are synthesized in a 7th.

Since man is a microcosm, the interlaced triangles or number 6 must ever manifest in him. The Kabalists call it the Supreme Triangle and its reflection. The Supreme Triangle they said was composed of Necessity, Liberty and Reason, referring Reason to *Kether,* Necessity to *Chockmah* and Liberty to *Binah.* The triangle reflected in man they designated Fatality, Will and Power. "Fatality is the inevitable sequence of effects and causes in a determined order. Will is the directing faculty of intelligent forces for the conciliation of the liberty of persons with the necessity of things. Power is the wise application of will which enlists fatality itself in the accomplishment of the desires of the sage."[5]

The △ pointing upward symbolizes *Siva*, fire, light and heavenly powers, also the Divine Trinity or upper triad in man, ever evolving upward after its incarnation in matter, seeking more perfect expression; the source of aspiration in man. The 2 lines of force, Law and Will, descending from the focus above (apex) and spreading out to include the base line, indicate that man is overshadowed by and included within the Divine, also that he can receive the positive and negative forces from above and correlate (unite) them on the physical plane or base line. The upward-pointing triangle also symbolizes the stability and poise which man can attain when he looks to the Divine Trinity within.

The downward-pointing triangle ▽ is dark, symbolizing the waters of Chaos in which the Divine Germ (Vishnu and the hosts of the lower worlds) is laid, also the instability of man's lower nature, "unstable as water." This triangle symbolizes that the 2 ascending lines of force can ascend from their focus (apex),

---

[5] *Transcendental Magic,* Lévi, 69.

on earth and reach up to and embrace the Divine. The interlaced triangles therefore symbolize the reflection of the Divine completed and man assuming his responsibility. For only by the perfect blending and balancing of the 2 natures, human and Divine, can man attain Wisdom and Perfection. In other words, man can attain Wisdom only as he can correlate his consciousness with both the realm of the Divine and with the realm of nature, whose symbol is 6.

According to the Kabalah the 1st trinity is called the Macroprosopus and the 2nd trinity, making up the 6, the Microprosopus, the 2 constituting the Vast and the Lesser Countenances. The Macroprosopus is all brilliancy and dazzling light, while the Microprosopus or lesser countenance shines only by reflected light. Thus must the 2 triangles, the Light and its reflection, be interlaced to form the 6 pointed star, the symbol of the macrocosm. The 6 days of creation correspond to the 6 forms of the Microprosopus. The 6th Sephira is called *Tipherath,* beauty or mildness, the divine name Eloah Va-Daath, and the angelic names Shinanim and Melakim. This 6th Sephira completes the 2 trinities; the 1st, the divine Father-Mother-Son, the 2nd, Power-Greatness-Fortitude, also Strength-Beauty-Clemency. Being the reflection of the Godhead on earth, these are magic forces which manifest through the interlaced triangles. In short, the Divine Reality back of this mighty symbol is that when the God attributes are not only reflected but interlaced and balanced in man's life, he becomes a mighty magician and all the forces within himself and nature must obey him. While this symbol has a certain power in itself, its full potency is manifested only when its dual forces are interblended and used to bring forth The Christ-man in the life.

The early Christian church gave a somewhat different meaning to the ✡. God, considered as the Father, has Nature for His daughter; considered as Son, has the Virgin for His mother and the Church for His Bride; considered as the Mother or Holy Ghost He regenerates and redeems humanity. These attributes are assigned to the various points as follows:

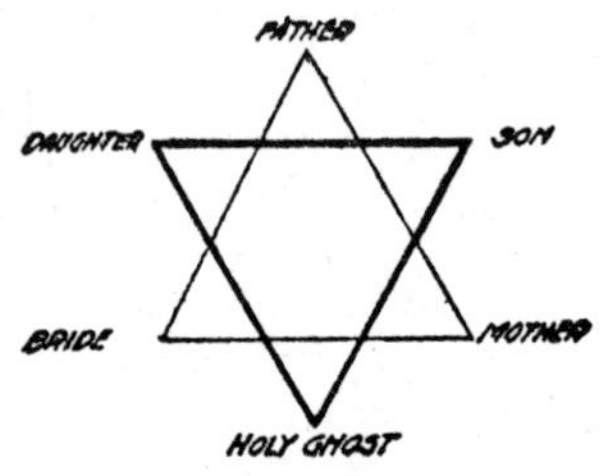

By some authors 6 is called the number of "co-operation, marriage, reciprocal action, counterpoise, psychology, divination, telepathy, psychometry and alchemy," all of which are based upon its primary significance as the Number of The Christ-force, the informing principle of the Soul, pushing through nature and man to perfection in number 7, Super-man.

The Druids held the number 6 in deep reverence and many of their sacred ceremonies were based upon it. They began their year upon the 6th day of the full moon, and the 6 days within the full moon—3 before and 3 after—were held especially sacred. Also when the sacred mistletoe was cut 6 priests performed the ceremony.

An astronomical period of 600 years was held in reverence and is often referred to in the Mysteries. It consisted of 31 periods of 19 years each and 1 period of 11 years. This cycle was known to the ancient Chaldeans, who declared it the most perfect of all astronomical periods. For instance, it was held that if on a certain day at high noon a new moon appeared at a designated place in the heavens, it would appear again at the expiration of 600 years in precisely the same place and relations, with all the planets in the same positions.

The Egyptians, like the Druids, had 6 High Priests, and a certain Aseshra is mentioned as the "Mother of the Mysterious Words of 6." Also a statue of Ei-meri has been found on which is carved the title, "Chief of the Dwelling of the Great 6."

Among the ancient Semites on Saturn's day (Saturday) 6 priests clothed in black ministered to the god Saturn in a 6 sided temple, the walls of which were hung with black. By some Saturn is considered as sinister, but the above incident only proves that the priests had a deep understanding of the esoteric position of Saturn as the Great Initiator. For esoterically black symbolizes that which is unmanifested and not, as vulgarly supposed—because Saturn was farthest from the sun—that which is cold, dark, evil and the bringer of malign influences. Saturn as Lucifer is the Unmanifested falling from heaven into manifestation, but the Star of the Morning as he rises, through perfected and tested evolution, to his heavenly home. Saturn is therefore often referred to as the hidden god with 2 faces, 1 white and 1 black.

Number 6 is magically related to the circumference of the circle, which contains 6×60 degrees, each containing 60 minutes of 60 seconds each.

Let number 6 remind you of the upspringing power of nature; of the universal Urge Toward Perfection which is inherent in the soul of all things; of the power of The Christ-force working in you toward more and more perfect expression through you. Let it ever remind you that the divine Trinity is reflected within you ◇, but that the lower triangle must be lifted up until it balances the upper and forms the ✡ , your life interlaced with the Divine. Also that by the power of The Christ within you must unfold the 6 sided cube and balance the cross.

CHAPTER 23

THE 6TH LETTER, *Vau* (ו).

> "He produced Vau, predominant in mind, crowned it, combined and formed it with Taurus in the Universe, Aiar (May) in the year, and the right kidney of man."
>
> —*Sepher Yetzirah,* 24.

The 6th letter of the Hebrew alphabet is Vau (V). It is a simple letter connected with Taurus, and its meaning is an "eye." At 1st glance it is hard to connect this meaning with the zodiacal sign Taurus, yet a little thought will reveal a wonderful significance; for it is the star Aldebaran, the eye of Taurus, which not only is the leader of this constellation, but which gives to it its great brilliancy. Taurus is composed of 2 brilliant constellations of 7 stars each—the Pleiades, which are ruled over by the 7 Rishis, and the Hyades, called the sisters or feminine aspect of these 7 great expressions of elohistic force, the Rishis. The Hyades form the head and neck of the Bull, which the Grecian myth says bore Europa across the seas to Crete, and was afterwards raised to the heavens by Jupiter as the sign Taurus. Another myth is that these constellations were raised to the heavens as a reward for having brought up Zeus at Dodora and taken care of the infant Dionysos Hyas. Aldebaran, the eye of the Bull, is a Star of a brilliant reddish color, with a magnitude of ½, and is the principal object of the group. But its true occult significance is that when this star is in conjunction with the Sun it is from that point of the ecliptic that the calculations of new cycles are computed.

A similarity will at once be noticed between the 1st mother letter Aleph (ox) and Vau, which is also related to Taurus. The difference is that Aleph relates to the sign in its creative aspect, while Vau is the manifestation of its force upon the earth.

In *St. Matthew* (vi, 22) we read: "The light of the body is the eye. If therefore thine eye be single, thy whole body is full of light." As above so below. When the eye of man is in conjunction with the Sun of Righteousness, or is looking to that source of Light alone with singleness of purpose, from that point we can calculate a new era in his life; for he has completed his cycle of darkness.

Again, Taurus is an earthy, fixed sign and is looked upon as unfortunate. Its children are plodders, are often poor and find life full of vicissitudes and sorrows, brought about, however, largely from their own want of poise and balance. And it is in just such earthly conditions that we must learn to fix our eye upon the Sun, if we wish to reach into a new cycle or new condition. The eye is often spoken of as the window of the Soul, and in Taurus the Soul may be said to be shut in a dark dungeon. But in this dungeon there is a window facing the East through which the eye can see the rising Sun, whose beams shall fill the dungeon with Light. Hence the eye represents the force of the Soul struggling in its prison house of flesh to penetrate through the mists and find the Light, just as number 6 is The Christ-principle struggling in matter, but always upward towards the Light.

In Vau we also have another symbol, that of a "link" between the human and the Divine, just as the neck in the body connects the head with the trunk in which is located the heart.

The 6 is called the hexad, from the Greek word *hex*, meaning 6, the Latin of which is *sex*. Hence sex or number 6, The Christ Principle, must be considered as manifesting through the 2 expressions of sex in humanity, man and woman. Sex or 6 expresses a definite cycle of experience through which all creation either has or will pass, but through which man and woman are passing today. Therefore the letter Vau (or Vav as it is sometimes written, u and v being synonymous) must be considered in reference to man and woman, Vau being the link that unites the 2. In the newly born infant it is the umbilical cord which unites it to its mother, and over which the life-force is carried to it, but between man and woman it is the far more sacred line of magnetic and spiritual love-force (life) which alone is the link capable of uniting the 2 in true marriage.

THE 6TH TAROT CARD

THE LOVERS

Papus

MEDIEVAL

Papus

St. Germain
EGYPTIAN

Smith
MODERN

THE 6TH TAROT CARD, *The Lovers.*

In the 6th card of the Tarot we have the idea of Vau as a link strongly brought out. This card is called "The Lovers," and pictures a young man standing motionless at a point where 2 roads meet, the "Two Paths," the straight and narrow path which leads to life everlasting, and the broad highway leading to the City of Destruction. His arms are crossed upon his breast in an attitude of deliberation, for the hands always indicate ability to accomplish, hence they are crossed on the breast when work is done. The hands are thus crossed in moments of idleness, after accomplishment or in death. Before him stand 2 women, each with a hand upon his shoulder, while with the other hand each is pointing to 1 of the Paths. The woman on his right has a circlet of gold upon her head. She is true Love, pointing him to the Path of Duty which winds up hill all the way. The woman on his left is disheveled and crowned with vine leaves. She points him to the Path of Pleasure and dissipation. These 2 figures represent Virtue and Vice, or the angel messenger of Love to link him to the Divine and the messenger of evil, the link which will bind him to the seduction of the senses. Above their heads floats a radiant figure surrounded by the rays of the Sun, in whose hand is a bow and arrow drawn ready to strike.

This card is a true symbol of the sign Taurus, for at this point the Soul must meet all the seductions of the senses, which are ruled by Venus, the dual Planet. It also contains the figure of Justice with his bow and arrow pointed at Vice. This figure represents the star Aldebaran in conjunction with the sun, also the number 6 and The Christ-force, which will send out its arrows against vice and will utterly destroy all evil, even as the rays of the sun shoot out their arrows of light and destroy all germs of disease. Suffering is inevitably linked to vice, for "the wages of sin is death; but the gift of God is eternal life."[1] It is not the difficult climb up the mountain path that brings death, but the wages you have earned. We must stop earning death and allow the gift of eternal life to manifest. Hence if the young man chooses the Path of Vice, he links himself to death, which is his only savior, for at each death of the body we are saved from committing further sins and reaping further suffering. We begin to die the moment we turn away from Divine Love, and only when death has done its work can we, through the power of The Christ-force, be resurrected from the grave of matter and live forevermore. If the young man chooses the Path of Virtue The Christ will work with him and the arrows of Justice will prove to be shafts of fiery life pushing all that is in him upward into life eternal.

The symbol of Vau is love, and only love is the light of the eye. How dull an eye through which selfishness looks, but how bright and clear when love shines from it. Love is the only link that can unite us to the Divine. Human love, however, must be a golden link, and the 1 we love must be crowned with the gold of spiritual ideals, for if we substitute lust for love we find a link of heavy iron, chaining us to something loathsome, chafing our flesh, hampering our movements; a link indeed, but a link with death.

THE 6TH COMMANDMENT.

"Thou shalt not kill."

—*Exodus*, xx, 13.

The 6th Commandment, altho short and definite, nevertheless derives its esoteric significance from the meaning of the number 6, The Christ-force fighting its way through the limitations of matter into more and

[1] *Romans*, vi, 23.

more perfect manifestations. Since the 1 Life which animates all forms of life is immortal, the only thing we can kill is the *form* of manifestation of the Divine Spark, whether in humanity or in the lower kingdoms. As we have said elsewhere: "The only sense in which man can kill is to separate any form of life from this stream of the One Life-force, or to dam it up or refuse to permit it to manifest."[2] Therefore, anything that we may do to retard the manifestation of The Christ-force in humanity or in the world is killing in its true sense. The thing we are really killing or retarding, however, is our own manifestation, our own evolution. This is killing in the sense of separating our life from the 1 Life and pushing ourselves back into the darkness of ignorance, selfishness and personality. Death is separation from God or the Divine Life-principle, and our ignorance consists in the belief or delusion that we can stop the 1 Life from unfolding within another, and at the same time not retard its manifestation in ourselves.

Every evolving Soul passes through many deaths in many conditions, yet by the power of The Christ, and with The Christ, he must ultimately triumph over death and no longer either cause or suffer death. It is said that the last victory is over death and the grave, *i. e.,* we conquer by learning that every thought of antagonism toward another is helping to retard the manifestation of Divine Love and Life which is seeking expression through that 1. And since we can only strike or injure another through ourselves, by so doing we are bringing desolation and death into our own auras. Every jealousy, every desire to belittle the work of another, especially if the proper performance of that work will contribute to the betterment of humanity; every word of reproach or slander which helps to blast the reputation and kill the usefulness of

[2] *V. of I.,* Chapter xxxii.

a fellow mortal, discourage him in his efforts to conquer, and make him fail, are all so many germs of death to us which will retard or prevent the manifestation of the Divine through us. For as we harbor rivalry, jealousy, envy, hatred, etc., we kill out our finer feelings and perceptions, our sympathy and loving tolerance and kindness, and thus sow the seeds of death within our own lives. Therefore, though the forms through which we express our life may die many times, yet through the power of The Christ we shall live again and again until we conquer death and the grave, and with this last enemy conquered we, together with all the redeemed of mankind, shall live forever more.

The Command that number 6 brings us, therefore, is that we are to recognize the Divine in all things, both animate and inanimate, so-called; that we are consciously to work with The Christ; that we are not to kill, deaden or even blind the eyes of the world to its workings, but strive to live in The Christ forever more, knowing that only as The Christ lives and manifests in us can we live and manifest our Divine Selves. Only by recognizing The Christ in the 1 Life shall we be made alive in Christ. Thus shall we obey the Commandment, "Thou shalt not kill."

CHAPTER 24

THE NUMBER 7.

The Mystery of Creation.

"Number 7 is the festival day of all the earth, the *birthday of the world.* I know not whether anyone would be able to celebrate the number 7 in adequate terms."

—*The Secret Doctrine,* Blavatsky, I, 438.

"By these Seven letters were also made seven worlds, seven heavens, seven earths, seven seas, seven rivers, seven deserts, seven days, seven weeks from Passover to Pentecost, and every seventh year a Jubilee."

—*Sepher Yetzirah,* 22.

The number 7 is the most sacred of all numbers, and for several reasons is so considered in all theogonies. *1st,* because it relates to the mystery of the manifestation of the Godhead, the *Mystery of Creation; 2nd,* because number 7 governs the equally divine *Mystery of Gestation,* and *3rd,* because it is the *Number of Perfection.*

All the ancient mystery teachings agree that the Divine brought forth the manifested universe through a Deity having a 7 fold aspect, called in the Christian scriptures the 7 Elohim, the "Sons of God" spoken of by Job.[1] The Elohim are the spiritual progenitors of the 7 great Creative Rays or Hierarchies which constitute the manifested aspect of the Godhead, and which are focused or embodied in the Rulers or Deities of the 7 sacred planets. It was these 7 manifestations of the 1 God who said: "Let there be light," and the white Light, which resulted from the perfect

[1] *Job,* I, 6.

blending of the 7 color rays,[2] brought the earth and the universe into manifestation.

As we have said elsewhere: "At the first rebirth of our earth — for the law of cyclic rebirth applies to planets and systems as well as to men—it was brought into manifestation or 'created' by a ray of pure white light from the Absolute penetrating the chaotic debris of previous world-periods. As a ray of light in passing through a prism is separated into seven color-rays, so this Ray of Spiritual Light in passing through the prism of manifestation was separated into seven great differentiations or color-rays called Hierarchies."[3]

The Hebrew word used in *Genesis* and crudely translated "God" is not only plural, being the plural form of El-h, but many later references to creation also refer to this same "God" in the plural, showing plainly that the 7 fold nature of the Godhead was clearly understood by the writers of the various books of the *Bible*. For instance, "Let *us* make man in *our* image, after *our* likeness. * * * And the Lord God said, Behold the man is become as one of *us*," etc.[4]

> "The Elohim are seven in number, whether as nature-powers, gods of constellations, or planetary gods, * * * as the Pitris and Patriarchs, Manus and Fathers of earlier times. The Gnostics, however, and the Jewish *Kabalah* preserve an account of the Elohim of *Genesis* by which we are able to identify them with other forms of the seven primordial powers. * * * Their names are Ildabaoth, Jehovah (or Jao), Sabaoth, Adonai, Eloeus, Oreus, and Astanpheus. Ildabaoth signifies the Lord God of the fathers, that is the fathers who preceded the Father; and thus the seven are identical with the seven Pitris or Fathers of India (Ireneus, B. I., xx, 5). Moreover, the Hebrew Elohim were preëxistent by name and nature as Phoenician divinities or powers. * * * In the Phoenician mythology the Elohim are the seven

[2] The simple experiment in physics proves that if the 7 colors are placed on a disc and rapidly revolved they will blend into white.

[3] *V. of I.*, 179.

[4] *Genesis,* i, 26; iii, 22.

> sons of Sydik (Melchizedek), identical with the Seven Kabiri, who in Egypt are the Seven sons of Ptah, and the Seven Spirits of Ra in *The Book of the Dead.* * * * They are the leading stars of seven constellations which turned round the Great Bear in describing the circle of the year. These the Assyrians called the seven Lumazi, or leaders of the flocks of stars, designated as sheep * * * The Elohim, then, are the Egyptian, Akkadian, Hebrew and Phoenician form of the universal Seven Powers, who are Seven in Egypt, Seven in Akkad, Babylon, Persia, India, Britain, and Seven among the Gnostics and Kabalists."[5]

The 7 great Creative Rays or Beings are called in the Christian scriptures, "the sons of God * * * the seven Spirits of God * * * the seven angels which stood before God * * * the seven Spirits which are before his throne * * * the seven Spirits of God sent forth into all the earth * * * the angels of the seven churches"[6] etc. By the early church Fathers these Angels are spoken of as the Spiritual Beings who have direct charge of the creation and evolution of this planet and its inhabitants and were regarded as the Agents of God and the Guardians and Regents over the 7 divisions of the earth and mankind. St. Denys, the Areopagite, St. Thomas Aquinas and others all express these same ideas.

> "We meet with those seven in Egypt—also in the Babylonian legend of Creation, as the Seven Brethren, who were Seven Kings, like the Seven Kings in the *Book of Revelation;* and the Seven Non-Sentient Powers, who became the Seven Rebel Angels that made war in heaven. The Seven Kronidae, described as Seven Watchers * * * their work of creation being identical with that of the Elohim of the *Book of Genesis."*[7]

Since number 7 is the symbol which refers to these creative Hierarchies, something of their potency and power inheres mystically in it. And since this number

---

[5] *S. D.,* III, 194-5-6.
[6] *Job,* i, 6; *Revelation,* iii, viii, 2; i, 4; v, 6; i, 20.
[7] *S. D.,* III, 193.

has been and still is connected with Deity in the thoughts of many Races of mankind throughout the ages, a great power and force has thus been generated and attached to it.

Among the various nations these 7 Creative Forces of the Cosmos have been identified with the Rulers of the 7 sacred planets—Sun, Moon, Mercury, Mars, Venus, Jupiter and Saturn. Among the Kabalists the symbols for these 7 Planetary Spirits are as follows: the Sun, a serpent with the head of a lion; the Moon, a globe divided by 2 crescents; Mars, a dragon biting the hilt of a sword; Mercury, a caduceus and the Cynocephalus; Venus, a lingam; Jupiter, a blazing pentagram in the beak of an eagle; Saturn, a lone and aged man, or a serpent coiled around a sunstone.

Michael (the Sun) was called the Angel of Light; Gabriel (the Moon) the angel of Dreams and aspirations; Samael (Venus) the Angel of Love; Anael (Mercury) the angel of Progress; Raphael (Mars) the Angel of Destruction; Zachariel (Jupiter) the Angel of Power; Orifiel (Saturn) the Angel of the Wilderness.

The 7 virtues and the 7 deadly sins were also associated with the planets as follows: Faith, which in the weak degenerates into Pride, is associated with the Sun; Hope and Avarice with the Moon; Charity (Love) and Luxury with Venus; Strength and Wrath with Mars; Prudence and Idleness with Mercury; Temperance and Gluttony with Saturn; Justice and Envy with Jupiter.

Spiritually the 7 sacred planets constitute the 7 sacred centers in the body of the Grand or Heavenly Man, all receiving their life-force from His heart, just as physically they receive their life-force from the sun and send it forth again tinged with something of their own color and characteristic vibrations. Since man is the microcosm of the macrocosm he also has 7 physical, 7 astral and 7 psychic centers within his body, in each of which is focused the force of the planet to which it corresponds. These are the 7 Portals, having 7 golden keys, referred to in *The Voice of the Silence*[8] which man must guard and learn to open and close at will. "These centers, each with its 7 subsidiary centers, are sometimes called the '49 crucified saviors,' signifying that the vital power of these centers is at present misused and crucified, and ere they can become man's Saviors they must be resurrected from the tomb of matter and made to function in a higher state. They are called the '49 fires' because their light guides man to Superman."[9]

In the realm of other physical expressions we again find number 7 *ruling Creation* and *Manifestation.* The 1 white light splits up into the 7 colors of the solar spectrum—violet, indigo, blue, green, yellow, orange and red—the colors of the rainbow, from which all other colors are produced. Since each manifesting vibration has its sound as well as its color, we naturally find that the musical scale is composed of 7 notes—do, re, mi, fa, sol, la, si, the next *do* completing the octave and beginning a new. From this scale the ancient philosophers constructed a ladder of relative planetary sounds upon which they based their "music of the spheres." This scale was made up of the 7 true nature-notes which composed the sacred Word by which all creation was called into manifestation, and are not the notes of the modern musical scale, which it is well known do not give the mathematically correct number of vibrations, but are slightly modified to suit modern methods.

From the proportions existing between the vowel sounds assigned to the planets, the distances between

---

[8] *Fragment,* III.

[9] *V. of I.,* 165.

the planets were estimated so accurately by the ancients that they approximate very closely to the figures claimed as a result of the use of the most scientific instruments by modern astronomers. The scale of planetary notes and colors as given in *The Secret Doctrine* is as follows:

PLANETS,	MOON	MERCURY	VENUS	SUN	MARS	JUPITER	SATURN
Vowels,	a	e	ee	i	o	u	oo
Notes,	si	mi	la	re	do	sol	fa
Colors,	Violet	Yellow	Indigo	Orange	Red	Blue or Purple	Green

> "The best * * * Psychics, as shown by Galton, can also perceive colors produced by the vibrations of musical instruments, every note suggesting a different color. As a string vibrates and gives forth an audible note, so the nerves of the human body vibrate and thrill in correspondence with the various emotions under the general impulse of the circulating vitality of Prana, thus producing undulations in the psychic Aura of the person which results in chromatic effects.
>
> "The human nervous system as a whole, then, may be regarded as an Æolian Harp, responding to the impact of the vital force." [10]

Perception is located in the aura of the Pineal Gland. During the process of thought there is a constant vibration in the light of the aura, and those who can use the inner sight can plainly see the 7 colors in that aura, each color shading from darkest to lightest.

The scale of true nature-notes was well known to the priesthood of many ancient peoples and was used in their sacred chants and mantra, especially during the ceremonies of Initiation. Among the Hindus this scale was expressed on a peculiar instrument called the *vina* which is used to accompany the chanting of their sacred hymns and mantra. This instrument is made

[10] *S. D.*, III, 509.

of a bamboo rod having attached at each end a large hollow gourd, which acts as a sounding board. On the front of the rod 5 strings are strung side by side, with an additional string on either side of the rod below the level of the others, thus making 7 in all. The *vina* is probably the most ancient musical instrument known to man, having been given to him, so the legend tells us, by Brahma himself. Altho there are more than 2000 airs for the *vina*—each 1 said to have its special effect upon diseases, obsessions, insanity, elementals, etc.—it is said none have ever been written down, but are handed on by ear from father to son or teacher to pupil. We will repeat (from memory) the legend of the *vina* as told us by Mme. Desai, a dainty little Hindu lady who is said to be the only woman player of the *vina* in the world. After Brahma had created the world and its inhabitants, his wife Sarasavati complained 1 day that he had given man nothing to relieve his toil, the monotony of his existence nor his sorrows and suffering. Brahma recognized the justice of her complaint and told her to devise some plan for the amelioration of man's lot. She therefore took a bamboo rod and strung strings upon it which would repeat the vibrations of love and harmony of the 7 nature-notes with which her father had created the universe. And the instrument thus fashioned and given to mankind was the *vina*.

We find a similar idea expressed in the Greek legend of the 7 stringed lyre given to Orpheus by Apollo his father, Apollo being the god of the sun or of spiritual Light, and the lyre representing the 7 creative nature-notes or the 7 color-rays emanating from the 7 planets, while Orpheus typified the animating principle or The Christ-force which alone can draw divine harmony from the forces of Nature.

> This is "the hidden meaning of Apollo's Heptachord, the lyre of the radiant god, in each of the seven strings of which dwelleth the Spirit, Soul and Astral Body of the Kosmos, whose shell only has now fallen into the hands of Modern Science." [11]

These notes represent lines of force emanating from the sun, 1 of which is picked out, focused and concentrated by each of the 7 planets and again sent forth. It is because of these rays of force, acting upon the 7 sacred centers in man which correspond to the planets, that the planetary forces affect man. Hence man can sweep the strings of his golden harp in harmony, only as he correlates with the sun-force (The Christ) within, and can listen, understand and respond, to the 7 mystic notes only as he builds into his life the planetary forces and rules them. This same idea is the foundation of the Christian allegory of a heaven in which the saints stand before the throne (*i. e.*, the sun) and play on harps of gold and chant the song of the Lamb which was slain. The Lamb is none other than the Ram of Aries slain that the cosmic blood or life-force of its ruler, Mars, might be poured out to manifest as the vitalizing, pushing, overcoming power by which the sprout of The Christ-seed[12] in every heart shall put forth in spite of all obstacles, and ultimately bring to bloom the Rose of Divine Love whose perfume is immortality. Hence the song of the Lamb is the great pean of mastery of the forces sent out by the septenary sun to the planets and reflected in man. It is sung by those who have mastered and been redeemed and not by those who have merely passed out of incarnation.

While the music of Apollo's lyre is man's response to the 7 planetary forces, the pipes of Pan represent the response of nature to these same forces. This is

[11] *S. D.*, I, 190.

[12] See lesson *The Christ Seed.*

beautifully illustrated by the story of the contest between Apollo and Pan before the mountain god Tmolus who was chosen umpire. "The senior took his seat and cleared away the trees from his ears to listen. At a given signal Pan blew on his pipes, and with his rustic melody gave great satisfaction to himself and his faithful follower King Midas, who happened to be present. Then Tmolus turned his head toward the Sun-god and all his trees turned with him. Apollo rose; his brow wreathed with Parnassian laurel, while his robe of Tyrian purple swept the ground. In his left hand he held the lyre and with his right hand struck the strings. Ravished with the harmony, Tmolus at once awarded the victory to the god of the lyre, and all but Midas acquiesced in the judgment. Apollo would not suffer such a depraved pair of ears any longer to wear the human form, but caused them to increase in length, grow hairy, within and without, and movable on their roots; in short, to become the perfect pattern of those of an ass." [13] This settles the question so often brought up by those who retire from human habitations to become hermits in an effort to attain peace and conquer temptation. To them the harmony of The Christ-force manifesting in the lower kingdoms and interpreted through the nature-tones of Pan, seems all that is necessary to lift them to godhood. But let them mingle with their fellow men, with the right attitude of mind, and listen while Apollo sweeps the heart strings of humanity and they will soon acknowledge the supremacy of the higher manifestation, or will grow asses' ears. In other words those who exclude themselves from human society inevitably tend to degenerate into animalism. For even at the creation of man there was found no help meet for him; no animal was found worthy to be his companion save 1 created after his own kind.

[13] *The Age of Fable,* Bulfinch-Klapp, 60.

Number 7 was also sacred to Clio, the Muse of epic poetry and history (which formerly were recited instead of written), because associated with the voice and sound, as it was through the spoken Word that the universe was brought into manifestation. There are 7 tones to the human voice, each of which correlates with 1 of the 7 creative tones and hence must be harmonized with the music of the spheres. To an Adept the tones of the voice reveal the stage of a person's spiritual unfoldment. These examples should be sufficient to show that number 7 governs the Law of Creation, in man, nature and the Cosmos.

CHAPTER 25

THE NUMBER 7—*(Continued).*

The Number of Manifestation and Gestation.

> "Seven high mountains I beheld, higher than all the mountains of the earth * * * seven rivers * * * seven great islands I saw in the sea and on the earth. Seven in the great sea * * * when the moon rises, it appears in heaven; and the half of a seventh portion of the light is all which is in it."
> —*Book of Enoch,* Chapter lxxvii, 6, 7; lxxvii, 5.

In the study of cosmic evolution, not only do we find 7 sacred planets in our system, but each of these planets has a 7 fold manifestation. As is concisely expressed elsewhere: "Each visible planet is but the lowest, densest aspect of a seven-fold chain, called by occultists a 'World Chain.' A World Chain is composed of seven globes of differing states of matter and consciousness, all existing at the same time and all interpenetrating. The globes of any one chain must not be identified with the visible planets, for only one globe of each Chain is visible, each physically visible planet being the physical globe of its own Chain, just as the Earth is the physical globe of the Earth Chain. The other six globes of each Chain are composed of finer and more ethereal states of matter to which our physical senses do not respond. They are invisible and hence to us apparently do not exist.

"In its descent (involution) into physical manifestation life appears successively on each of the seven globes during one day-period called a Round, seven such day-periods or Rounds being required to complete the cycle of manifestation (involution—turning point

—evolution). 'Our Earth, as the (now) visible representative of its superior fellow-globes * * * has to live, as have the others, through seven Rounds.' * * * These arcane teachings, preserved in their purity upon imperishable records through all ages, tell us that during each Day-period or Round seven Great Races follow each other successively, each being made up of seven sub-races, which in turn are composed of many tribes, kingdoms and nations. These Races and sub-races do not begin suddenly nor end abruptly to make way for the next, but overlap for untold ages ere the old give way to the new. For example: 'The majority of mankind belongs to the seventh sub-race of the Fourth Root Race.' * * * altho humanity is already entering the sixth sub-race of the Fifth Great Race of the Fourth Round."[1] The 1st Great Race of this Round was the Polar, the 2nd the Hyperborean, the 3rd the Lemurian, the 4th the Atlantean, and the 5th is our present Aryan Race.

"The Great Law manifests in seven major aspects,[2] one of which is the main lesson to be worked out on each planetary chain, while all the others are represented as secondary factors. Thus, while the earth chain is working out The Law of Polarity as its main lesson, still this can only be learned by a blending of all the other aspects as subsidiary lessons, just as each of the seven colors of the spectrum, while manifesting its own dominant ray, still contains within it an expression of all the other rays."[3] "No one aspect manifests alone, but while each may predominate in turn all the others manifest at the same time as subordinate factors."[4]

Not only is number 7 the Law of Manifestation in the Races of mankind, but also in man himself. For, like the planet and the Race, man is a 7 fold being composed like number 7, of the 3 and the 4, the △

---

[1] *V. of I.*, 206, 229-30.

[2] As (1) Order, (2) Compensation, (3) Cause and Effect or Karma, (4) Vibration, (5) Balance, (6) Cycles, (7) Polarity or Opposites.

[3] See lesson *The Ancient of Days.*

[4] *V. of I.*, 193.

and the □. His *physical* body is the most dense and physical instrument through which the Soul, the Real Man, manifests. This physical body is but the outer covering of, and is built upon, a body composed of finer and more ethereal matter, the *astral* body, through which the body of desires *(Kama Rupa)* functions. The *mental* body *(lower Manas)* completes the □ of the 4 fold vehicle through which the Soul, composed of the △ of the 3 higher principles — Divine Mind *(Higher Manas)*; The Christ-Consciousness *(Buddhi)* and the Ray *(Atma)* from the Absolute—functions in the worlds of manifestation.[5] According to *The Secret Doctrine*[6] man has 7 states of consciousness—atmic, buddhic, higher manasic, lower manasic, astral, desire and animal or instinctive. He also has 7 kinds of perception, *i. e.,* physical, sense-perception, self-perception, psychic, vital, will and spiritual perception.

Man's physical body is 7 fold in its construction. There are 7 natural divisions of the body: head, thorax (chest), abdomen, 2 arms and 2 legs. The human embryo has 7 parts: the fetus, amnion, amniotic fluid, chorion, allantois, decidua and umbilical vesicle. There are 7 great tissue systems composing his body: epithelial, connective, muscular, nervous and the blood, lymph and reproductive fluids. Of connective tissue there are 7 kinds: gelatinous, areolar, fibro-elastic, cartilage, bone, reticulated and adipose. Of epithelial tissue there are 7 kinds: squamous, ciliated, goblet, neuro, columnar, glandular and pigmented. The body has 7 great functions: respiration, circulation, assimilation, excretion, reproduction, sensation and reaction. There are 7 great organs essential to life; brain, heart, lungs, liver, kidneys, spleen and pancreas. There are 7 layers to the skin: stratum corneum, lucidum, granulosum, germinativum, corium, hair and fat. There are 7 divisions to the eye: cornea, aqueous humor, iris,

[5] For further details see *The Secret Doctrine*, Blavatsky.
[6] Vol. III, 565-6.

lens, vitreous humor, retina and sclera. There are 7 layers to the retina: fibrous, ganglion cells, inner and outer nuclear layers, layer of rods and cones; pigment layer and the choroid. There are 7 divisions to the ear: auditory canal, tympanum, ossicles, semicircular canals, vestibule, cochlea, membranous labyrinth. The heart has 7 compartments or cavities: the right and left ventricles, right and left auricles, right and left auricular appendages and the sack of the pericardium which encloses the whole. Among the Hindus the heart is called the 7 leaved lotus or the "Cave of Buddha" with 7 chambers. There are 7 parts or natural divisions to the brain: cerebrum, cerebellum, optic thalami, corpora quadrigemina, crura cerebri, pons varolii and the medulla oblongata. There are 7 functions to the nervous system: olfactory, optic, auditory, gustatory, tactile, heat and pain sensations.

2nd only to the fact that it represents the idea of the Godhead and the *Mystery of Creation,* number 7 is sacred because, as the *Number of Gestation,* it has to do with the complete manifestation of the Godhead in all its various expression ($1+2+3+4+5+6+7=28=10=1$). We may expect, then, to find number 7 connected with all forms of life and force which have to do with birth and bringing forth. And so we find it. Cosmically, it required 7 "days" or creative periods of enormous length to complete the objective manifestation of this solar system, and its evolution will continue through 7 more such "days," in the 4th of which it is now living. Materially, we find that the chemical elements making up the world of matter arrange themselves according to a 7 fold principle called the Periodic Law. That is if the elements are arranged according to their atomic weights, from the lightest to the heaviest, the 1st 7 are found to have markedly different and characteristic properties, while the properties of the next (8th) element are not different and characteristic, but resemble those of the 1st. Similarly the 9th element resembles the 2nd, the 10th resembles the 3rd and so on until all the elements (with certain temporary exceptions) are arranged in 7 great groups, the elements composing each group having similar properties, functions and reactions.

> "We thus see that chemical variety, so far as we can grasp its inner nature, depends upon numerical relations, * * * we find a law of periodicity governed by the number *seven*. * * * The fact that this periodicity and variety is governed by the number *seven* is undeniable, and it far surpasses the limits of mere chance, and must be assumed to have an adequate cause, which cause must be discovered."[7]
>
> "It must be stated that Occult Science recognizes *seven* Cosmic Elements—four entirely physical, and the fifth (ether) semi-material, which will become visible in the Air toward the end of our Fourth Round, to reign supreme over the others during the whole of the Fifth. The remaining two are as yet absolutely beyond the range of human perception. They will, however, appear as presentiments during the Sixth and Seventh Races of this Round, and will be fully known in the Sixth and Seventh Rounds respectively. These seven Elements with their numberless sub-elements, which are far more numerous than those known to Science, are simply *conditional* modifications and aspects of the One and only Element. This latter is not Ether, not even Akasha, but the *source* of these."[8]

Number 7 is called the "Master of the Moon," because the moon changes its appearance every 7 days. It is well known that the phases of the moon not only rule the tides and vegetation, but in the higher forms of life regulate both the periodic functions of woman and gestation in general.[9]

---

[7] *S. D.*, II, 663-4.

[8] *S. D.*, I, 40-1.

[9] "The moon is the Giver of Life to our Globe; and the early races understood and knew it, even in their infancy." *S. D.*, I, 415.

> "The birth, growth, maturity, vital functions, healthy revolutions of change, diseases, decay and death, of insects, reptiles, fishes, birds, mammals and of even man, are more or less controlled by a law of *completion* in weeks (or 7 days)."[10]

For instance, the embryo of the pigeon hatches in 2 weeks, the chicken in 3 weeks, the turkey and duck in 4, the goose in 5, the rhea in 6, the ostrich in 7 and the cassowary in 8 weeks. Being the most complete of all forms of life, the human embryo or fetus, while viable at the 7th month, requires the complete cycle of 10 for its development before birth, thus, 10 months of 28 days or $4 \times 7 = 28 \times 10 = 280 = 10$. Also the average weight of the human fetus is 7 pounds.

Both Hippocrates and Pythagoras held—and this is confirmed by the experience of modern physicians—that a child born at 7 months or at the full term of 9 months could live, because each of these numbers was composed of a male (odd) and a female (even) number, thus $3 + 4 = 7$; $5 + 4 = 9$; but children born at 8 months could not live because born under a purely feminine number, thus: $4 + 4 = 8$. The umbilical cord dries up and drops off by the 7th day; the teeth begin their development in the 7th week of intra-uterine life, the 1st teeth appear during the 7th month after birth and the full set, which last for 7 years, are attained in the 4×7 or 28th month, while the sex functions begin in the 2×7 or 14th year.

> " 'With the Egyptians number 7 was the symbol of *life* eternal', says Ragon, and adds that this is why the Greek letter Z, which is but a double 7, is the initial letter of Zaô, 'I live', and of Zeus, the 'father of all living'."[11]

The 7th letter of the Egyptian alphabet is called Zenta and means life.

---

[10] *S. D.*, II, 658.

[11] *S. D.*, II, 616.

The cells of our bodies are continually changing, the old dying and being replaced by new, so that it has been estimated that every 7 months the soft tissues are completely renewed, while every 7 years we have an entirely new body, even to the composition of the bones.

> "The physical body of man undergoes a complete change of structure every seven years, and its destruction and preservation are due to the alternate functions of the Fiery Lives, as Destroyers and Builders. They are builders by sacrificing themselves, in the form of vitality, to restrain the destructive influence of the microbes, and, by supplying the microbes with what is necessary, they compel them under that restraint to build up the material body and its cells. They are Destroyers also, when that restraint is removed, and the microbes, unsupplied with vital constructive energy, are left to run riot as destructive agents.[12]
>
> "The facts I have briefly glanced at are general facts, *and cannot happen day after day in so many millions of animals of every kind, from the larva or ovum of a minute insect up to man, at definite* periods, from a mere *chance* or *coincidence* * * * Upon the whole it is, I think, impossible to come to any less general conclusion than this, that, in animals, *changes occur every three and a half, seven, fourteen, twenty-one and twenty-eight days, or at some definite number of weeks,"*[13] or septenary cycles.

[12] *S. D.*, I. 283.

[13] *S. D.*, II, 659.

CHAPTER 26

THE NUMBER *7—(Continued).*

The Number of Perfection.

"When thou hast passed into the seventh, (stage) O happy one, thou shalt perceive no more the sacred Three, * * * They have become one star, the fire that burns but scorches not, that fire which is the Upadhi of the Flame."
—*The Voice of the Silence,* Blavatsky, 19-20.

In considering number 7 in its aspect of *completeness* and *perfection* we find that the Hebrew word for 7 is composed of the 3 letters S B O and has many interpretations, but all are connected with the fundamental idea of completeness and "Satisfied abundance." It means "age" or "cycle," hence Sabbath is the rest of old age or the completion of the life-cycle. It is connected with the gray-headed, and the 7th or Sabbath day is presided over by Saturn, who is represented as an old man, Cronus or Father Time. In the Greek the word *septos,* from the verb *sebo,* to venerate, is connected with the idea of Father Time as a venerable old man as commonly depicted.

The 3 periods which complete man's life are composed of 3, 4 and 3 groups (total 10 groups) of 7 years each, thus: youth extends $3\times7=21$ yrs; prime extends $4\times7=28$ yrs; age extends $3\times7=21$ yrs; total $7\times10=70$ yrs, or the biblical "threescore and ten" or $3\times20+10=70$ years.

"During the first half of a man's life, the first *five* periods of seven years each, the Fiery Lives—the 7th and highest sub-division of the plane of matter—are directly engaged in a process of building up man's material body; Life is on the ascending scale, and the force is used in

> construction and increase. After this period is passed, the age of retrogression commences, and, the work of the Fiery Lives exhausting their strength, the work of destruction and decrease also commences."[1]

Number 7 is complete and sacred because it is composed of the triad (3) and the tetrad (4) or God and nature, combined in man. Pythagoras says number 7 has a body composed of the 4 principles and a soul composed of 3 principles. 3 as the Number of *Light* is wedded to 4, the Number of *Life,* and 3 as the Number of *Spirit* is wedded to 4 as the Number of *Matter,* and these 2 couples are both combined in 7. Again 3 is spiritual and Divine while 4 is physical and human, hence man as 7 is both human and Divine, the □ overshadowed and protected by the △. In number 5 the 1 God descends into the midst of the pairs of opposites of humanity thus: 2-1-2, but in number 7 the Divine Trinity has unfolded its triple aspect within the 2 pairs thus: 2-3-2, the effect of which is to transmute the mundane twos into divine threes, thus: 3-1-3 or has perfected the work begun in number 5 as 2-1-2. That 7 is an expression of Perfection is also shown by the fact that the sum of the first 7 digits equals 10, thus: $1+2+3+4+5+6+7=28=10$.

> "The number seven," says the Kabbalah, "is the great number of the 'Divine Mysteries'."[2]

According to Cornelius Agrippa, "Seven, being the sum of the Primary Numbers, is a diameter of *all* number. A diameter of 7 has a circumference, in whole numbers, of 22. The action of life is a dividing of this circumference of 22 by its diameter of 7, resulting as: 3.142857,142857∞ the residuum eternally repeating 142857. * * * Hence, by reason of these prop-

[1] *S. D., I,* 283.

[2] *S. D., I,* 68.

erties of 7 * * * to numerically interpret Infinite Nature is to divide its number (999,999,999∞) by 7. This gives us, again, the Number of Infinite Evolution: 142857,142857,142857∞."[3]

It requires 7 members to form a Free Mason's Lodge (altho 5 may hold it after organization), thus symbolizing that man to be the Master Man must manifest number 7. While he can hold a "lodge," *i. e.,* can be a man and live his life as a 5 fold being, yet he must always remember that this is but a stage of growth, a place of incompleteness, and that he must ultimately prepare and add 2 more members (senses and powers) to his "lodge," ere he can be a true Mason. The Knights of Kadosh symbolize the masonic ideals of the relations between God and man by a double ladder having 7 steps of ascent and 7 steps of descent. The former are called *Ohed Eloah, or Love of God,* while the latter are termed *Oheb Kerobo,* or *Love of thy Neighbor.* These symbolize that to give true brotherly love to your neighbor you must first ascend in love to God.

Just as the truths of the Wisdom Religion have been preserved through the Dark Ages in a game of cards —the *Tarot,* from which our playing cards were derived —so has the importance and fortunate nature of number 7 been handed down from the days of the Chaldeans in the game of dice, the opposite sides of which always add up to 7, thus: 1 is opposite to 6, 2 is opposite to 5 and 3 is opposite to 4.

The method of calculating cycles in the *Bible* is by systems of weeks, weeks of days, weeks of years, etc.

From the Goth's names for the 7 Planetary Deities we derive our names for the days of the week, thus, the Sun's day (Sunday), the Moon's day (Monday), Tuisco's (Mars') day (Tuesday), Wotan's (Mercury) day (Wednesday), Thor's (Jupiter's) day (Thurs-

[3] *The Mystic Thesaurus,* Whitehead, 47-8.

day), Friga's (Venus') day (Friday), Seatur's (Saturn's) day (Saturday).

The Zuni Indians built their villages in clusters of 6 tepees surrounding a 7th. Their mystic sacerdotal gatherings were composed of 6 "Priests of the House" who drew their inspiration from a 7th who was always a woman called the "Priestess Mother." While officiating at their annual festivals each was arrayed in a robe of the color sacred to 1 of the 7 sacred planets, and when so robed each was considered to be the representative of the planetary deity whose color he wore, hence gave his judgments as from that deity. These priests received an annual tribute of corn of 7 colors from the members of the tribe.[4]

The city of Thebes had 7 gates built by Amphion. "The most famous monument of ancient Thebes was the outer wall with its seven gates, even as late as the sixth century B. C., it was probably the largest of artificial Greek fortresses." "The seven gates of Thebes, attacked and defended by seven chiefs who have sworn upon the blood of victims, possess the same significance as the seven seals of the sacred book interpreted by the seven genii, and assailed by a monster with seven heads." [5]

Westcott calls attention to the fact that "The number 7 was curiously related to H. P. Blavatsky and the Theosophical Society. 'Lucifer' was first published in 1887, and 1887 is the sum of 17 hundreds, 17 tens and 17 units; H. P. B. lived at 17 Lansdown Road, and 17 Avenue Road; 'Lucifer' was published at 7 Duke St.; 7 volumes were completed at her death; Colonel Olcott first met her at 7 Beckman Street, and later at 71 Broadway, New York. Anna Kingsford was elected president first of the London T. S. Lodge in 1877, and the Third volume of 'The Secret Doctrine' was published in 1897, after her death."[6]

---

[4] *S. D.*, II, 665.
[5] *Transcendental Magic*, Lévi, 14.
[6] *Numbers*, 84.

Besides the passages already quoted, both the *Old* and the *New Testaments* are filled with references to the number 7 which show the great regard in which it was held in Israel. These again exhibit the fundamental idea of completion, rounding out, also, the binding and unalterable nature of a thing repeated 7 times. Thus Naaman was told to dip 7 times in the river Jordan to be cleansed of his leprosy (II *Kings* v, 14). This is a symbol of the potency of number 7 in evolution, for only as man has dipped at least 7 times into the Stream of Life—which like the river Jordan is muddy and turbulent—and has cleansed himself from all loathsome carnalities can he emerge as conqueror and be ready to pass on through number 8 to his Great Initiation in number 9.

Noah was commanded to take into the ark of all clean beasts by sevens, and of the unclean by pairs *(Genesis,* vii, 2). The clean beasts were those used for food, and as food is the material from which the tissues and energies of the body are elaborated, it is naturally ruled by 7. The unclean beasts not used for food refer to mundane forces which are ruled by the pairs of opposites. In the tabernacle a golden candlestick with 7 branches was a notable feature *(Exodus,* xxv, 31.) This again symbolizes man with the fires in his 7 sacred centers lighted, each of which must emit the flame of Divine Love ere his tabernacle (body) is a fit dwelling place for the Holy Presence. Abraham made a covenant with Abimelech *(Genesis,* xxi, 28) by presenting him with 7 ewe lambs, thus making the covenant complete and binding. Jacob served 7 years for Rachael, was deceived with Leah and served yet 7 other years for Rachael (*Genesis,* xxix). Pharoah dreamed of 7 "well favored kine and fatfleshed" and of 7 "ill favored and leanfleshed kine that did eat up the 7 well favored and fat kine." He also dreamed of

7 ears of corn upon 1 stalk, and 7 thin and blasted ears which devoured the full ears. Both of these dreams Joseph correctly interpreted as 7 years of plenty followed by 7 years of famine (*Genesis,* xli).

There were 7 days of unleavened bread (*Exodus,* xii, 15), and 7 Sabbaths were ordained (*Lev.,* xxiii, 15). The children of Israel followed 7 priests blowing 7 trumpets for 7 days in their march around the city of Jericho and on the last day encompassed the city 7 times ere its walls fell (*Joshua,* vi). Wisdom buildeth her house out of 7 pillars (*Rev.,* ix). There are 7 "gifts of the Spirit" mentioned by *Isaiah* (xi, 2) as follows: Wisdom, Understanding, Counsel, Might, Knowledge, Fear (Awe) of the Lord (Law), and Righteous Judgment.

In the *New Testament,* as we have pointed out elsewhere,[7] "The Man upon the cross spoke seven sentences symbolizing the seven steps of Initiation." "Father forgive them; for they know not what they do. * * * Today shalt thou be with me in paradise. * * * Woman, behold they son. * * * My God, my God, why hast thou forsaken me? * * * I thirst. * * * It is finished. * * * Father, into Thy hands I commend my spirit."

"Man has his seven Principles, each of which is derived from and ruled over by one of these seven Planetary Angels, called by St. John 'the angels of the seven churches.' Also, 'you have the seven Angelic Planes, whose "Host" collectively are the Gods thereof.' "[8] Man and Nature are akin, and while each man contains emanations from all the 7 creative Rays[9] manifested through his 7 Principles, still in each man 1 influence or Ray predominates. This fact naturally divides mankind into 7 main classes of thought, designated by St. John, as we indicated in a previous lesson,[10] as the 7 "churches." "These 7 great

---

[7] See lesson *The Meaning of the Cross.*
[8] *S. D.,* II, 251.
[9] *V. of I.,* Chapter xiii.
[10] *The Revelation of St. John.*

modes of viewing Truth are subdivided ad libitum. * * * The many subdivisions agree with the manifold character of the planetary influences, which vary with each hour of the day."

"This idea of the seven fold division of the universe is esoterically represented in *Revelation* by 'the seven churches which are in Asia.' These were at Ephesus, Smyrna, Pergamos, Thyatira, Sardis, Philadelphia and Laodicea. These names were made use of more to illustrate the inner truth than as applying to the historical cities, altho the churches in those cities may have manifested the types of thought indicated, just as Wall Street in New York is used to symbolize the power of money. The inner truth so symbolized has, of course, seven keys by which it can be read, one interpretation being that the seven churches refer to the seven principal ganglia or centers of the human nervous system, another to the seven steps of Initiation."[11]

"A 'church' signifies an aggregation of people of similar thought, and here we find all humanity divided into seven great classes or types called 'churches.' The words 'which are in Asia' are merely an euphonious blind, for we find that these seven 'churches' or types of humanity have existed in various parts of the world for ages. And they always will exist, for, as we have shown in the lesson on Evolution,[12] mankind is the progeny or emanation from seven great Creators or, as the Bible terms them, the Elohim. * * * And as we showed in that same lesson, all mankind are emanations from one of these seven great spiritual Progenitors or, as St. John terms them, 'The seven Spirits which stood before his throne.' This throne, which is spoken of later on[13] as 'a great white throne,' is the perfect white light of the Divine into which all its manifestations (rays) are ultimately indrawn and

---

[11] See lesson *The Seven Churches.*
[12] *V. of I.,* Chapter xiii.
[13] *Revelation,* xx, 11.

enthroned. Hence, of necessity, there must be in the world seven distinct classes of religious thought, each trying to manifest the characteristics of the Ray of which it is an expression."

"Not only have there been, since the world began, seven representative schools of thought—first under one name and then, as times change, under another—but every child is born with a type of mind over which the influence of one of these great Rays predominates. * * * Therefore, to confine the seven 'churches' to the handful of apostolic adherents in the historical cities whose names are mentioned, is to lose the universal significance of the revelation."

"The seven golden candlesticks which St. John saw symbolized the outer garments or the physical vehicles or methods by which the seven manifestations of the Light of Truth are placed before man. The seven candles symbolize the seven different types of teaching which the seven candlesticks (churches) uphold before the world, and by which the Flame or Spiritual Light is given to humanity, the Light in all cases being identical, altho produced by different candles."[14]

---

[14] See lesson *The Revelation of St. John.*

CHAPTER 27

THE NUMBER 7—*(Continued).*

The Number of Perfection—(Continued).

"And I saw in the right hand of him that sat on the throne a book written within and on the backside, sealed with seven seals. * * * And I beheld, and, lo, in the midst of the throne and of the four beasts, and in the midst of the elders, stood a lamb as it had been slain, having seven horns and seven eyes, which are the seven Spirits of God sent forth into all the earth."

—*Revelation,* v, 1-6.

The book of *Revelation* abounds in the use of 7 in reference to completion, such as the 7 vials of the 7 last plagues; the 7 trumpet calls; the 7 thunders; the sounding of the 7 angels; the 7 kings, 5 of whom are fallen; the beast with the 7 heads, etc.

As we have said elsewhere: "The book mentioned in our text is the great Book of Life (Akashic Records), with its seven fold manifestations, so frequently referred to in scriptural and occult literature. Within this Great Book is written all that is to manifest during the cycle which begins when the word is spoken, 'Let there be light', and the Spirit of Life moves upon the face of the waters of Chaos. The seven seals are the seven manifestations of the One Life; in the solar system, the seven cosmic centers of force or powers of the Heavenly Man and the seven great Day-periods or Rounds; in humanity the seven Great Races, and in man, made in the image of the seven fold Elohim, the seven sacred centers of his body and his seven stages of growth. Just as a stone thrown into a calm pool sets up ever widening waves of vibration, so the Light shot out into the darkness of Chaos causes a seven fold wave of manifestation throughout the Cosmos.

"The Great Book as applied to man is his body with its seven sacred centers. It is sealed with seven seals because, altho individually man can open these centers as he evolves godward, for humanity as a whole they open only as it passes through the seven Great Races, each of which opens to man a new sense, new conditions and new experiences. These centers are the avenues through which man comes into conscious communion with the higher realms, but they are sealed until through normal growth he has evolved to a point where he can control and utilize them."[1]

The fact that the Great Book of the Akashic Records is sealed with 7 seals which no man is worthy to open, should effectually dispose of the claims of those who say they have transcribed certain works directly from the Akashic Records. There is, however, a reflecting medium which is mistaken by many psychics for the Akashic Records. This reflects both from above and below, but looked at from the earth it reflects more from present day conditions than from the Akashic Records, thus mixing the 2.

Number 7 when complete in man may be called The Christ-Gift (the prototype of the Christmas gift) which is sealed with the 7 seals of Love, Patience, Purity, Trust, Perseverance, Endurance and Devotion. These are the King's seals which must be opened and manifested 1 by 1. For even if 1 remains sealed the Neophyte will not bear the mark on his forehead which seals him as 1 of the Elect.

"The lamb had seven horns and seven eyes. The horn is an universal symbol of power. Horns are the principal defense and strength of many animals, enabling them to maintain their supremacy over those having no horns. For this reason the Ram becomes

[1] See lesson *The Great Book,* Part I.

the leader and defender of the flock, the sheep being without horns. A horn symbolizes a ruler, a king or military power. To 'exalt one's horn' or 'cause it to bud' or grow is to strengthen and prosper. To 'lift one's horn' is to become arrogant, to 'cut off one's horn' is to weaken or be crushed. The horn is also a symbol of plenty, both in the physical and spiritual life, showing that the Ram, although slain and reborn as the Lamb, must still lead and feed the flock through the plenteous outpourings from its seven horns. The seven horns symbolize the seven great powers of man,[2] whose attainment are steps upon the Path to Mastery along which The Christ-light must lead him. * * * The seven eyes, 'which are the seven Spirits of God sent forth into all the earth', in this connection symbolize that spiritual insight which is the accompaniment and reward of such conquering,"[1] or the perfected clear seeing upon all planes, as well as the watchful care of the Spirit.

"The seven stars in the right hand of the Ancient of Days are the seven Cosmic Forces or Planetary Deities. Another aspect of these same Forces is symbolized by the lights of the seven candles, but in this case they are confined to an earthly vehicle, the Light merely shining through a limited earthly conception —for although the candlesticks are golden (pure) they rest upon the earth—while in the case of the stars the Light shines direct from the Absolute. It also indicates that the Great Law holds even the planets and the Planetary Deities in its hand. 'As above, so below,' the one Light in both stars and candlesticks. Do not confuse this teaching with Pantheism, for it is not. We do not teach that there are many co-equal gods, but that there are many divine, Entitized Manifestations of the one God, the Absolute."

"The Great Law has two aspects, one represented

[1] See lesson *The Great Book,* Part I.
[2] See *The Voice of Isis,* Chapter xii.

by the seven stars—the seven manifestations of the Great Law in its purity—and the other represented by the seven candlesticks or its chosen vehicles of expression on earth. These vehicles, while of gold and originally reflecting the light of the seven stars in its purity, are nevertheless susceptible to contamination by the mire of earth, as the rebukes given to the seven churches in the next chapter will show."[3] A candlestick is a specially created (manufactured) instrument for the 1 purpose of holding a candle that the Light may shine out to illuminate and guide humanity.

The *Sepher Yetzirah* agrees with occult philosophy when it states that out of the 7 letters and the 7 numbers, colors, tones and the planetary forces with which they are identified, there were created the 7 worlds, the 7 heavens, 7 earths, 7 seas, 7 rivers, 7 deserts, 7 days, etc. The 7 worlds are the 7 globes which compose a World Chain. Among Kabalists these 7 worlds are called the Original, Intelligible, Celestial, Elementary, Lesser (astral), Infernal (Kama Loka or Hades) and the physical or Temporal. The 7 heavens are the 7 divisions or sub-planes of the Astral[4] (*i. e.,* the reflective, etheric, vital, desire, mental, inspirational and ecstatic). The 7 earths are the 7 states of consciousness experienced on earth, *i. e.,* primitive animal consciousness; self-consciousness; tribal or class-consciousness; ethical or duty to others; astral or psychic; spiritual or Christ-consciousness, and Universal or Cosmic Consciousness. The 7 seas refer to the 7 states of illusion. The 7 rivers are the 7 streams of force in man, *i. e.,* blood, nerve, pranic, astral, mental, psychic and spiritual. The 7 deserts are the barren wastes of doubts, fears, misconceptions, disappointments, disillusions, poverty and ill health.

> "It is on account of his septenary nature that the Sun is spoken of by the ancients as one who is

[3] See lesson *The Ancient of Days.*
[4] See *Realms of the Living Dead,* Curtiss, 49, 50.

> driven by seven horses equal to the meters of the Vedas; * * *as also that he has Seven Rays as indeed he has. * * * The Seven Beings in the Sun are the Seven Holy Ones, self-born from the inherent power in the Matrix of Mother-Substance. It is they who send the seven principal Forces, called Rays, which at the beginning of Pralaya will center into seven new Suns for the next Manvantara." [5]

The 7th Path in the *Sepher Yetzirah* is that of Occult Intelligence, a combination of Faith and Intellect. In Hinduism the Path of Perfection is made up of a series of 7s, each 7 marking a definite step or a victory won by the Neophyte. These steps are spoken of as Portals or Gates because the Neophyte must pass through experiences and enter states of consciousness which are closed to him until he brings the Golden Key to each or until he has attained the mystic power which will open them. These 7 keys are as follows: to the 1st Portal, Charity and all-embracing Love; to the 2nd, Harmony and Fearlessness; to the 3rd, Patience; to the 4th, Indifference to pleasure as to pain; to the 5th, dauntless Energy; to the 6th, ceaseless Contemplation, and to the 7th, the Key which opens the final gate, whose entrance makes of man a God.

Number 7 is held to represent magic in its fulness. Éliphas Lévi says: "The virtue of the Septenary is absolute in magic for the number is decisive in all things; hence all religions have consecrated it in their rites." [6] In other words man (5), through the power of The Christ-force (6), in number 7 has claimed his heritage. He can now stand upon the Foundation Stone (4) and allow the Divine Triangle (3) to pour down its triune blessings upon his head. The 5 pointed star has gained 2 more points—the rod by which man holds his 5 powers in his right hand, and the Dot in

---

[5] *S. D.*, I, 310.

[6] *Transcendental Magic*, 79.

the center which synthesizes all his powers, the true magic pentagram. (Fig. 7.) It is man's mind reinforced by all the elementary potencies.

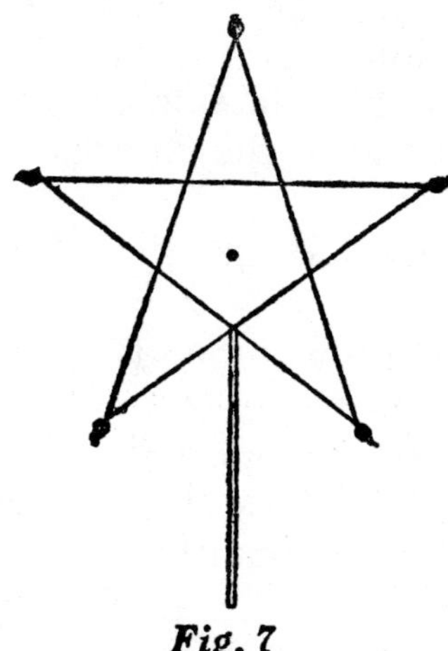

Fig. 7

"Viewed as a compound of 6 and 1, the Senary and the Unity, number 7 was the invisible center, the Spirit of everything, as there exists no hexagonal body without a *seventh* property being found as the central point in it." [7]

The symbol of a star with 7 points was sometimes used in ancient temples and Schools of Mysteries, but it was used as an exoteric blind; for it was well known by the initiated Priests that a 7 pointed star was not a true symbol. A star with 7 points would necessarily focus the forces which the points contacted into a central point, thus giving the figure an 8 fold power. This symbol was used to instruct the Neophyte in the perfection of number 7 and to instill into his mind a reverence for its potencies, while the force invoked was that of number 8, which is both evolution, balance and poise, all of which are qualities necessary for Initiation. But until he had passed his Initiation the

---

[7] *S. D.,* II, 616.

6 pointed star with its central Dot could not be entrusted to him, lest he misuse its potencies and powers. Hence in true esoteric symbolism there is no 7 pointed star, as it cannot be formed by the combination of any 2 simple geometrical figures, altho it is sometimes seen in exoteric emblems. The geometrical symbol of number 7 is the interlaced triangles with the Dot in the center ✡, the Dot being the same germinal point we found within the circle, or the creative nucleus of the mundane egg which has evolved during its 6 day-periods of creation through nature and man and become the synthesized focal point for the forces of its 6 manifestations. As ⊙ represents Deity as the source of all so ✡ represents Deity manifesting through the perfect unfolding and balancing of the positive and negative triangles described under number 6. The 6 points represent the 6 days required to bring forth the microcosm, while the Dot within is the Throne upon which the Deity rests on the 7th day and pronounces all His works good. As the Dot in the circle represents the Throne of Deity in the macrocosm, so the Dot in the 6 pointed star represents the Throne of Deity established and manifesting in the microcosm. The Dot in the center represents the Soul of all things, as the star represents the body, for there is no body which 6 lines or the 6 directions of space—north, south, east, west, up, down—will not enclose, and which is not an outward manifestation of the 7th point in the center. This symbol therefore represents the perfected spiritual or *Nirmanakaya* body when attained.

> "In its Unity, Primordial Light is the seventh, or highest, principle, Daiviprakriti, the Light of the Unmanifested Logos. But in its differentiation, it becomes Fohat, or the 'Seven Sons.' The former is symbolized by the central point in the Double Triangle; the latter by the Hexagon itself, or the 'Six Limbs' of Microprosopus, the Seventh being Malkuth, the 'Bride' of the Christian Kabalists."[8]

By the Essenes this symbol is called the Seal of Solomon, for they recognized Solomon as the personification of esoteric Wisdom. And to this day, even among Christian peoples it is still looked upon as a powerful talisman, especially in Russia and Poland. The Pythagoreans called it the symbol of creation and the Egyptians similarly looked upon it as the union of fire (3) and water (4) or generation.

The 7th Sephira is called Netzach, "Firmness and Victory, corresponding to the divine name Jehovah Tzabaoth, the Lord of Hosts and the angelic names Elohim and Tharshism, the Brilliant Ones." Hence man can evolve intellectually to a point where he can unfold the 6 Sephira, that is, he can intertwine the divine attributes with the physical and thus become the magic symbol of Solomon's Seal, the Seal of Wisdom. But until he has unfolded or manifested the 7th point and gained a complete Victory; until he has fixed his gaze upon the Star of Initiation, The Christ-sun, and made that the center from which all his works proceed, he may be a magician with mighty power, but he is not accepted as a White Magician. The 6 represents wonderful intellectual development, but it must recognize, accept and respond to the Spiritual Overshadowing or the Divine Illumination of the Dot in the center, ere the perfection of 7 is reached.

> "The seventh key is the hieroglyph of the sacred septenary, of royalty, of the priesthood (the Initiate), of triumph and true result by struggle.

---

[8] *S. D.*, I, 236.

> It is magic power in all its force, the true 'Holy Kingdom.' In the Hermetic Philosophy it is the quintessence resulting from the union of the two forces of the great Magic Agent (Akasha, the Astral Light)."[9]

In the Greek legend Minas, King of Crete, demanded every 9th year a toll of 7 youths and 7 maidens who were sacrificed to Minatour, a monster with the body of a man and the head of a bull. This monster was confined in a labyrinth, in whose passages any of the victims who attempted to escape lost their way and were eventually devoured. When the time for the 3rd sacrifice drew near, Theseus, taking the place of the youths and maidens, went to Crete to slay the Monster. At his landing, Ariadne, the daughter of Minas and granddaughter of the Sun-god Helios, fell in love with Theseus and gave him a thread which he unwound as he proceeded and thus was enabled to find his way out of the labyrinth after slaying the Monster.

This myth symbolizes the positive (masculine) and the negative (feminine) aspects of the 7 planetary Hierarchies through which the great tests of humanity are brought out. Since the bull symbolizes the sign Taurus and the generative power, the meaning is that the man whose passions (bull) rule and dominate the body (occupy the seat of government, the head), is confined and shut in on every side by the labyrinth of earth conditions. In other words, animal man while evolving through the lower aspects of forces symbolized by the 3 decans of Taurus, degrades and devours the most beautiful planetary influences, until the close of the 3rd cycle or 3rd great Initiation, when the Real Self (Theseus), by following the thread of Love and Intuition given him by the feminine aspect or daughter of the Sun (the 3rd decan of Taurus being

[9] *S. D.*, III, 106.

ruled by Venus), is able to slay the Monster and set the planetary influences free from the domination of the animal-man, that they may accomplish their true mission of opening to the initiated man the gates of Paradise or the New Jerusalem.

Among the Greeks the sun is portrayed as a chariot drawn by 7 horses, representing the 7 planetary Hierarchies or Rays. And, in the myth, Phaethon, the mortal son of Helios the Sun-god, essays to drive this chariot of the sun, with disastrous results. The meaning of this allegory is that man must perfect his 7 principles and his 7 powers on earth and become more than mortal ere he can safely hold the reins and control the 7 planetary forces. It also refutes a popular modern teaching, *i. e.,* that because man has a divine Father he is therefore, *now in his present undeveloped state,* a god with all the powers of a god successfully to negotiate the circle of the zodiac in his own strength. The fate of those who espouse this doctrine is as certain as was Phaethon's, for like him they must face all the monsters of the zodiac, especially Scorpio which caused the disaster to Phaethon. As the legend reads, "Here the Scorpion extended his two great arms, with his tail and crooked claws stretching over two signs of the Zodiac (Virgo and Scorpio which were formerly one sign and represented in Syrio-Chaldean magic as God and the Devil). When the boy beheld him, reeking with poison and menacing with his fangs, his courage failed and the reins fell from his hands."[10] The test of Scorpio—the test of sex—is thus fitly described. It is under this test that so many self-styled gods in mortal frame fail. And as with Phaethon the fiery steeds of thought run away with them and they are dashed to earth.

The dragons and serpents of antiquity were all 7 headed, as was the Beast of the *Apocalypse,* a head for

[10] *The Age of Fable,* Bulfinch, 54.

each of the 7 Races, and had 7 hairs on each head, representing the 7 sub-races of each Great Race. The 4 Dragons of Wisdom were composed of 7 constellations each. The 7 Northern constellations made up the Black Warrior; the 7 Eastern, the White Tiger; the 7 Southern, the Vermillion Bird, and the 7 Western, the Azure Dragon. The 7 headed Akkadian Serpent whose heads multiplied from 7 into 1000, fitly symbolizes the 7 Principles of man and nature, with their manifold aspects. Number 7 was also held sacred to several gods, for instance, Osiris, whose body was cut into 2x7 pieces; Mars and his 7 attendants; Apollo and his 7 stringed lyre, etc.

CHAPTER 28

THE 7 PRINCIPLES OF MAN.

The One Life is, as explained, a Film for creative or formative purposes. It manifests in seven states, which, with their septenary subdivisions, are the Forty-nine Fires mentioned in the sacred books. To Man it gives all that it bestows on all the rest of the manifested units in Nature; but develops, furthermore, the reflection of all its 'Forty-nine Fires' in him. Each of his seven principles is an heir in full to, and a partaker of, the seven principles of the 'Great Mother'."
—*The Secret Doctrine,* Blavatsky, Vol. I, 310.

The 7 Principles of which man is composed, from the densest and most material to the highest and most spiritual, are as follows:

The 1st Principle. The Physical Body.

While the physical body is the lowest expression of the Real or Divine Self it is 1 of the most important. Altho at the opposite pole from Spirit it nevertheless has within it the centers in and through which each of the higher Principles must focus to manifest on earth. The body therefore should not be looked upon as a hampering garment to be despised and escaped from as soon as possible, for it is an instrument which is *absolutely necessary* for the manifestation of the Higher Self and without which it cannot accomplish its mission in the physical world. The viewpoint of Christian Mysticism is therefore just the opposite to much teaching that passes for true Oriental philosophy. Because the animal body is passionate, seductive, self-willed, hard to train and control until it has been purified, spiritualized and made the willing servant of the Real Man, many Eastern students seek to weaken it, maim it, or even kill out its natural forces, that they may ultimately escape from the bondage of the flesh and from rebirth. But the Christian Mystic seeks to perfect it in every part and have every function in its highest state of activity that it may be a perfect instrument, well knowing that rebirth must continue until he has built up a perfected and spiritualized organism through which perfectly to express The Christ-force for the redemption of himself, his fellow-men and the lower kingdoms.

The physical body is made in the image of the Spiritual Body of the Real Man. It is therefore an organism in which all the creative energies of the 7 fold Elohim are synthesized and through which they must manifest. Hence the Soul must again and again build a physical body, until ultimately it builds 1 which can perfectly express the Divine Man. It may be compared to a switchboard containing terminals for the ramifications of a mighty electrical system, some of its currents connecting it with the higher Principles and all parts of the universe, even the distant planets, all of which affect and manifest through the physical body.

*The 2nd Principle, The Astral Body and Its Double.**

The Astral Body projects its shadow or double from the Astral World into the mother's womb as a pattern, and into the meshes of this pattern the physical materials composing the flesh and bone of the future man are built. Its focal point in the physical body is in the spleen. The Astral Body is the seat of sensations, which are transmitted to and from the physical body by its double, and operate through the nerves. The Astral Body and its double are material bodies of a sort, so material that, under certain conditions, they can be photographed with an ordinary camera, but the matter composing them is more tenuous, ethereal and of a higher rate of vibration than physical matter. It

* For details see *Realms of the Living Dead,* Curtiss 57.

is so plastic that it is capable of being acted upon from within by the Real Self, from the mental world through thought, from the passional world of the Animal Soul through the emotions and from the physical world through the nerves. It is also easily affected by the vibrations from the beings and forces in all the realms of the astral world.

It is the semi-material substance (called ectoplasm) of this astral double which exudes from a medium at a materializing séance, its plastic condition allowing it to be moulded into a model of itself by the discarnate entity who desires to manifest, or it can even be moulded into form by the thoughts of the sitters. The form thus materialized is connected to the medium by a cord of ectoplasm the rupture of which would mean death to the medium. Hence it is dangerous to pass between a materialized form and its medium. The astral *double* is connected to the body of the medium by an umbilical cord which prevents its extrusion beyond a limited distance, while the astral *body* itself is not so limited, but can travel to great distances, always connected to the physical, however, by a line of force.

The 3rd Principle. The Life-force.

This Principle is that aspect of the 1 Life which is sometimes called the sun-principle or *prana*. This force has its seat in the physical body in the solar plexus, its point of contact through the umbilicus and its action through the lungs, blood and spine. Since this Principle is a stream of force from the universal Cosmic Life-principle or the Breath of Life, it is a connecting link which binds all the Principles, not only together but, through the 1 Life, to all that is in manifestation. It is through a perfect understanding and control of this Principle that the Adept rules all his lower Principles and while still in the physical body learns to make conscious contact with the Higher Self. This force must act according to the laws of harmony and purity and be under the guidance of the Divine Will or it will be like steam escaping from leaks in a boiler. 1st, it fails to give its power to the engine (body), which consequently slows down, grows weak, devitalized and ultimately stops; 2nd, it acts as a destroyer, just as escaping steam fills the engine-room, rusts the engine and becomes a menace to the engineer (the Real Self). Therefore this Principle of the Life-force is the creator or bringer of life to the physical and astral bodies, the preserver and regulator of life and vitality, and finally the destroyer. During the lower stages of development—as in the animal and undeveloped man—this force is guided by the subconscious mind according to the law of harmony. But in the higher stages where mind is more active, its normal currents and actions are interfered with by man's impure thoughts, habits and desires, also by anything that defiles the breath. Hence we have physical inharmony, sickness and disease, as manifestations or stages in the process of disintegration.

The 4th Principle. The Desire Body or Animal Soul.

This Principle, together with the physical and astral bodies and the life-force, completes the 4 fold Foundation Stone laid by the Higher Self in the physical world. For only as the Divine Ray sent down into matter can find a foundation composed of the elements belonging to the worlds in which it seeks expression, can it manifest there and garner the experiences of those worlds. Therefore its earthly instrument of manifestation is built up just as is a house. 1st, the plan or pattern is conceived and the framework erected, the outer structure is built around it, the life-force warms it and then the Animal Soul, like a janitor, takes charge. Then it is ready for occupancy by the owner, the Real Self.

The Animal Soul *(Kama)* includes the animal desires, passions, sensations and the subconscious mind, together with the desires, passions and emotions brought to it from the astral and mental worlds; for the astral can transmit both the good from above and the evil from below. The subconscious mind, composed of the synthesis of the consciousness of each cell, organ, nerve center and force in these lower bodies, is the means by which the Animal Soul rules over all the bodily functions. It is also the regulator and ruler of the waves of life-force and the breath in the body, and through them keeps the body in health. It also correlates all the desires, emotions and sensations which will cement the 4 lower Principles together and make a firm foundation on which the 3 higher Principles may build their Temple of the Living God. In short, this is the Stone which the builders—both Oriental and Christian teachers—have heretofore rejected, because apparently so hopelessly perverted by man's wrong thinking and so impregnated with disintegration and death, but which ultimately must become, 1st for the individual and then for the Race, the "headstone of the corner."

The Animal Soul has its seat in the liver and a point of contact in the sex centers, while it rules the body through the brain of the subconscious mind, the Solar Plexus. It must gather strength and power from all sensations, desires and experiences and devote all its life-forces to the 1 end, namely, toward erecting the Temple in which The Christ may dwell among men, and from which The Christ-radiance may send forth its redeeming power to all the kingdoms. The Animal Soul is, therefore, the synthesis of the 4 lower Principles, overshadowed by the Rational Mind

(*Lower Manas*). But when it attracts to itself and holds captive the Rational Mind through animal desire, it becomes the personal tempter (*Kama-manas*). The desires and appetites of this Animal Soul, which in the animal kingdom are perfectly normal when ruled by the Group Soul of the species through instinct, in the human kingdom must be ruled by the Rational Mind. But under the liberty allowed by human free-will they tend to run wild and follow their own inclinations. They thus often enhance and magnify the normal animal instincts and seduce and drag man down below the level of the beasts. This is the great fight in man; the Animal Soul seeking to gratify unrestrainedly its natural appetites, and the Higher Self endeavoring to make it follow the higher path through the guidance of the Rational Mind. It is this Animal Soul that must be curbed, made to occupy its true place and become the faithful servant of the Rational Mind, as the latter must be the faithful servant of the Super-conscious Mind or the mind of the Higher Self.[2]

The 5th Principle. Mind (Manas) or Spiritual Self-Consciousness.

Mind is the 3rd aspect of the Divine Triangle or Trinity, *Atma-Buddhi-Manas,* the Immortal Self, the Soul, the Father-in-heaven, which overshadows the human personality; "the three-tongued Flame that never dies." The true Mind, therefore, transcends its lower expression, Intellect, to a far greater degree than Intellect transcends Instinct. This Principle is usually presented only in its dual aspect of Higher and Lower Mind or *Manas*. While this division is correct as far as it goes, it leaves much to be desired; for in reality Mind, like all the Principles, is septenary, with 3 main divisions corresponding to body, mind

[2] For further discussion of the subconscious mind, see *V. of I.*, 90, 167, 206.

and Spirit, *i. e.*, the Subconscious, the Rational and the Spiritual or Super-conscious Mind.

Much confusion has been caused by exoteric writers classing all mental and psychic manifestations not attributable to the mind of the ordinary waking consciousness, as belonging to the subconscious mind, thus trying to account for both animal instinct and the most spiritual inspiration and ecstasy as coming from the same source. Such a manifestly absurd conclusion is easily avoided if we remember that the prefix *sub* means under or below. Therefore the word *sub*conscious should be used to designate only those aspects of Mind which lie below the threshold of the Rational Mind. These include the consciousness of the individual cells and organs, together with animal instinct, which constitutes the mind of the Animal Soul, and from which we can never expect to receive inspiration and spiritual guidance, for *the latter must come from above.*

The Rational Mind is the ordinary waking consciousness which functions through the Intellect, and has its seat in the cortex of the brain. It is the middle aspect of Mind, and like the middle number (5) it marks the difference between the human and the lower kingdoms, but overshadowing and blending into them through its subconscious aspect, just as it in turn is overshadowed by, and is capable of blending into, the Super-conscious Mind.

All the lower kingdoms are under the dominion of man's thought. When self-consciousness awoke, the Rational Mind was given control over instinct, and should therefore stand upright on the Foundation Stone and guide all the lower Principles. But until the Rational Mind is enlightened from above and realizes its responsibility, it only too often revels in the desires of the Animal Soul and lends its higher intellectual powers to enhance and degrade what should be but a normal animal instinct.

The Spiritual or Super-conscious Mind is the real 5th Principle which overshadows the personality, and whose informing ray makes man an intellectual and rational, instead of an instinctive, animal. Hence only when its 2 lower and limited aspects have become united with the higher, and the Higher Self or Soul has perfect control over its instrument, the personality, has man reached number 10. From 1 to 5 the lower kingdoms struggle toward self-consciousness, but from 5 to 10 man fights the battle allegorized in all scriptures under various names, such as the war in heaven, Armageddon, etc., but all referring to the war between the Higher and lower selves for the control of the personality. The 1st great battle is won when the Spiritual Mind is able to inspire—not force—the personality to respond to its overshadowing love and wisdom, and the Rational Mind sees the desirability and logical necessity of setting out in earnest to climb the heights to its Father's home. Thus life after life the Spiritual Mind reaches down into the experiences of earth life, sifting and weighing them and storing up the good, the beautiful and the true to be blended with the 6th Principle, overshadowed and illumined by the 7th, the 1 Ray of the Divine. When thus blended and illumined it becomes the Immortal Self, the Higher Self, the personal god, the highest point of attainment for each individual. When thus blended with the 6th and 7th Principles the Mind is also the Reincarnating Ego "with a form (rupa), which prevails during the whole life cycle of the Fourth Round, while its *Sosie,* or resemblance, the personal Ego, has to win its immortality;"[3] for the 4 lower Principles, since they pertain to the physical world, are mortal and perishable until redeemed.

[3] *S. D.,* II, 519.

The Higher Self, being purely spiritual, can have no direct consciousness in the physical world. Hence to enable it to complete its manifestation in all worlds and to become a redeemer it must send down a Ray of itself into the human-animal body that through this expression in matter it may complete its Destiny. This Ray is called the Antaskarana, the bridge which joins the lower to the higher, the earthly to the Divine. It is also called the bridge across the "Great Abyss" over which the pilgrim must cross to the "eternal shore," for it is over this Ray from the Spiritual Mind that the Rational Mind of man must send every aspiration of the heart, together with the ultimate lesson of good out of every condition experienced by it or the Animal Soul. During each life the Higher Self thus garners all the spiritual experiences of its Ray or reflection, and upon its withdrawal rests in the bosom of the Father, while the Animal Soul, with all that has not been redeemed, disintegrates.

> "The essence of the Divine Ego is 'pure flame,' an entity to which nothing can be added and from which nothing can be taken; it cannot, therefore, be diminished, even by countless numbers of lower minds, detached from it like flames from a flame."[4]

The story of the crucifixion is an allegory of the fate of the 5th Principle, for just as the Divine must take upon itself *individuality* in the World of Formation by embodying a Ray from Itself in the Spiritual Mind or Higher Manas, so in turn must this divine Son take upon itself *personality,* become flesh and temporarily be separated from its Father. It is this Ray, therefore, which makes itself responsible (through its lower expressions) for all the sins of its various personalities. This is the real vicarious atonement. Hence the "abyss" is often described as inhab-

[4] *S. D.,* III, 511.

ited by monsters of evil seeking to clutch the pilgrim Ray and pull it down as it strives to cross the bridge to its Father's home. Again, the Antaskarana is the cross by means of which The Christ-principle is expressed in matter. It is diagrammatically expressed thus:

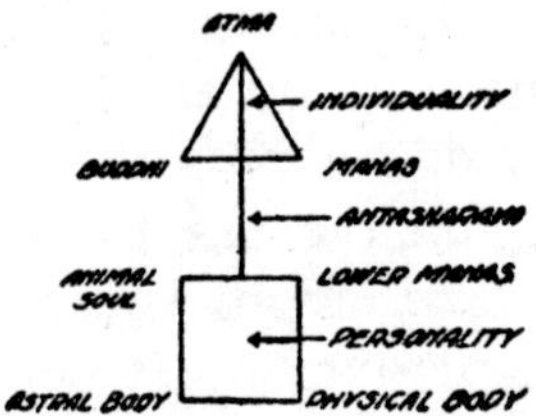

This truth, altho for ages holding a most important place in mysticism, was suppressed by the early Church as bearing too close a resemblance to the story of Jesus, which is but an allegory expressing this same truth.

In another sense the Spiritual Mind is the mansion in heaven prepared for its lower expression or son, that where the Father is there may the son be also. But it is the son or personality who must furnish this mansion by the pure thoughts, aspirations and lessons which the Rational Mind of each personality is all the time storing up in the Spiritual Mind. At the next incarnation the Spiritual Mind again sends down a Ray and builds up another personality which embodies as inherent faculties all the experiences gained and powers unfolded during the previous incarnation.

In the gospel allegory the Trinity or Spiritual Soul is called the Father who sent his only begotten Son (*lower manas* or Rational Mind) into earth conditions, not only to express the divine attributes of his Father, but also, when 1 with his Father, to become the Redeemer by giving up his life or Christ-force that literally, "whosoever believeth on him, shall not perish but have eternal life." That is, whosoever believeth that the Mind is a Ray from the Divine Mind given to man as a means by which he can garner wisdom out of experience; through whose illumination he can uplift, inform and redeem all beneath him; also as a means to find and become 1 with his divine Father; such an 1 can never perish or be separated from his Father, and will ultimately cross the Antaskarana in safety and dwell forever in the bosom of the Father. Then the abyss will no longer exist for him, for it has been swallowed up and he has become "the way, the truth and the life."

The Spiritual Mind has its seat in the body at the Spiritual Heart, a secret point back of the breast, which corresponds to the physical heart; the heart being the seat of physical life and the Spiritual Heart being the seat of the spiritual life. Its organ in the body is the pineal gland.

The 6th Principle. The Christ-Principle or Spiritual Soul (Buddhi).

Strictly speaking, the Spiritual Soul is the highest Principle, as the Divine Ray is no Principle, but an outpouring of the all-pervading and universal Essence of the 1 Flame, the Absolute, the Cause of all the Principles. Just as the Rational Mind is a vehicle for the Ray from the Spiritual Mind, so the Spiritual Soul is the vehicle for the Ray from the Divine. While it is generally classified as The Christ-principle this is more or less of an exoteric blind, for The Christ-principle is the Great Creative Principle or aspect of the Divine on all planes. It becomes the creator of spiritual differentiation only when individualized and manifesting through the Spiritual Soul and Spiritual Mind or Higher Self. It manifests in the Divine World as creative ideation, in the mental world as the creative power of thought and in the physical world as the power of fertilization or sex.

The Spiritual Soul can have no manifestation or consciousness in the lower worlds except through the Spiritual Mind and its various Rays. When the Spiritual Soul and the Spiritual Mind are blended and illumined by the Divine Ray they become the Divine Trinity, the Higher Self, or Reincarnating Ego. The Spiritual Soul stands to each of its expressions or personalities in the same relation that the Universal Soul stands to each individualized Spiritual Soul. It is not human but Divine and therefore immortal, "a Pillar of Light," an incarnation of 1 of the 7 Flames. It cannot complete its expression in the lower worlds and become a redeemer, however, until it clothes itself with and manifests through a human body.

Its seat is not in the physical body, but in the astral body. It contacts the physical body directly only when the psychic center in the middle of the forehead —the radium center (Realization)—is awakened.

The 7th Principle. The Divine or Atma.

This is called the 7th Principle merely for purposes of exoteric classification, as it is not a Principle of Man, but a Ray of pure Spirit from the Absolute. It can contact the human body only as the higher astral centers are consciously awakened and then made subservient to reaching into the higher realms where the Divine holds sway.

Just as the 7 notes of music are completed and synthesized in the 8th note, which leads into a new octave, so are the 7 Principles of Man synthesized in the Aura. This is sometimes called the 7th Principle, but in reality it is the synthesis of all, having a point of contact in each.

CHAPTER 29

THE 7 PLEIADES AND THE 7 RISHIS.

"Canst thou bind the sweet influences of the Pleiades, or loose the bands of Orion?"

—*Job,* xxxviii, 31.

"There I beheld seven stars, like great blazing mountains, and like spirits entreating me."

—*Book of Enoch,* xviii, 14.

The constellation Taurus, the Bull, contains over 400 stars, among which there are said to be more bright stars than in any other constellation, and chief among which are the 7 Pleiades and their sisters the 5 Hyades. And since in every age this constellation has been a favorite theme for myth and allegory, we may well expect to find an important occult significance connected with it.

One myth is that these 12 sisters saw their brother Hyas killed by a snake while hunting in Lybia.[1] They lamented his death so passionately that Zeus, out of compassion, translated them into stars—5 into the Hyades in the head and 7 into the Pleiades in the neck of the Bull. The Hyades are called "the rainy ones" and the greatest importance is attached to this group when it rises at the same time as the sun, namely during the month of May, at which time the rainy season begins. We therefore find that among the ancients the Hyades represent the fertilizing principle of moisture. They symbolize the feminine or astral aspect of the 5 senses, which lament that their brother (the physical senses) is so deadened by the snake of matter and the perversion of the creative powers, that they are cut off from him and must remain in the higher

[1] *Fasti,* Ovid, v, 165.

realms; that he can no longer commune with them except as he reaches up into the heaven world. They continually exert, however, the gentle moisture of their fertilizing principle which like dew falls from heaven or the astral world and helps man to find the 7 spiritual senses represented by the Pleiades. The physical and astral senses should be in such harmonious accord and development that when we see a physical object we should also see its astral counterpart; when we hear a physical sound we should also hear its astral expression, and so on with each of the other senses.

Another myth has it that the 7 Pleiades and their mother met the hunter Orion 1 day in the woods. The sight of their beauty so inflamed his desires that for 5 years he pursued them through the dense forest, now losing sight of them and now seeing them flying before him. Finally Zeus in pity turned them into white doves which flew to heaven and were translated into stars, altho during the flight 1 dove was lost among the "wandering rocks." Homer in the *Odyssey* (xii, 6) alludes to them as "The doves who brought ambrosia from the West." Since doves always symbolize the Spirit, we have no difficulty in connecting the Pleiades with spiritual forces or the perfection and spiritualization of man's 7 senses. While the Spiritual Sun rises in the mystical East we are told that it must shine "even unto the West." And it is man who, by the unfoldment of his 7 spiritual senses, must bring back from the farthest point of manifestation (matter) the ambrosia or sustenance of the gods with which to nourish his immortal body.

Orion is represented in mythology as a giant with a girdle, a sword, a lion's skin and a club, while his dog Sirius follows him and the Pleiades fly before him. Orion here represents man in pursuit of the higher attainments of the spiritual senses. He is indeed a giant girded with strength. A girdle is a symbol of a priestly office. Thus, when Aaron and his son were anointed as priests (*Exodus* xxxix, 29) they received the girdle of linen thread of 3 colors, blue, purple and scarlet, as does the Brahmin boy in India today when initiated into his caste. "As the Celtic word for a Belt is 'Crios,' so the Celtic name for Christ is 'Crios-d,' meaning 'Belt-God.' This Belt named all Druids, who were identified with the Sun and his continuous activity. * * * All words like Belt, Gir-th, Ban-d and Gir-d name the same daily orbit of the sun, which in the picture-language costume of the Druids was the Gilded Belt."[2] The girdle is also a covenant of strength and represents the current of spiritual force which circles around man's body just below the breasts. Thus Isaiah says: "I will clothe him with thy robe, and strengthen him with thy girdle" (xxii, 21). Again, "And righteousness shall be the girdle of his loins, and faithfulness the girdle of his reins" (xi, 5). Also, the Son of Man who stood in the midst of the 7 candlesticks is described in *Revelation* (i, 13) as "Girt about the paps with a golden girdle." For when man can hold the 7 stars in his right hand, his girdle will be a visible current of spiritual life-force passing through his heart, through the life-center in the right breast and through the center of illumination in the spinal cord opposite the heart.

The sword of Orion symbolizes the power of man's dominion over the earth, obtained by fighting and struggling with the density of physical conditions. This is the Sword of the Spirit through whose right use man may win his way back to his former high spiritual estate in Eden. The lion symbolizes spiritual courage, strength and love, the only forces—represented by the Lion of the tribe of Judah—found worthy to open the seals of the Great Book of Life (*Revelation*

---

[2] *The Jarvis Letters*, Chapter xi.

v, 5). We have already explained the aspect of man represented by the lion,[3] but Orion represents man as he is today with his 5 fold development, forever pursuing his 7 spiritual powers with eager passion, yet never quite able to attain them. Hence, instead of having attained the real, inner powers of the lion, he is able to manifest only their lower or outer expression, *i. e.,* the lion's skin. In other words, with courage, strength and love man persistently follows the flashing wings of the spiritual doves through the shadows of the forest of life, yet because his courage partakes of recklessness, his strength is tainted with cruelty and his love inflamed by passion he never fully attains, and will not until he, too, finds his place in the heaven world. Orion's club symbolizes man's physical power and personal will. For, alas, man too often hopes to claim his heritage through mere physical prowess and personal will, instead of by the use of the Sword of Spirit. His dog Sirius represents man's animal nature, trained to keep its appointed place; for like a faithful dog it should follow where man leads and be his friend and helper. As Orion unsuccessfully pursues the heavenly doves for 5 years, so will man unsuccessfully pursue his higher spiritual attainments through the 5 periods during which his physical senses rule. Only when his 6th and 7th senses begin to unfold and Zeus transforms him into a star and he enters the heavenly realms, will he find the doves.

The Pleiades appear in the Northern heavens at the beginning of Spring, and wield a mighty influence over the earth and its inhabitants. Not only do we find Job recognizing the power of their influence, but it was generally taught by the ancient Sages that this group ruled over the 7 Races and sub-races of mankind, determining also the great changes which ac-

[3] See lesson *The Great Book,* Part I.

company the beginnings and endings of the racial and planetary cycles.

The Hottentots worship the Pleiades, celebrating their annual appearance above the Eastern horizon with great rejoicing. As soon as the constellation appears all the mothers, with their children, ascend the nearest hill and teach the children to stretch out their arms toward the friendly stars. They also worship the Hyades under the name *Tusib,* the Rain God. They call the stars the Souls of the deceased.

According to the Greek legend the Pleiades are the 7 daughters of Atlas and Pleione.[4] In 1 version, all save Merope married gods and became mothers of the famous heroes who founded cities, nations and subraces. Merope married a mortal (Sisyphus) and hence is said to hide her head in shame.

> "They are * * * regarded by Madler and others, in Astronomy, as the *central group* of the system of the Milky Way. * * * The Pleiades (Alcyone, especially) are thus considered, even in Astronomy, as the central point around which *our universe of fixed stars revolves,* the focus from which, and into which, the Divine Breath, Motion, works incessantly during the Manvantara."[5]

These influences, however, must always be considered in connection with their positive aspects or executors, the 7 stars in the constellation Ursa Major or the Great Bear.

> "There were two constellations with seven stars each. *We* call them the Two Bears. But the stars of the Lesser Bear were once considered to be the seven heads of the Polar Dragon. * * * In Egypt the Great Bear was the constellation of Typhon."[6]

These stars are called the *Sapta Rishi* or 7 Rishis.[7] Altho Ursa Major was catalogued by Ptole-

---

[4] Their names are Maia, Electra, Taygeta, Alcyone, Celeno, Sterope and Merope.

[5] *S. D.,* II, 582.

[6] *S. D.*

[7] Their names are *Amba, Dula, Nitatni, Abrayanti, Mahayanti, Varshayanti* and *Chupunika.*

my as having 8 stars and by Hevelius as having 12, nevertheless its 7 brightest stars constitute 1 of the most characteristic figures in the Northern sky, and are called by the Hindus "the husbands of the Pleiades." The fact that so many of the ancient writers mentioned only the Pleiades, the Rishis, the Hyades and Orion, led modern astronomers for a long time to believe that these were the only constellations known in those ancient days. But recent scientific discoveries are corroborating so many of the old myths, legends and allegories, that it is easily understood that only these groups were mentioned by the ancients, because these were of the greatest importance from a mystical and occult standpoint. Modern research has plainly shown that the stars surrounding us do not constitute a simple, but a double system; a fact that was well known to the Sages. For it has been shown that many stars widely separated and apparently belonging to separate systems, are mysteriously related to each other, especially the Pleiades and the Great Bear. "It seems difficult to account for the very remarkable and unsystematized distribution of the motions, unless we suppose that the stars form two more or less separate systems superimposed; and it has been found possible by assuming two drifts with suitably assigned velocities to account very satisfactorily for the observed motions."[8] During the present Iron Age it is the masculine, positive force of these Rishis that has been dominant, rather than the feminine force of the Pleiades. For the influence of the Pleiades is exerted less upon the immediate events in the mundane sphere than upon the higher planes, yet it is always the feminine force which brings forth the great changes which appear on earth as the dominance of the cycle of 1 subrace gives place to the next. For corresponding reasons, during this cycle only the masculine Masters of

[8] *Encyclopedia Britannica,* Vol. XXV, 79.

Wisdom manifest in earth conditions, the feminine Masters working in the higher realms.

> "Meanwhile it is the seven Rishis who mark the time and duration of events in our septenary Life-cycle. They are as mysterious as their supposed wives, the Pleiades."[9]

In fact, it is largely the positive and negative powers emanating from these 2 constellations that give to number 7 its mystical significance.

> "Again number 7 is closely connected with the Occult significance of the Pleiades * * * the 6 visible, or the 7 actual sisters, the Pleiades, are needed for the completion of this most secret and mysterious of all astronomical and religious symbols."[10]

The importance of this constellation in laying the foundation of the universe is illustrated in the book of *Job*[11] when Saturn, the Great Initiator, demands of the candidate the mystery-questions which will reveal his knowledge of the secret cycles and the spiritual significance of the influences emanating from the Mazzaroth (zodiac). The ability to understand, correlate with and bind the sweet influences of the Pleiades is there indicated as a necessary requirement for Initiation of both man and the planet. As the Pleiades are connected with the closing of cycles—as their number 7, perfection, indicates—they have to do with the tests which each Soul must pass ere it can evolve out of 1 cycle of spiritual unfoldment into the next. Hence to "bind" their influence means that the candidate must have gained the power to face the Karma of his old or closing cycle and successfully pass through the changes which the steps of Initiation inevitably bring. This power is gained by assimilating the sweet influences of love, compassion, faith, intrepidity, action, patience and devotion focused by the Pleiades.

---

[9] *S. D.*, II, 579.
[10] *S. D.*, II, 654-5.
[11] xxxvii-viii-ix.

By the Hindus the Pleiades are called the nurses of the planet Mars, the Commander of the Celestial Armies.

> "In India they are connected with their nursling, the war God, Kârttikeya. It was the Pleiades (in Sanskrit, Krittikâs) who gave this name to the God, Kârttikeya being the planet Mars, *astronomically*."[12]

This should give to the student of astrology an insight into the deeper significance of that greatly maligned planet Mars; for as the Commander of the Celestial Armies we must look to his influence for the courage, fortitude, strength and the dauntless energy that will carry us on to final victory. In fact the true mystic teachings in regard to that planet will be revealed to man only when the 7th Sister comes from her hiding and begins to unroll the scroll of the 7th Great Race.

The allegory of Niobe, the sudden death of whose 7 sons and 7 daughters—symbolizing the 7 sub-races of the Atlanteans and their 7 branches—also refers to the cataclysms which occur at the close of the great Race cycles, for she was a daughter of 1 of the Pleiades.

Investigation by modern astronomers has confirmed the occult teaching that at the time the Pyramid of Cheops was built the Pleiades were directly overhead. These were the forces drawn upon by the Giants who accomplished that work over 31,000 years ago.

According to Stinson Jarvis: "The 7 branches of the (Druid) Church and the accompanying colonies were recorded through the descent from the 7 Daughters who named the stars of the Pleiades. The reader will remember that the great Fire Signal which exhibited the deity's Consent for further life on earth was not given until the Pleiades were exactly overhead in

---

[12] *S. D.*, II, 654.

the night sky. The constellation was a center of the priestly heavens, and had the most honorable position, on the neck of the constellation TAURus, who represented the BULL and Thunder-god of England. * * * and when Homer names this famous constellation, he writes the name to make it fit the metre, as 'PE. LE. IA. DES," using the whole word PE, to make another syllable, and also to name the DOVE which was always the name of Venus and the sign of divine LO.Ve. The Druid college which prepared the missionaries was on the island called the Island Dove of Heaven, and the Greek name of the Dove or Pigeon was specially made as PELEIA, and Homer's writing it as PELEIA-DES names these stars as the 'Dove Gods,' or Priests because all Druid missions carried a message of Love, referred to in *Job* as the sweet influences of these stars.

"The geographical uses of the Peleia-Des were partly as follows: The 7 parts of the early church, as spread out over the world, were here named and pictured in one cluster; each S.T.AR or 'Sign of Honor' (Anglian AR, 'Honour'), being named as a Daughter. These Daughters are married to the male British deities who name our week days, and they bear children whose names are the patronymics or father-names of great and well-known peoples, such as Dardanus, Lacedaemon, etc.; and in this way it becomes clear that the whole arrangement about to be described was a part of the memory systems which the Druids and their Branch priests used to record all kinds of information. * * * It was the invention and memory-system of the one Church, the one Candlestick of Seven Branches, which as a picture was not exclusively Hebraic. As we know that the Pleiades were held sacred from Peru to Java, and that these 7 stars received the names of the 7 branches of the church, it is clear that the system embraced the earth." [13]

With all this symbolic myth and legend we must conclude that the sweet influences of the Pleiades are something that every Soul should expect as a part of its heritage. But they can be attained only when the Soul is able to face the Great Initiator Saturn and answer his questions, "Canst thou bind the sweet influences of the Pleiades, or loose the bands of Orion?" Those sweet influences can never be ours until we can loose the bands which hold us to the limitations of the personality. In fact it is the loosing of these bands which is the great purpose of evolution, and which is indicated by the digits from 1 to 9. Only when we reach number 9 and face our Initiation and successfully answer these questions can we become more than man.

---

[13] *The Jarvis Letters,* Chapter viii.

CHAPTER 30

THE 7TH LETTER, *Zain* (ז)

> "He produced Zain, predominant in Movement, crowned it, combined and formed it with Gemini in the Universe, Sivan (June) in the Year, and the left foot of Man."—*Sepher Yetzirah,* 24.

The 7th letter, Zain (Z), is 1 of the simple letters and is connected with the sign Gemini. Its radical meaning is a "sword" or "weapon," while hieroglyphically it means an "arrow," both the meanings suggesting the idea of conquest. Just as number 7 is the perfection of the 1st great step or period in man's cycle of unfoldment, so this letter indicates that the forces represented by the letters we have already studied have reached the end of the 1st arcana, the outbreathing of the 1st mother letter, air, and have laid down certain principles which are shown in action by the letter Zain.

Zain represents man when he has reached a step where he can understand the underlying principles of life, and by the power of his perfected manhood grasp them in his hand as a weapon with which to carve his own destiny. Only so can he rule, for the meaning of Zain is also a "scepter." At this step in his perfected manhood man must become a conqueror, with the kingly ability to rule 1st himself then all nature, and with the power to defend, preserve and use the mystical weapon bestowed upon every Victor, namely, the Sword of the Spirit, or the "Fiery Sword" of the magician.

Thus Zain is the fulfillment or perfection of that which was breathed out by the mother Aleph, for the

Victory of number 7 is attained by a complete mastery of the breath. The words that are spoken must be words of love and words of healing. The Victor who holds the Sword or Weapon Zain in his hand must have gained absolute control of his speech. For in 1 sense this weapon is the mighty weapon of the tongue, to which so many allusions are made in the *Bible*. In *Psalms* (lvii, 4) we read: "Whose teeth are spears and arrows, and their tongue a sharp sword." Again, "Who whet their tongue like a sword and shoot out their arrows, even bitter words." And again in *Proverbs* (xii, 18), "There is that speaketh like the piercing of a sword, but the tongue of the wise is health." Again, "Death and life are in the power of the tongue." Also at the Great Initiation we hear Job asking, "Is there iniquity in my tongue?" Hence it is quite fitting that, as the manifestations of the 1st septenary may be called the children of the 1st mother, Aleph (air), they should be completed and the Victory gained by a Mastery of the tongue.

As we have said elsewhere: "Speech is one of the greatest powers, for it includes the powers of sound, number, color and, when written, form. * * * To bring to your minds some of the practical effects of this power, we would ask you for one day to note carefully the effect your words have on those about you. Many pupils ask for something *practical* to do to develop occult powers and manifest the higher life. Noting the effect of your words is *practical* and most important, and a practice which can be indulged in without fear of dangerous consequences. And until at least some conception of the power of speaking kindly and lovingly but to some purpose and *some degree of mastery over it has been attained,* the development of other occult powers will be retarded if not actually prevented." [1]

---

[1] *V. of I.*, 174-5.

The relation of Zain to the sign Gemini is in the idea that Gemini rules the arms and represents also the masculine and feminine qualities combined. Only he who has raised his arms in blessing and has blended the masculine and feminine qualities within himself can be called the victor over the power of the tongue. Another aspect of Gemini is the 2 opposing forces to which man in his unregenerate state is bound, as St. Paul said: "When I would do good, behold evil is present with me." Hence the Victor must have found the perfect blending of these pairs of opposites and must know how to use them to help on his further advance, the ability to accomplish which is symbolized by the arms. "When thou hast passed into the Seventh, O happy one, thou shalt perceive no more the sacred Three, for thou shalt have become that Three thyself." [2]

---

[2] *The Voice of the Silence,* Blavatsky, 19.

THE 7TH TAROT CARD

THE CHARIOT

Papus

MEDIEVAL

Papus

St. Germain
EGYPTIAN

M

Smith
MODERN

THE 7TH TAROT CARD, *The Chariot.*

In the Tarot the 7th card is called The Chariot, and is represented by a conqueror crowned with a coronet, composed of 3 pentagrams of gold. He stands in a chariot having the form of a cubic stone, having over him an azure canopy supported by 4 columns, and having 14 stars over his head. He has 3 right angles upon his breast, and upon his shoulders the Urim and Thummin, represented by 2 crescent moons, 1 on either side. He carries in his right hand a scepter surmounted by a globe, a square and a triangle. In his left hand he has a fiery sword. Upon the square front of his chariot is a lingam and the winged sphere of the Egyptians, while 2 sphinxes, 1 black and 1 white, draw the chariot, each straining in an opposite direction yet both looking toward the right and under the absolute control of the driver.

This card symbolizes the main characteristics of the sacred septenary. It represents man who has become the Conqueror, master both of himself and the elements, making the cube—now become the Philosopher's Stone—his chariot; the heavens his canopy; the 2 sphinxes—the forces of the Great Agent, black and white magic—his servants to bear him onward. His cuirass is the "breastplate of righteousness" or his knowledge of the manifestations of the Divine which makes him invulnerable to assaults from either the human or elemental kingdoms. The Urim and Thummim upon his shoulders indicate his priestly power to answer all questions through direct inspiration from the Divine. The globe on the scepter, surmounted by the square and triangle, indicates the 7 fold powers of man arising from the ○. The scepter corresponds to the Magic Wand mentioned above, while the Fiery Sword is the "Sword of the Spirit" with which he has gained the Victory.

THE 7TH COMMANDMENT.

7. "Thou shalt not commit adultery."
—*Exodus,* xx, 14.

Since we know that number 7 is the Number of Perfection, especially that perfection of humanity which will prevail when, through the power of number 6 the 5 senses have evolved into the 7, we can readily understand that to commit adultery has a far greater significance than the 1 generally ascribed to it. For to adulterate is to add some foreign and inferior substance to the thing adulterated. Also a thing is said to be adulterated when not absolutely pure and exactly what it purports to be.

It has been the custom to confine this 7th Commandment exclusively to the creative functions; but, while we concede the importance of obeying its literal meaning, still we must not make the mistake of confining it solely to that meaning.

The fact that 7 is the Number of Perfection and yet deals with the creative powers of man is, to say the least, significant. A perfect humanity is 1 in which the creative powers have not been adulterated, but while fully functioning and under the absolute control of the Will are used in love, purity and wisdom to create that which is needful, unadulterated by lust or any of the lower carnal desires, and with a full recognition that the Great Creative Force is creative on all planes, and that it becomes sex-force only when it functions through the sex centers. And as we are responsible for the use of that great Force through all the centers, it must be kept pure and unadulterated if we would conquer death and the grave. In itself it is the mightiest agent entrusted to humanity; in fact, its use is the great test of the humanity of this globe. In its true esoteric significance it is so far above man's present conception of it that only as he evolves the 6th and 7th senses can he understand and master all its possibilities. Mankind of today, in dense ignorance of its divine origin and purpose, is wallowing in the mire created by the perversion of its lowest aspect. Only when we know, really know, its true essence and functions, through our own divine illumination, and have tested and proven them from experience; in fact, only when we have been able to look this mighty problem in the face with a pure heart and an understanding mind and know it in its pure and unadulterated state, can we take the 7th step. We must create each step ere we can take it, and if we confine the Great Creative Force to its functions in the flesh, we live in the flesh. And so long as we presume to judge the God who made us and gave us this force, and say that all use of the creative force is evil and belongs only to the unregenerate man, we must remain unregenerate; for we have turned our backs on the very power given us to bring about our regeneration and create our next step. Therefore, let us cease to adulterate our conceptions of this Divine Power with the misconceptions which have their origin in ignorance, asceticism, fear, prudery and the self-righteous thought that we are better able to judge of what is pure than the God who made us, and use for their highest ends all the powers given us. Nor must we adulterate the Divine Wisdom handed down throughout the ages. Only thus can we truly obey the 7th Commandment.

Since we never try to kill anything that we do not consider harmful or vile, the very fact that the unenlightened place this mighty force at the head of all evil things and give it over to what they are pleased to term the Devil, helps to make the Devil an actual entity, built up through the ages by man's perverted thought forces, and vivified and strengthened daily by the votive offerings of those who create him out of the very forces which should make man a god. Is it any wonder, then, that the Devil lives and thrives and exerts a vile, degenerating and disintegrating influence upon mankind? For every outpouring of life-force which the unenlightened mind of man brands as vile, goes to prolong the life and strengthen the powers of "the devil and his angels." For the thought of evil creates evil thought-forms, hence that power given to man with which to reach divinity, which should bring him to number 7 and make him perfect even as his Father in heaven is perfect, has been adulterated and used to bring about imperfection and death.

Therefore, until we learn the real essence of this 7th Commandment by heart, and exemplify it in thought and life, the Angel with the Flaming Sword will forever bar us from returning to our spiritual home in the Garden of Eden.

CHAPTER 31

THE NUMBER 8.

> "Where is thy individuality, Lanoo, where the Lanoo himself? It is the spark lost in the fire, the drop within the ocean, the ever present ray become the All and the eternal Radiance."
> —*The Voice of the Silence,* Blavatsky, 20-1.

Number 8 is the Number of Evolution and is connected with the spiral motion of cycles. It is the Number of the inevitable and onward rush of Time. Its symbol is the hour glass, also the balance. It is also the Winged Globe of the Egyptians and the Bird of Life of the Hindus which carries man from the realm of earth (the lower o of the 8) to the higher realms (the upper o of the 8).

According to Stinson Jarvis: "Our word E I G H-T names the Horse-God (his Celtic name is E I G H) and the eight hours. * * * These eight H O R-Ses, or Hour-Signs, are still shown harnessed abreast, in the carvings of Java which illustrate our D A Y-god's car. * * * The Eigh-T chambers name the eight Hours, eight H O R-Ses, eight notes, eight divisions of the compass, and every other eight or the O C-T, or Oak-God, who is 'O C T,' or Eight. * * * The same naming of the Eight-god, or O C-T, was continued in the great tower and temple of B-E-Lus in Babylon. * * * This was divided into Eight separate towers. * * * The Greeks have two O's, naming the sun as the 'Great O,' or O-MEGA, and the moon called O-micron, or Circle Small. * * * These two O's name the Sun and Moon on which all time calculations were made; and the Oak God, or

OC-T, was supposed to be both of them in one. Consequently, he was fully named by the figure 8, and OC-T, OCH-D and OCH-T name Eight in the Celtic, Gaelic, Latin and Greek. * * * Therefore we see that they were all the one deity under different names, but fully represented by the figure 8, which shows the small Moon above the large Sun, or the o-mi-cron above the O-mega, and thus names the deity who was both Moon and Sun in one. Father Smiddy wonders why the Druids seem to pay such deep respect to number Eight; but this proceeded from their science, because their service of praise was nearly all vibrational, to produce unity of mind through song, and the 'Oc God Song,' or OC-T-AVe, was composed of Eight notes."[1]

Many writers give to number 8 a most sinister interpretation. They attribute to it all that is unfortunate—imperfection, privation, loss, ruin, decay, corruption and death. While it may present such aspects, they are fearsome only to those who do not know the meaning and object of evolution, those who refuse to face conditions which the Great Law brings for their instruction and unfoldment. For evolution means ever becoming. That which has fulfilled its cycle of manifestation must give place to something higher; that which is imperfection, because only "in part," must be superseded by the more and more perfect. The less evolved forms of life suffer the lack of only that which must be the ultimate result of the step, as the child is deprived of the ripe wisdom of the man, altho it has all the faculties by which to acquire that wisdom in the course of growth. That which is lost is that out of which the law of evolution has absorbed the life-force, as a rind of an orange is thrown away when the substance of the orange is extracted. Ruin, decay, corruption and death are all phases of life ex-

[1] *The Jarvis Letters*, x, v.

pression. The rind of an orange may decay, become corrupt, and seemingly die, yet the life substance in it is reabsorbed by the elements, from which there will again be evolved a new form of life. "For we know in part, and we prophesy in part, but when that which is perfect is come, then that which is in part shall be done away."[2] To those who bestride the Bird of Life and boldly face each step in evolution, no matter what it may hold for them, number 8 is the symbol of the Good Law.

> "The wheel of the Good Law moves swiftly on. It grinds by night and day. The worthless husks it drives from out the golden grain, the refuse from the flour. The hand of Karma guides the wheel; the revolutions mark the beatings of the karmic heart."[3]

Since evolution can advance only by reaping that which is sown, number 8 is a perfect symbol of Balance or cause and effect. It is the Number of the ceaseless Breath of the Cosmos, the outbreathing and inbreathing by which the equilibrium of the Soul is attained. It breathes into man the ideals from the higher spheres and draws up from the lower spheres of personality his lower ideals. Man's ideals are therefore but the divine ideals deformed and colored by his limited conception and understanding of them, just as man breathes in pure air, and breathes out the same air tainted and more or less polluted by the volatile waste products of his system. According to the health and purity of his body is man's outgoing breath pure and sweet. And according to his oneness with his Higher Self and the purity of his thoughts, can man breathe out or manifest the ideals indrawn from the higher realms.

The path of the psychic breath in the body forms a perfect figure 8. This, however, must be understood

---

[2] *I Corinthians,* xiii, 9-10.

[3] *The Voice of the Silence,* 28.

from its esoteric aspect, for there are many mysteries connected with the breath, all of which pertain to man's evolution.

In number 4 we have squared and laid our corner-stone, as far as our physical expression is concerned, and in number 7 have erected our Temple of the Living God, and are now ready to inaugurate the priestly office in it, by means of which we are enabled to enter into the higher circle of number 8 where, behold! all things to us become new; in short, we are now ready to die to the old, for which reason the Ancients called number 8 death. But like so-called physical death, this death is but an evolution into a higher state of life. Another conception of number 8 is that of the perpetual and regular flow of the life currents of the universe, the evil being consumed to make way for the good. If we find a bad crop this season, we plow it under and sow a better crop next season, thus working with the Law of Eternal Motion or Evolution, toward ultimate completion.

The Gnostic teachings postulate 7 interpenetrating spheres surrounded by an 8th, which is composed of the left-overs or unredeemed forces left behind by the 7 fold chain of spheres in their onward rush of evolution. This 8th sphere is 1 of absolute darkness, hence is often called the "dark star," and its motion is so much slower than the earth-chain to which it belongs that it greatly retards that chain's progress. It is out of this 8th sphere that, at the dawn of the next great world-period, the materials will be gathered to form a new 7 fold earth-chain, just as the 8th note in music, while a repetition of the 1st, is nevertheless the beginning of a newer and higher octave. This process is alluded to in the teachings of the Gnostic Marcus, as follows: "Now the motion of these seven spheres is exceedingly rapid, whereas the eighth sphere is much slower than the motion of the seven mutually interpenetrating spheres, and as it were balances [the Balance of number 8] or checks their otherwise too rapid motion by pressure on their periphery."[4]

Number 8 may be compared to a power belt which transmits the power from the drive-wheel of the engine to the power-wheel of a machine. And curiously enough such belts are usually crossed in the exact shape of a figure 8. Nearly all symbols or objects having the shape of number 8 convey the fundamental idea of evolution, *i. e.*, the transmission of the force of 1 cycle or form into the next higher expression.

It is at the point of crossing over, therefore, that we must expect to meet the dread Dweller on the Threshold who will bar our way until our courage has been proved. Only fortitude and determination at this step can prove that we have learned the lessons of the lower wheel and have demonstrated our fitness to pass on and receive the Initiation which must precede our entrance into number 9. This is the crucifixion, or the dying upon the cross of the personality, that The Christ, the only begotten Son of God, may rise and sit forever at the right hand of his Father. Only by the way of this cross, *Via Crucis*, can man become more than man.

The Dweller who awaits us at this threshold of our New Life is the synthesis of all those mistakes and unredeemed creations which we have pushed behind us during our struggle to reach the Perfection of number 7. For in our lower evolution there are many things which we have not the strength completely to conquer. Yet we progress in spite of them, for such things are mercifully held back until we grow to spiritual manhood. But ere we can pass this crucial step we must meet and redeem them in the person of our

[4] *Fragments of a Faith Forgotten*, Mead, 379.

"Dweller" on the threshold of the new life, just as they await us in a lesser degree at every new step upon the Path. But here they must be faced, recognized, conquered and transmuted ere we can enter the ○ of the higher evolution.

By some writers this Dweller is described as a frightful monster of so terrible a mein that at sight of him the candidate is either paralyzed by fear or in rare cases is driven mad from horror. This occurs, however, only in extreme cases where the pupil has failed to conquer fear during the earlier steps or where he has persistently denied all evil and refused to face and recognize his faults and failings, hence has made no effort to redeem them. But the student who has lived close to Divine Love and who has recognized his power to redeem his creations, will have little to fear at this step; for by the recognition of the power of The Christ within the student has learned how gradually to redeem the Dweller in his daily steps along the Path; in fact, has grown familiar with his face, hence is not appalled. He knows that he can conquer all that his evolution brings to him.

Many students are puzzled to know how they will meet the Dweller or know when they are upon the Threshold of Initiation, but there are many experiences which, to 1 who is truly watching, will indicate it, and many ways to meet the Dweller will appear. Some have a symbolic dream or vision, or an experience in life itself brings it to their recognition. 1 student relates that he had the following dream: He dreamed he stood before a small entrance which seemed to lead into a vast Hall. He was eager to enter, but at the door stood a monstrous Giant with drawn sword barring the entrance. Seated near the doorway behind a small table was a huge Mongolian noble. The student sought to enter, but the Doorkeeper demanded a fee. On asking how much he was to pay, the student was told 70 cents. He handed the Doorkeeper 75 cents, but the Mongolian would not let him in until he had paid the exact amount, telling him it was impossible to pay more than was demanded. Then the Giant lowered his sword and let the student enter. The symbology here is very plain, for 70 cents symbolized 7 complete cycles of 10. And only when the candidate for Initiation can give to the Doorkeeper the value of 7 complete cycles can he enter the Narrow Gate which is the crossing point of number 8.

1 fault which gives the Dweller great power, and which is a great shock when 1st realized by the candidate, is self-righteousness and spiritual pride. The person whose Dweller has been built up through the grosser sins of selfishness, greed, drunkenness, lust, etc., knows all along that he is violating the Law and rather expects to pay the penalty some time; in fact, has in all probability had many glimpses of his Dweller and knows full well it is his own creation, hence is not so appalled at his handiwork when seen in full. He is therefore far more ready to recognize it as his own creation than the self-righteous person who has lived so long in his artificial sanctity that he cannot believe the Dweller to be his.

Once having successfully faced the Dweller and entered the higher circle of evolution in number 8, we now meet Saturn, the great Tester and Initiator, whose number is 9. "For Satan (Saturn) is the magistrate of the Justice of God (Karma); he beareth the balance and the sword. For to him are committed *Weight and Measure and Number*."[5] The Initiator should not be confused with the Dweller, for the latter is an entity of our own creation, while the Initiator is 1 of the Elohim or Sons of God spoken of by Job. He 1st appears to us as grim Death, the Reaper,

[5] *Book of Hermes,* quoted by Kingsford. Appendix of *The Perfect Way.*

but as such he comes 1st to teach us to conquer fear, and 2nd that we may prove to ourselves the power of man, uplifted and sustained by the Divine within, to conquer even Death; to prove that there is no death; for if we rest in the 1 Life, the Divine Breath manifesting through number 8 will sweep us safely past this point of crossing. "Perfect love casteth out fear," hence long ere we reach this step we should have learned "in whom we trust." Then is death swallowed up in Victory.

If we do find the spiral of evolution, like number 8, manifesting to us decay and dissolution, this merely proves that only as the old and useless husks decay can the seed sprout and bring forth. It is ruin only in the sense that the breaking of the shell by the evolving sprout means ruin. Only as the shell is broken can the kernel of the nut be extracted. Number 8 should not be regarded as privation, imperfection, corruption or loss, except as we gladly lose the lower or lesser to obtain the higher and greater, or just as a child breaks and ruins or is deprived of its old toys when the time comes in its evolution to take up the serious business of life. Here we gladly lay aside the old thoughts, the old bonds of flesh, even our old ideas and beliefs, especially the thought of our greatness and power; the ability of the unaided personality to meet and conquer all physical conditions. For only as these old conceptions fall away from us 1 by 1, decay and return to their original elements, are we ready to pass through the Narrow Gate and be weighed in the Balance of Perfect Justice.

CHAPTER 32

THE NUMBER 8—*(Continued)*.

"My heart, my mother—may there be no parting of thee from me in the presence of him that keepeth the Balance."—*Book of the Dead,* Budge, xciv-v.

The effect of number 8 may be compared to that of a Balance in which the Soul must be weighed. This balance was an important symbol among the Egyptians. "The Vignette of Chapter xxx of the *Book of the Dead* represents the deceased sitting in one pan of the scales and being weighed against his heart which is placed in the other." In another Vignette "we see the heart of the deceased in one pan of the balance, and a feather, emblematic of Right and Truth *i. e.,* 'what is straight,' in the other."[1] In fact, in its ancient form number 8 (∞) resembles a balance.

In number 7 man (5) attains his 2 higher faculties and sees himself not as a 5 fold personality, but as a 7 fold Being made in the image of the 7 Elohim. But in number 8 he must see himself not even as a perfected personality, but one with the Universe of Being. Here he must of his own free-will throw into the scales all that he has attained and put it to the test, just as the alchemist who, after long and laborious efforts has obtained his gold, will 1st put it to the acid test to see if it is indeed gold, then cast it into the scales to be weighed ere he can truly say, "I have attained." The very personality we have so laboriously perfected in number 7 must now be left behind. Our own power, our judgment, our self-reliance, our own guidance, all these are necessary that we may recognize and understand the greatness of the self we have perfected,

[1] *Book of the Dead,* Budge, xciv-v.

yet having completed the cycle of limitation within that lower self, we must now lay it aside as we would lay the body aside in the grave, and face our Initiator ere we can evolve into the upper o of the 8, the Higher Self.

But number 8 is more than a Balance, it is the purifying Flame of the Divine Breath which sweeps round the Soul to consume its dross, and only that which is pure gold can withstand it.

Pythagoras calls number 8 the 1st evenly even number, for both sides of the balance must be made equal or there must be a cubic stone (4) on each side of the scale; in other words, in number 8 we must find perfect balance. St. Paul tells us to "Prove all things; hold fast that which is good," which is but another way of saying weigh, measure and test. But the student does not have to create his own tests. All he has to do is to strengthen his will, quicken his love and be ready for all that comes; for life itself will bring the tests. We therefore warn all students who are seeking the balance which precedes Initiation, not to be over enthusiastic or rash in asking for tests. Do not demand that all your Karma descend upon you all at once, even in 1 life. Just rest in the knowledge that the Great Law is Divine Love, hence the fires of purifaction will be no hotter than you can bear, provided you let the loving Christ walk with you in the fiery furnace of purification and testing. Many prolong this period of weighing and testing by the pride they take in being able to pass through it so bravely. Since pride and personality are the 2 things which most require purging from the Soul, and since number 8 is Absolute Justice, of necessity the fires must be made the hotter until these impurities are consumed.

The crossing point in number 8 is the valley between 2 attainments, the valley between the Mount of Crucifixion and the Mount of Ascension, the Valley of the Shadow of Death spoken of by the Psalmist: "Yea, though I walk through the valley of the shadow of death, I will fear no evil (the Dweller); for thou art with me; thy rod and thy staff they comfort me."[2] It is only the Rod of Power—the power of The Christ—and the Staff of the 1 Life that can carry the candidate safely through this deep experience. For those who are filled with spiritual pride this is the Valley of Humiliation, for ere they can make this great transition their pride in their spiritual superiority and righteousness must be humbled until they become as little children. This point of crossing is also the straight and narrow gate referred to by Jesus, up to which each Soul is brought by evolution. "Enter ye in at the straight gate;—because straight is the gate and narrow is the way, which leadeth unto life, and few there be that find it." It is also the gate referred to as the needle's eye, through which it is so difficult for the man attached to this world's goods to pass.

To enter this gate we must make straight our Path; must straighten out all the devious and winding paths of the old life so that as we enter the higher cycle of evolution the lower o of the 8 will be straightened out to form the upright stem of number 9. If we fail at this point we enter the broad gate and go down and round and round the circle of the old life. "Wide is the gate, and broad is the way, that leadeth to destruction, and many there be which go in thereat."

If the circumscribing conditions of our old life are straightened out and we pass onward and upward, we can rest assured that we have passed the tests of number 8. But if our life goes over and over the same old conditions without advancing us; repeating the same old mistakes, thinking the same old thoughts, etc., we will know that we have been weighed and tem-

---

[2] *Psalms,* xxiii, 4.

porarily found wanting, hence have missed the narrow gate and must go round the circle of the old conditions until we again find ourselves facing the Dweller. Even if our old problems do seem to fall from us, yet we seem to have lost interest in spiritual things, are seemingly switched off into worldly pleasures and excitements, we may know we are upon the broad path, the lower o of the 8.

THE 8TH LETTER, *Heth* (ח).

> "He produced Cheth, predominant in Sight, crowned it, combined and formed with it Cancer in the Universe, Tamuz (July) in the Year, and the right hand of Man."—*Sepher Yetzirah,* 24.

The 8th Hebrew letter is Heth or Cheth (ch). It is 1 of the simple letters and is related to the zodiacal sign Cancer. This letter should not be confused with the letter Hé which is somewhat similar in name and closely allied in occult significance. Its hieroglyphic meaning is a cultivated "field" in which a crop is brought forth. It thus suggests labor and effort, as well as the idea of increase and wealth. The field of endeavor may be 1 in which to cultivate and produce the fruits of peace and plenty, or a field of strife and battle. But in either case it is the field in which the Conqueror of the previous (7th) letter must use his Weapon, either as a sharp sword or arrow, to gain the supremacy over the forces that would retard his further evolution, or as an implement to cultivate the field that it may bring forth abundant crops. Only when through victory he has beaten his sword into a plowshare and his spear into a pruninghook, can they be used to make the field bring forth her increase to bless both the Conqueror and all mankind.

The field is the field of his own nature and consciousness. Hence the step indicated by the 8th letter should bring to him the increase of evolution. This can be attained only through effort, battle, victory and balance, and by sedulously cultivating the soil of his field. The Conqueror must prove his power to balance the forces of good and evil which are contending in his field and come forth the Victor. He must also demonstrate his power as an husbandman to make his field produce to its utmost. Generally the Conqueror has to fight with his sword until he has equilibrated the positive and negative forces. Then will he find his field enriched from the very struggle and bloodshed which at 1st seemed only to devastate it. Thus Perfect Justice is attained; for that from which we suffer most and whose adjustment and fulfillment our rebellion and struggles delay, when once we have truly learned our lesson, the Law as Justice and Compensation yields us a harvest, which is all the richer because of the struggle that has drenched our field with the blood of our heart.

As with the individual, so is it with the world. There must come an era, even as prophesied by Isaiah,[3] when "He shall judge among the people—and they shall beat their swords into plowshares, and their spears into pruninghooks; nation shall not lift sword against nation, neither shall they learn war any more." This is the inevitable result of evolution. 1st 1 here and there grasps the idea that war is unnecessary, then gradually a mighty current of thought-force embodying that idea sweeps around the world and, appealing to and fostered by woman, is impressed upon the consciousness of the unborn children which will make up the future humanity.

Again, since we find this letter in the *Sepher Yetzirah* expressing the underlying force of the sign Cancer—Cancer being the great mother-sign and governing the breasts from which all are nourished—

---

[3] ii, 4.

we must expect to find a similar meaning in Heth. And this we do, for it is both the productive, nourishing, mother-force, which is 1 of the main factors in evolution, and also the masculine force which accomplishes by the use of the hand. Also July is the month of increase, when the fruits are ripe and ready for the harvest. "O sing unto the Lord (Law) a new song; for he hath done marvelous things; his right hand, and his holy arm, hath gotten him the victory." (*Psalms,* xcviii, 1).

This is the field in which humanity must bring forth victory for the individual, the race and for the planet, through perfecting the fruits of equilibration in Mother Earth, upon whose ample bosom all her children shall find enough, not only to sustain life, but to balance all economic problems. And through the balancing of supply and demand they shall take the next economic step in the evolution of the Race. Just that which is impressed upon the unborn children and what they draw in from their mother's breast, will the Race express. Just so must humanity imbibe from the breasts of the Great Mother the forces of the sign Cancer, which shall give them the power to bring forth the higher ideals in the field of their evolution. Only as we turn to the Great Mother, like tired children, will we find sustenance and to spare.

It is therefore not at all remarkable that the 8th letter should stand for a "field" and be connected with the maternal sign Cancer. For we have seen that number 8 is the step at which humanity must find its Balance and where the Conqueror of number 7 must turn his weapon into an instrument with which to bring forth increase in the higher o of the 8, instead of destruction in the lower circle.

THE 8TH TAROT CARD

JUSTICE

Papus

Papus

MEDIEVAL TYPES

St. Germain
EGYPTIAN TYPE

Smith
MODERN TYPE

CHAPTER 33

THE 8TH TAROT CARD, *Justice.*

"Thou canst create this 'day' thy chances for thy 'morrow.' In the 'Great Journey' causes sown each hour bear each its harvest of effects, for rigid justice rules the World."
—*The Voice of the Silence,* Blavatsky, 35.

The 8th card is called Justice, and is represented by a woman seated upon a throne between the 2 columns of the Temple, Jakin and Boas. This card symbolizes the Great Mother through whose love, care and perfect Justice alone can the children of men find equilibrium. Here we see her seated and at rest between the positive and negative, giving her fostering love to both alike; she is "Wisdom who sitteth in the gates." (*Prov.,* viii).

She wears an iron coronet. Iron being the metal of the planet Mars, this symbolizes that only through the force of that planet, balanced and enthroned, can the equilibration of the sexes take place. This is not the force of Mars in its militant and destructive aspect, but its energy, strength and push. The force of iron, not fashioned into swords and guns, but into a coronet to crown the Great Mother, must be the Urge back of evolution (∞). But iron must undergo a very drastic experience ere it can be put to its highest uses. It must be melted in the hot fires of the blast furnace (the fires of Karma) and be chilled by being plunged into earth conditions again and again, and hammered by the Great Law, ere it can be welded, transformed into steel and become fit to make the rails and the bridges over which the trains of commerce annihilate distance and weld people together through association and common interest.[1] Just so must the force of Mars be transmuted and utilized to make a line of communication from heart to heart and join both man and woman in the oneness of common interests.

In 1 aspect the force of Mars may be compared to the circulation of the blood, governed by the breath. It is also the life-force of the breath of evolution; for as the Soul inbreathes it draws in its inspiration and its ideals, while as it exhales it manifests the inspiration and ideals as speech and works. Hence, the Great Mother being crowned with the force of Mars shows that she has gained the victory and is balanced and poised, ready to lead her children into a new day of manifestation.

She holds in her right hand a sword with its point upward, again a sign of victory. This is again the Sword of the Spirit that ever cleaves asunder the false from the true. In her left hand she holds a Balance. This is again the Balance of number 8 in which each Soul must be weighed ere it can receive its Initiation.

THE 8TH COMMANDMENT.

8. "Thou shalt not steal."—*Exodus,* xx, 15.

As 8 is the Number of Evolution, while allowing the exoteric meaning to stand in its literal sense, to understand the esoteric meaning of this Commandment we must consider the relation which stealing bears to evolution.

Esoterically this Commandment means that the personality shall not steal from the Higher Self; must not be allowed to steal the scepter and usurp the place of the Higher Self as the ruler of the life. It means that physical conditions and circumstances must not be allowed to steal from the personality its opportunities

[1] See lesson *The Iron Age.*

for meditation, realization, unfoldment; its opportunities for expression and manifestation of the Higher Self in the life. For to do so is to sap and weaken the very source of all evolution, *i. e.*, the pressure of the inner or ideal state for outward expression, modified by the limitations imposed by the environment. Nor must these same opportunities be stolen from others who are seeking expression through personality. Evolution is retarded until humanity as a whole awakens to the importance of the fact that every Soul must have freedom of opportunity to find its own place, perfect itself in its work and follow out the inner guidance of its Father-in-heaven.

The Great Law as Karma gives to every Soul the portion of goods belonging to it and sends the Soul forth into this far country of earth life to see what use will be made of its inheritance. Each Soul is a cell in the Grand Man, an atom in the Soul of the Universe, and has its own place in the Grand Plan. The goods which are given to the Soul are all the faculties, powers, knowledge and wisdom gained through past experience, expressed in this life as inherent faculties, powers and abilities, together with the as yet undeveloped possibilities which the experiences of this life are intended to unfold and perfect. Only by this unfoldment and perfection through evolution can the Soul be fitted to take its true place in the Grand Plan; a place which no other Soul can fill, and which must remain empty or be imperfectly filled until that individual Soul has consciously correlated with, and become an unobstructed channel for, the manifestation of the 1 Life.

When the human law puts a man in jail for stealing money, or perhaps a loaf of bread, if it deprives him of his freedom and his opportunities without due consideration of the motives, circumstances and causes of his act, it is not administering or correlating with the Law of Exact Justice; for it is stealing from him far more than he stole from society, and is retarding and often pushing back evolution. If we punish without justice and mercy; coerce, domineer or in any way steal away the rights and freedom of others, we steal from them their Soul opportunities. And the Great Law will imprison us, individually and collectively, in the prison of limited and unhappy conditions and at hard labor, until we see our error and learn to help our less fortunate brothers and sisters through the exercise of tolerance, love and compassion, which are all a part of real Justice. All these, together with such other help as we can give toward its highest unfoldment, is due every Soul from every other Soul. If we withhold these we are stealing from that other forces which are rightfully his, and we must remain in bondage to selfishness just that much longer.

To steal mere physical things is punishable by physical Karma. That is, we must suffer, either in this or another life, from conditions that will open our eyes and bring us to a realization that it is both inherently wrong and causes suffering to take even the physical things that belong to another. Karma does not mean that if you steal a man's watch in this life, in the next life he must steal a watch from you. If this were true the Soul-quality whose lack prompted the stealing would never be developed, the spirit of stealing would be perpetuated, and there would be no end to the vicious circle. In the above case Karma would mean that you must pass through certain experiences—say the loss of things your personality valued highly—which will develop in you a recognition of the rights of others to the enjoyment of that which is rightly theirs. The Great Law shuts up a Soul who steals in the prison house of limited environment, to labor under the oppression of physical conditions until the lacking Soul-quality is developed.

Since all evolution tends to develop more and more perfect organisms through which greater and greater degrees of freedom from the bondage of external conditions can manifest, we can be truly free from the bonds of Karma only as we work with evolution, through the seeking of those things which are our own and following those things which will perfect and thus hasten our evolution. This is not attained by selfishly trampling on the freedom or rights of others that we may advance—for to do so is to develop selfishness—but through harmonious co-operation for the good of all.

Therefore, we see that nothing will so retard our own evolution as to steal from another that which has been given to him and not to us, be it a thing, a thought, an opportunity or a life. For the Great Law of Exact Justice will keep us in bondage to physical limitations, in the prison house of flesh, in the treadmill of Karma, incarnation after incarnation, until we have fulfilled every jot and tittle of the Law we have broken, and have repaid to humanity a 1000 fold that which we have stolen.

CHAPTER 34

THE NUMBER 9.

> "The Ninth Path is the Pure Intelligence, so called because it purifies the Numerations, it proves and corrects the designing of their representation, and disposes their unity with which they are combined without diminution or division."
>
> —*Sepher Yetzirah,* 29.

Number 9 is primarily the Number of Initiation. As we have previously pointed out: "It is that most mysterious number which never changes. No matter how multiplied or added the sum of the resulting digits will always equal 9, *i. e.,* 9+9=18=9, or 9×9=81=9, etc. In it all numbers are swallowed up to emerge once more in a new cycle, 10."[1] In this sense it has the same symbology as the serpent swallowing its own tail, namely, the ending of a cycle. It is Cronus or Saturn devouring his children. Thus it is truly the Number of Initiation. For while there is a minor initiation at each step in the Soul-life, "no matter how you have multiplied sensation, experience, knowledge or attainment, you cannot pass your Great Initiation until you have returned to that from which you started, just as all multiples of 9 return to 9." [1]

As number 9 is the square of the 1st odd number or trinity, 3, it represents Deity descending into humanity and evolving through man until squared, or until through Initiation man has manifested the Divine in each of the 3 worlds. Number 9 is also the Number of Initiation because it is a trinity of trinities—God, man and nature—man, woman and the magnetic link between them—love, truth and understanding—each trinity of which, no matter how we deny or try to

---

[1] *V. of I.,* 368.

escape it, brings us face to face with Deity (3) in the 3 worlds and ultimately completes our Great Initiation.

The 9th Sephira completes the 3rd trinity, or the trinity of trinities. It is called in *The Kabbalah* "El Chai," the mighty Living 1, also Shaddai, the foundation or basis, because only as this 3rd trinity is unfolded and made the base for the other 2, is the disciple ready to pass his great Initiation. It is here that the Mystic Rose may be said to bloom in his heart. This Rose is represented in a conventionalized form with 9 petals on the outer edge, 6 on the next row and 3 around the center. Its angelic name is "The Flames."

Every step by which we evolve from 1 number to the next is a minor initiation, but after each 3 such minor steps there is a Major Initiation which when passed admits us into a new cycle (10) and realm of consciousness (See Table 2, page 136). At each minor initiation we must face our personality, but at each Major Initiation we must face our own Soul or Deity (3). These 3 Major Initiations, which complete the Great Initiation of number 9, are represented mathematically thus:

$0+1+2+3+4=10$, the *Cycle of Nature* or physical conditions, whose symbol is the Staff.

$(10)+5+6+7=28=10$, the *Cycle of Man* or The Christ-force, whose symbol is the Robe.

$(28)+8+9+10=55=10$, the *Cycle of Super-man* or the Higher Self, whose symbol is a lighted Candle or Lamp of Hermes.

The Staff is the Staff of the Patriarchs by the use of which we tread the Narrow Way of Initiation leading to the heaven world. The Robe is the Robe of

The Christ or the Mantle of Nature. When clothed in it we are 1 with all manifested life. The Lamp of Hermes is the Light of Wisdom which lights the way of the Super-Man. "Number nine is that of divine reflections; it expresses the divine idea in all its abstract power, but it also signifies extravagance in belief, and hence superstition and idolatry. For this reason Hermes has made it the Number of Initiation, because the Initiate reigns over superstition and by superstition and alone can advance through the darkness, leaning upon his staff, enveloped in his Mantle, and lighted by his Lamp. * * * The Lamp of Trismegistus enlightens past, present and future, lays bare the conscience of men and manifests the inmost recesses of the female heart. The Lamp burns with a triple flame, the Mantle is thrice-folded, and the Staff is divided into three parts."[2] Again the 3×3=9.

As we have already said: "In 9 we find again the cipher with which we started, but with a straight line (the evolution of the lower o of the 8 completed and straightened out) descending from it. Later when the Initiation is completed this line will take its place to the right of the cipher making 10, thus completing the cycle and making man more than man."[3] According to Éliphas Lévi: "Initiation is a preservative against the false lights of mysticism; it equips human reason with its relative value and proportional infallibility, connecting it with supreme reason by a chain of analogies. Hence the Initiate knows no doubtful hopes, no absurd fears because he has no irrational beliefs; he is acquainted with the extent of his power, and he can dare without danger. For him, therefore, to dare is to be able * * * He knows, he dares, and is silent."[2] The Initiates are the Sons (Suns) of God, and in the world of men hold the same relation as the Stars (Suns) do to the Cosmos.

---

[2] *Transcendental Magic,* Lévi, 88-9.
[3] *V. of I.,* 369.

While number 9 has always been considered the Number of Mystery, it is said to embody the power of Silence or that sacred hush in which all activity is swallowed up in the initiation of new life; the darkness just before the dawn; the magnetic thrill as the sun sinks below the horizon; the hush before a storm; the pause at the turn of the tide.

Apollonius of Tyana, the Greek Neo-Platonic philosopher, was an Initiate and hence fully understood the significance and importance of this number. He instructed his disciples specifically concerning it. He required strict observance of the 9th hour as a time for silence. He also forbade his followers to mention number 9 aloud. "This number, says Apollonius, must be passed over in silence, because it contains the great secrets of the initiate, the power which *fructifies the earth.* * * * the mysteries of *secret fire;* * * * the universal key of *languages;* * * * the second sight from which *evil-doers* cannot remain concealed."[4]

When number 9 was met with in their calculations it was therefore passed over in silence, and a deep obeisance was made as a recognition of its sacred character. This, of course, was but a ceremony intended to impress upon the minds of the Neophytes the great importance of Initiation, its sacredness and the folly and danger of even speaking lightly concerning its mysteries. We quite agree with this teaching, for the mystic 9th hour, both as a period of the day and as a period of the Soul's evolution, is a cycle of most sacred and mysterious import. At high noon all the forces of life are focused on the physical plane, hence great activity is going on in the physical body. This is therefore the best time to eat a hearty meal; for just as the Sun has its greatest power in nature at high noon, so is it in man's body. Noon is also the best time to send out our spiritual blessing to the world,

[4] *Transcendental Magic,* Lévi, 407.

upon the physical plane, since it is the time of greatest activity and impressionability. From noon until 3 P. M., or during the 9th hour, should be a time of quiet rest and digestion, both of the physical food taken at noon and also of the spiritual forces impressed on the physical body in the noon meditation and prayer service.

In response to this need the Order of Christian Mystics has established a noon-day silence and healing service which is open to all, and with which all are urged to unite.[5] In this service, just as the clock strikes 12, strive to enter the great Temple of Silence, don the Seamless Robe of The Christ and become 1 with your brothers and sisters throughout the world.

As it is noon in some part of the world all the time, and as our pupils in all parts of the world are sending their love and force to the Center of the Order as the clock strikes 12, it makes a continual stream of force sweeping around the globe every moment of the day and night. Their love adds a touch of human sympathy and comfort to the great currents of spiritual force which are poured into humanity from the higher realms through this Order and which sweep Westward around the globe from this Center, carrying Light and Love, health and prosperity to all who are in need; burning up the chaff and unfolding the blossoms of love and unselfishness in the hearts and lives of each 1 who correlates with them. All that is necessary to partake of this stream of spiritual force and love is mentally to unite yourself with the band of devoted brothers and sisters who are joined hand in hand and heart to heart in an endless chain which reaches around the globe, for the purpose of rendering unselfish service for The Christ to humanity. And as you give of your force for the good of all, to that extent do you partake of the power and force of all.

---

[5] See *V. of I.*, 410-11.

Each student should set aside at least 10 minutes during the day for silent meditation upon the Divine, and should faithfully keep this tryst with his or her Higher Self. If possible make this time at noon. If this is not possible at least send your thoughts of love and helpfulness to this Center at that time and contribute the force of your love and devotion to the upliftment of all. This is an exercise in *practical occultism* which has far-reaching effects.

At the conclusion of the silence period we mention the names of all who have sought the help of the Order, and mentally lay them in the radiant Light of The Christ-force in the mystic Temple of Silence[6] that they may receive a spiritual blessing. We will repeat each day for 1 week, all names sent us, at the end of which time they will no longer be mentioned unless by special request. All who ask this special help should make a determined effort to correlate with us at this hour and should report the experiences or results which follow.

Long ere man passes his Great Initiation he must consciously correlate his consciousness with those intelligent forces of nature brought to the earth at noon by the Sun's direct rays, which Apollonius called *genii,* but which are known to the Hindus as the *Devas,* and to the Christians as "the principalities and powers in heavenly places" (*Eph.,* iii, 10), whose function it is to guide the forces of the 1 Life into expression through the various planes of evolution, both in nature and in man. Each hour has its presiding Genius or "power," the Genius of the 9th hour being concerned with gathering out of the 3 realms—nature, man and God—all the forces which the 1 Life has perfected (initiated), and with them laying a square foundation upon which a new and more perfect cycle (10) can be erected. Hence ere man can pass number 9 he must

[6] See lesson *The Temple of Silence.*

understand how, not only to harmonize with the forces of nature, but also how consciously to direct them. Thus will he work with the Genius of the 9th hour. "God works in a mysterious way His wonders to perform." It is a step towards this great achievement when we set aside a few moments each day at noon and try to gather The Christ-force, which in Nature is Sun-force, and to send it forth in blessing and healing to the world.

If something of the reverence for Initiation taught by Apollonius were inculcated in modern students their spiritual unfoldment would be markedly quickened. So many today with irreverent tongues talk glibly of the many so-called "initiations" through which they have passed, while all the time their very garrulity and their lack of real understanding, power and helpfulness, proves to those who know the Law, that such boasters have never passed a Major Initiation. For since number 9 is the Number of Silence and creativeness, of working with nature-forces, the Initiate can always be recognized by his silent power. He never babbles, for he knows that in nature the babbling brook has no still depths in which the mystery of a new life can be brought forth. It also shows that such boasters have little understanding of what even a minor initiation signifies. Such claims lay their authors open to the suspicion that they have been deluded either by their own ambitions or have been deceived by astral impostors or both, or that at best their experience was but the astral ceremony of a minor initiation which was to work out later on in the physical life. This illustrates the folly of such claimants trying to make a great impression on their hearers.

The danger of boasting concerning such mighty experiences of Divine Realization is that the Great

Law, under the guidance of the Lords of Karma, must make the claimant prove every assertion. The law as stated in the *Bible* is, "For by thy words thou shalt be justified, and by thy words thou shalt be condemned" (*St. Matthew,* xii, 37). Hence a babbler will soon find himself plunged into troubles and tests for which he is unprepared, and will perhaps wonder at his uncommon run of ill luck, as he may call it, coming at a time when, according to his flattering astral guides and the assurance of his ambition, he should be enjoying the fruits of his exceptional worthiness. "Be humble, if thou wouldst attain to Wisdom. Be humbler still, when Wisdom thou hast mastered."[7]

It should be clearly understood that Initiation occurs 1st in the higher realms and then gradually descends to manifest in the physical world, thus following the law of all manifestation.

"Having taken this step alone, apparently in the darkness, the pupil will be brought to the Initiation which his demand will surely bring about. He will meet this Initiation either unconsciously through natural worldly events (events, however, which he will have no difficulty in connecting with this great step), or consciously in the higher astral. The experiences met with at this period will not consist of a few great Soul-stirring events, which when once passed entitle him to admission, but will consist of events which will bring to him a repetition of experiences which will force him to face himself and bring to his consciousness every secret and open fault; events which will force him to gaze into the eyes of the self that he has created out of the personality which his Real Self (or Ego) has created to train and function through; the self built up out of the thought-forms he has created. * * * There can be no dodging the issue or turning back from these events, for it is a mathematical law that he

[7] *The Voice of the Silence,* 39.

cannot pass on until he has acquired strength to conquer these faults, one by one, as they are presented to him. If he refuses, or is unable to conquer, his Soul must wait and work in the lower Orders until it grows stronger, and another cyclic opportunity for advance is afforded."[8]

The Soul may experience and pass an Initiation in the higher realms (5th and 6th) of the astral world,[9] and some realization of the event may be brought down into the waking consciousness in the form of a well remembered dream or psychic experience, but it may be many years ere the Initiation descends into manifestation and is worked out on the physical plane; for the same tests which the Soul successfully passed in the higher realms are presented to the unsuspecting personality by life itself. Generally the dream ends ere the final step is taken, leaving the dreamer uncertain of the end, because the end is not decided until by his own free-will he has chosen to manifest it in his daily life. The consummation of the Initiation on the physical plane is often pushed back and delayed, sometimes for a whole incarnation, by the refusal of the personality to follow the guidance of the Higher Self or by its refusal to face, recognize and strive to conquer the events in life as they are presented to him day by day by the Great Initiator. All depends upon how the personality meets these tests. Life brings these tests upon the aspirant at his weakest points, but since he has already passed them in the higher realms, he has the strength and Soul-power to conquer them if he will allow that Soul-power to manifest through him. "Let not him that girdeth on his harness boast himself as he that putteth it off." (I *Kings,* xx, 11). As illustrated in the case of Benhadad, King of Syria, in the story referred to above, the very boasting brings the battle upon the aspirant long before it would

[8] *V. of I.*, 63-4.
[9] See *Realms of the Living Dead*, Curtiss, xix, xx.

have otherwise descended and before the intermediate steps have prepared him to meet it. But until the inner experience has really descended into the physical world and conditions analogous to those which the dream or vision symbolically outpictured have actualized into life problems, can he be said to have passed his tests. Such occurrences are not fables nor mere imagination, but actual life experiences. The candidate must meet them without being told that they pertain to his Initiation, except as his own Higher Self endeavors to prepare his waking consciousness for the experiences which are to follow. In reality all are warned and prepared interiorly, but alas all do not remember or heed or attach due importance to such warnings. After the Great Initiation has been exemplified in the life, the victorious candidate will consciously meet his Initiator face to face and receive the assurance that he has indeed been admitted into the Brotherhood.

In occult stories pertaining to Initiation, that mystical experience is usually treated in an allegorical or symbolic manner. The candidate is made to pass through the most phantastic experiences and the most harrowing and grewsome trials of his courage, faith, and obedience. Such stories are purposely intended to stimulate the desire for Initiation, yet are blinds which do not reveal to the profane any of its secrets. The candidate may pass such fantastic experiences in the astral world, but ere he is truly an Initiate he must meet in real life that which they symbolize. Remember that true Initiation gives real balance, real power and real spiritual growth, which will manifest in the daily life.

CHAPTER 35

THE NUMBER 9—*(Continued)*.

"It is on this 'knowledge' that the programme of the Mysteries and of Initiations was based: hence the construction of the Pyramid, the everlasting record and indestructible symbol of these Mysteries and Initiations on Earth, as the course of the stars in Heaven."

—*The Secret Doctrine,* Blavatsky, Vol. I, 333.

Among the disciples of Apollonius and other ancient philosophers many mystic potencies were ascribed to number 9. It was frequently worn as an amulet, 1 method being that of having it engraved upon a sardonyx stone set in a silver ring. Such a ring was worn upon the 2nd finger of the left hand (the Saturn finger) as a sign of having passed a certain Initiation. In such a case it was said to possess the power of making the wearer invisible at will. The ring, however, had to be presented to the successful candidate at the time of the Initiation, after having been made under the special conditions necessary. Many curious and authentic tales are told, even today, of the mysterious power of invisibility possessed by certain highly advanced individuals.

The power of number 9 was also said to prevail against plagues and fevers. But since all amulets, talismans, etc., derive their powers largely from the currents of force focused in them by the will of the maker and the thought-power of those who believe in them, it is quite understandable that those Great Souls who were working among the densely ignorant and superstitious masses during the Middle Ages, found it helpful and admissible to have some object upon which to focus the attention, belief and thought-power of their followers. Nevertheless, each number has a potency of its own which is inherent in that which it represents. A sardonyx stone also has its own magnetic and other mystic potencies, as do all jewels, minerals, etc. The oriental sardonyx consists of 3 distinct layers, a black base, a white intermediate zone and a deeper superficial layer of reddish brown. Thus it is said to typify the 3 cardinal virtues necessary for a true Initiate, the black of his unmanifested possibilities which he is to unfold and express, the white of chastity and purity of body, mind and heart, and the brown of that humility which puts aside all personality, mixed with the red of Mars which gives the courage to face martyrdom if necessary rather than to reveal the sacred Mysteries of Initiation to the profane. Also the setting of this talisman in silver (the metal of the moon), gives to it the power of intuition and psychic unfoldment. Number 9 was also said to bring health and long life if carved upon any kind of amulet and worn upon the bosom. But wisdom and an understanding of the laws of health and the power of will and thought, will prove the best amulet for this purpose in the present day.

Plato, the greatest pupil of Pythagoras, lays great stress upon the importance of number 9. By the power of his will he is said to have so ordered his life that he passed away at the square of 9 or $9 \times 9 = 81$ years of age, in full vigor of intellect and power. It was his death occurring at that particular age which was largely responsible for bringing 81 into disrepute and causing it to be dreaded by his later and uninitiated followers.

Being the last of the digits, number 9 is the symbol of that which brings things to an end and prepares for a new manifestation. Just as the intra-uterine life of the child is brought to a close at the 9th month and the new cycle of life begins with the breath of number 8 entering the lungs at birth, so does Initiation sum up all the lessons learned through past experiences and initiates the consciousness of the candidate into a new life. It was at the 9th hour that Jesus is represented as breathing his last upon the cross, and we are told that "from the 6th hour (from 9 A. M. until noon), there was darkness over all the land until the 9th hour," or from noon until 3 P. M. This allegorically represents the Initiation of every true disciple of The Christ; for as long as the personality hangs on the cross—from the time The Christ (No. 6) is conceived in the heart (the 6th hour) until the Initiation is completed (9th hour)—there is darkness over the earth or the human understanding. And only at the 9th hour, when the personality gives up the ghost or resigns its life to the Father-in-heaven and cries with a loud voice: "Father, into thy hands I commend my spirit," is the veil between the 2 worlds rent and the real birth into the higher Divine Consciousness accomplished.

The 6th hour is The Christ hour, the period during which the rays of the sun are struggling toward complete expression at the zenith. And just as in nature, from 9 A. M. until noon, so in the disciple during the 6th hour, he is striving to let the Spiritual Sun dominate and reach the zenith of his life. From noon until number 3, while the light seems to be waning, in reality it is passing into the mysterious depths of nature and being alchemically transmuted into new growth, and at number 3, the divine number, the indrawing is complete. During the 11th hour, or from 3 to 6 P. M., nature is resting, and during the 4 watches of the night a new day is taking form in the womb of nature. As the 4 divisions of the day lay the foundation of Initiation, so the 4 watches of the night lay the foundation of a new day, number 10.

In Grecian mythology number 9 was consecrated to the "music of the spheres" and to the Muses. There were 9 Muses, daughters of Jupiter and Mnemosyne (memory). Each was assigned to preside over 1 particular department of literature, art or science. *Calliope* presided over epic poetry, *Clio* over history, *Euterpe* over lyric poetry, *Melpomene* over tragedy, *Terpsichore* over choral dance, *Polymnia* over sacred song, *Erato* over love poetry, *Urania* over astronomy and *Thalia* over comedy. Again, 9 combines the 3 Graces *(Euphrosyne, Aglaea* and *Thalia),* who preside over the joys of life, the banquet and the dance; the 3 Fates *(Clotho, Lachesis* and *Atropos),* who spun the Thread of Destiny, and the 3 Furies *(Alecto, Tisiphone* and *Megaera),* who punished by their secret stings the crimes of those who escaped or defied public justice, into a trinity of trinities, which illustrates the tests and trials of Initiation. For the candidate must prove his mastery over the social pleasures of the Graces, must courageously take from the Fates his 3 fold Thread of Destiny and meet with unruffled equanimity the 3 Furies and accomplish the Karmic adjustment of his secret sins.

The great Eleusinian Mysteries began on the 6th day of the month and continued for a period of 9 days, during which time the Initiation of the candidates took place. Number 9 played an important part in the life of the Romans. They celebrated a Feast of Purification for all male infants on the 9th day after birth. This rite was called "mudina." They buried their dead on the 9th day, and also held a feast called "Novennalia" every 9th year in memory of the dead. The Roman Catholic Church still holds the Feast of Neuvaines, a service of prayer and devotion celebrated on 9 successive days, during which the worshippers pray for such special blessing as may be indicated by the condition of the church or the needs of the times, but always the idea is to pray the Soul out of Purgatory. There can be little doubt as to the efficacy of such a ceremony; for if a number of persons pray earnestly for 9 consecutive days for anything upon which they all agree and concentrate, they will surely bring it into manifestation, be it a blessing or a curse. The Jews were forbidden to wear either the Talleth or the Phylacteries on the 9th of the month Ab until the close of the day, and were strictly enjoined to spend the entire day in fasting and repentance; for they believed that no good thing could come of any work done on the 9th day.

It is claimed by certain authors that number 9 pertains to Black Magic and sorcery, as well it may, for when the Candidate fails to pass his Initiation there is a temptation to use such powers as he has already won for selfish purposes. We find number 9 alluded to in this connection by Shakespeare in *Macbeth* (Act 1, scene 3), where we find it conspicuous in the spells of "the sisters three."

> "Weary, sev'n-nights, nine times nine,
> Shall he dwindle, peak and pine * * *
> The weird sisters, hand in hand,
> Posters of the sea and land,
> Thus to go about, about;
> Thrice to thine, and thrice to mine,
> And thrice again, to make up nine.
> Peace! * * * the charm's wound up."

Number 9 was dreaded by the candidate who had not mastered fear, for at Initiation all the evil influences of man's lower nature come up before him to tempt or appall him. But number 9 is also the number which gives to the brave and true Knight the courage to dare all such conditions, as well as the wisdom to transmute them into good.

We often meet with number 9 in old myth and fairy tales where, if not connected with black magic, it is looked upon as the enchanter's number. In the story of *Kilhweh* and *Alwen* the castle was constructed with 9 gates and 9 portals, beside which sat 9 dogs. There was also an inexhaustible basket from which it is said that thrice 9 men at a time could each find the meat that he most desired. King Arthur is said to have fought with an enchanted pig for 9 days and 9 nights. These are but 2 more references to Initiation, as are many other seemingly meaningless fairy tales; for the pig represents man's lower animal nature and its appetites, which the candidate for Knighthood or Initiation must conquer.

The Tartars hold number 9 in great reverence. It is said that the Great Khan was told in a vision to go to a certain mountain overlooking the sea and there kneel 9 times toward the East. He did so and the sea separated and exposed a pathway 9 feet broad, over which all the Tartar hosts passed dry shod. This is but another version of the myth of the passage of the Israelites through the Red Sea in a similar fashion. Both these myths symbolize the desire of the Soul, after harkening to the voice of the Law Giver, to come out of and away from the land of spiritual darkness (Egypt), where it and all its faculties (the Children of Israel) have been in bondage to King Desire (Pharaoh) and the sensations of the lower self. They both refer to the 1st *conscious* steps that lead toward Initiation.

The Masons have an Order called "The Elect of the Nine," in which 9 roses, 9 lights and 9 knocks enter into the ceremonies. This degree is consecrated to "bravery, devotedness and patriotism." All of these are summed up in the simple mandate, "Protect the oppressed against oppression; and devote yourself to the honor and interests of your country." This degree also inculcates self-renunciation and self-control, both necessary qualities for Initiation. While the Masons in general may not place as great a spiritual significance upon Initiation as does the mystic, nevertheless the very term "The Elect of the 9" refers to those who have passed a certain Initiation.

"The nine regular pictures of the universal Druid Church * * * are as follows: (1) The naming of the Time-keeping priest by the TEMpl and the Rope; (2) his ears being shown in the form of their Celtic name 'O'; (3) the picture of the Ape, pointed out as his name; (4) the blazing Sun on his breast, containing the face of the human deity; (5) the Serpent, which was also worn on the robes of the Celtic Druids; (6) the two Doves used in biblical sacrifice; (7) the Belt which named all the Druid Belt priests; (8) the Feathered head of the Chief to name the rank of this High Priest; (9) the Two Eight spoked Wheels of universal use in naming the Solar God and his Car."[1]

Milton represents Satan and his rebellious angels as requiring 9 days to fall from heaven. Milton, like all inspired poets, is mystical in spite of the orthodox twist he gives to his great conceptions. Lucifer, instead of being a "fallen" angel, was 1 of the Elohim who consciously descended into the realms of human consciousness to bring to mankind the Divine Light and, in his aspect of Satan or Saturn, to become the great Initiator.[2]

Number 9 is the greatest single number or the Master Digit, because it manifests the ultimate power of 1 place. 2 nines (99) express the ultimate power of 2 places, 3 nines the ultimate power of 3 places, etc. The Number of the Manifested Cosmos is therefore

[1] *The Jarvis Letters,* xi.
[2] On this point see *V. of I.,* 243-7 and 333-6.

a series of nines extending to infinity, thus: 999,999,-999∞. In other words only by passing the Initiation of number 9 can the cycle of any manifestation or dispensation or circle of 360—which adds up to 9—be completed.

The mystical number of the 144,000 Saints gathered from the 12 tribes of Israel—which closes the cycle of that dispensation—also adds up to 9. This is but another expression of the unity of all mankind in Adam whose number is 144=9.

> "The cycle of Initiation was a reproduction in miniature of that great series of cosmic changes to which astronomers have given the name of the Tropical or Sidereal Year. Just as, at the close of the cycle of the Sidereal Year (25,868 years), the heavenly bodies return to the same relative positions as they occupied at its outset, so at the close of the cycle of Initiation the Inner Man has regained the pristine state of divine purity and knowledge from which he set out on his cycle of terrestrial incarnation."[3]

The digits 1+2+3+4+5+6+7+8+9 = 45 = 9. Therefore 9 is called the basis of the unit value of all numbers and the key to the mensuration of all chances. Divide any number by 9 and if there is no remainder the digits of the number so divided will add up to 9. In other words, the sum of the digits exactly divisible by 9 equals 9; for instance, 7641 is exactly divisible by 9 and 7641=18=9. When dividing a number by 9, if there is a remainder the number will add up the same digit as the remainder, for example: 921 divided by 9 leaves a remainder of 3 and 921=12=3. Number 9 also reproduces itself in all multiples, thus: 7×9=63=9; 4×9=36=9, etc. Added to itself or its multiples, 9 always remains, thus: 9+9=18=9; 27+9=36=9. But added to any other number it is lost, thus: 9+8=17=8; 28+9=37=10. An exam-

[3] *S. D.*, I, 334.

ple of the persistence of number 9 is seen in the following table:

1 digit 9	or	9×	1=9×1	=9		
2 digits 9	"	99×	11=9×11×1	=99×	1×99	=18=9
3 " 9	"	999×	121=9×11×11	=99×	11×1089	=18=9
4 " 9	"	9999×	1221=9×11×111	=99×	111×10989	=27=9
5 " 9	"	99999×	12221=9×11×1111	=99×	1111×109989	=36=9
6 " 9	"	999999×	122221=9×11×11111	=99×	11111×1099989	=45=9

The sum of the Seal of Solomon is also 9, thus:

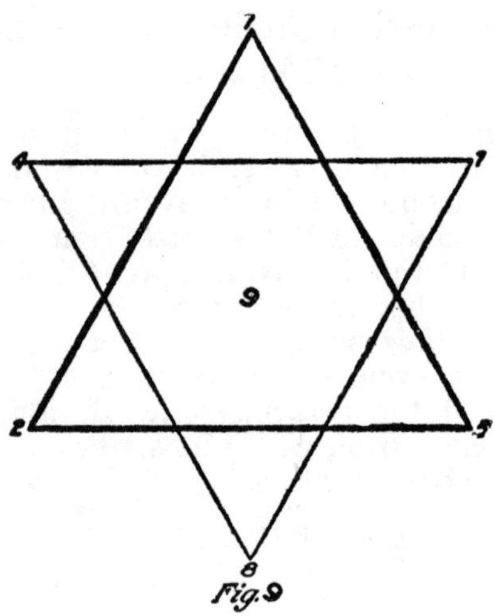

Fig. 9

The sum of any 2 points joined by a line through the center equals 9, and added to the central point equals 18=9.

In the philosophy of Henry Cornelius Agrippa, who wrote extensively concerning numbers and magic early in the sixteenth century, some extremely interesting mathematical relations involving number 9 are given. "Take any number, reverse it to obtain a second number, subtract one number from the other, and the digits of the remainder will always by addition reduce into 9 and the remainder itself will always be 9 or a multiple of 9. This operation is a spiral movement of the numbers employed, and the 9, therefore, represents a circle. An eternal spiral motion may be properly represented by an endless row of nines, each 9 symbolizing one complete revolution of the spiral movement. * * * By reason of these properties of 7 and 9 to numerically interpret Infinite Nature (999,999,999∞) is to divide it by number 7 (the Interpreter of Nature). This gives us, again, the Number of Infinite Evolution—142857,142857,142857∞. * * * There are 9 points to a cube—its 8 corners and its center, the only point where its 7 dimensions intersect each other. The cube itself is an Ego or One. This One, plus its 9 points, shows the cube to be a Raised One or 10. By dividing this Raised One by its 7 dimensions we obtain 1.42857-142857,142857∞."[4] This number 142857 also equals 27=9.

"Multiplying 142857 by 7 gives, of course, 999,999, the original nines returning. Multiplying the first 6 digits gives a 'magic square,' every line and column of which contains all the original digits of the number. The sum of each line and column is 27, or 3 times 9; also 4 times 7, *minus* 1, here a diameter correction.

"The Magic Square of 142857 is as follows:

142857×1=15873 nines or 142857=27=9
142857×2=31746 " or 285714=27=9
142857×3=47619 " or 428571=27=9
142857×4=63492 " or 571428=27=9
142857×5=79365 " or 714285=27=9
142857×6=95238 " or 857142=27=9

"The *lines* of the square show external rotation only. The *columns* show internal transposition only, and the digits are so transposed that each one *always* adds into 9 with its co-ordinately placed digit.

"The whole number of nines in the square is 333,333. The total of the square is 2,999,997, in which 7 goes exactly 428571 times, and 9, of course, 333,333 times."[5]

[4] *The Mystic Thesaurus,* Whitehead, 45-6.
[5] *The Mystic Thesaurus,* Whitehead, 49-50.

A surprising series of rotations which result when the figures 12,345,679 are multiplied by 9 and by multiples of 9 is given by the German mathematician, Albert Neuberger, as follows:

$$12345679 \times 9 = 111111111$$
$$12345679 \times 18 = 222222222$$
$$12345679 \times 27 = 333333333$$
$$12345679 \times 36 = 444444444$$
$$12345679 \times 45 = 555555555$$
$$12345679 \times 54 = 666666666$$
$$12345679 \times 63 = 777777777$$
$$12345679 \times 72 = 888888888$$
$$12345679 \times 81 = 999999999$$

CHAPTER 36

THE 9TH LETTER, *Teth* (ט)

"He produced Teth, predominant in Hearing, crowned it, combined and formed with it Leo in the Universe, Ab (August) in the Year, and the left Kidney in Man."—*Sepher Yetzirah,* 24.

The 9th Hebrew letter, Teth (T), is 1 of the simple letters and is connected with the zodiacal sign Leo, the heart of the Grand Man. The actual meaning of Teth is a serpent, and as 9 is the Number of Initiation an Initiate is called a *Naga* or Serpent of Wisdom. Another reason for the application of this term is that just as the serpent changes and renews his outer skin, so the Initiate changes and renews his personality; that is, he shakes off and emerges from the limitations of the old personality as he becomes an Initiate. Number 9 also completes and shakes off the old digits—which might be compared to the personality—and emerges in the new number, 10. As with the serpent, however, the new skin or personality is built up by the digestion and assimilation of all that was contained or experienced in the former, so that the 2nd cycles of digits (10, 20, 30, etc.) are the same as the 1st, but with the power of 10 added to each. And just as the newly emerged serpent is the old serpent grown longer and more perfect, so does the Initiate retain the old but perfected personality, with all the unfolded powers added. For in his long pilgrimage toward the 9th Gate he has little by little transmuted the old body, and atom by atom has cast off the seeds of decay and death, until now it is a glorious body of immortal life, for he has overcome death.

The hieroglyphic meaning of Teth is a "roof," the idea being that of a covering or protection. Another meaning of the letter is "El Chai," the Mighty Living 1, for it is the force of the 1 Life manifesting in man as an electro-dynamic force, the Kundalini or serpent power, which when lifted up and dominated by the spiritualized Will makes of man an Initiate. In this sense Teth indicates that only as we have passed the Great Initiation of number 9 and have become "wise as serpents and harmless as doves," can we consciously express the power of the Mighty Living 1. The sentence quoted above is another allusion to the mystic Initiation, for the candidate has 2 great tasks to perform in his physical body ere he can gain perfect control over it, and without which the Great Initiation cannot be passed, namely, the control of the serpent power and the attainment of the wisdom it brings. For only as this power—under control of the spiritualized Will—is lifted up and guided until it reaches the sacred center between the eyes, can Realization be attained and the candidate become as wise as a serpent.

Another task is to find that center within the body where the Bird of Life has its nesting place—the Heavenly Dove whose head is Wisdom, whose body is Humility, whose right wing is Life Immortal, and whose left wing is Divine Love—and having found this nest attain sweet rest "between the wings of that which is not born, nor dies." Among the precepts found in *The Voice of the Silence,*[1] written for the guidance of those who are nearing the 9th Gate and not applicable to nor intended for the guidance of those not definitely seeking Initiation, we find the following: "Bestride the Bird of Life, if thou would'st know * * * let not thy 'Heaven-Born' * * * break from the Universal Parent (Soul), but let the fiery power retire into the inmost chamber, * * * then from the

[1] Pages 5-9-10.

heart that Power shall rise into the sixth, the middle region, the place between thine eyes."

This Universal Parent Soul is the same as the Mighty Living 1, or the "fiery power," in its universal aspect, or as we would say, the Great Creative Christ-force. Hence the main point in occult development is not to break away from this Christ-power which is the mediator between man's personality and his Divine Self and the Redeemer of the lower nature. As we develop this power we blend with and come under the conscious protection of the Mighty Living 1 of the Cosmos, who now lives in and acts through us as our protector and sustainer, instead of merely overshadowing and influencing us as in the earlier steps.

The lesson to be learned from the Bird of Life is that of poise. Just as in Initiation there must be an absence of all fear and a quiet resting between the equilibrated forces of love and life, so must the Soul rest between the 2 wings of the Bird of Life. Hence to "bestride the Bird of Life" means to be master of life, and like the Bird be able to rise at will into the higher realms in thought. We can never be a Master of Life until we have gained this equilibrium; so that no matter what disturbs us we can rise above it. We must hold the picture of ourselves fearlessly standing on the back of the Great Bird, holding the reins and guiding it, so absolutely poised that we and the Bird are 1.

Another meaning of Teth as a "roof," is that as we advance spiritually and approach our Initiation we develop a center called by the Hindus the "Siddhis center." As this center develops it forms a real protecting roof of glory over the head of the aspirant, from which there pours down a golden rain of force like a fine golden mist which forms the Veil of Protection. It is the Banner of Love held over the Saints by the Bridegroom spoken of in the *Song of Solomon* (ii, 4). "He brought me to the banqueting house (number 9), and his banner over me was love." In all pictures of the Saints we see this Banner depicted as a circle of gold or a *halo* of light placed *horizontally* just above the head. This should not be confused with the *nimbus* which is placed in the *vertical* plane and represents the scintillating colors of the aura. This Banner and Veil of Protection can be consciously developed through certain advanced exercises which are given to the candidate only by his Guru or teacher.

The letter Teth is also connected with Cosmic Electricity.

> "The Ancients represented it (cosmic Electricity) by a serpent, for *Fohat hisses as he glides hither and thither,* in zigzags. The Kabbalah figures it with the Hebrew letter Teth (ט), whose symbol is the serpent which played such a prominent part in the Mysteries. Its universal number is 9, for it is the ninth letter of the alphabet and the ninth door. It is the magical Agent *par excellence,* and designated in Hermetic philosophy 'Life infused into Primordial Matter,' the essence that composes all things, and the Spirit that determines their form."[2]

In short, Cosmic Electricity is the Initiator of Matter.

As Teth is connected with the sign Leo, the heart, it is only by overcoming the forces of the heart and making Leo the Lion tame and obedient to the will, that the little Christ-child, who is now growing stronger and stronger day by day, may lead him and make him lie down with the lamb. Only thus can we pass the Initiation of number 9. Yet the Lion which has become tame and obedient must have lost nothing of his strength or virility. This is symbolized in the myth

[2] *S. D.,* Vol. I, 105.

of Samson who when he slew the lion found in the carcass much honey.[3] So when the candidate has slain the passion aspect of the heart-forces which rave like a lion, he finds the honey, which is both sweetness and food.

The 9th letter also expresses the idea of Wisdom, for the protection or roof must be the result of the Wisdom of the Initiate himself. When he has reached this step we are told that he must lay down every weapon, both of offense and defense. He can no longer seek protection from the power of his strength, nor can he ask that any being outside of himself shall protect him, yet he who has attained unto Wisdom is protected from every ill. In *Ecclesiastes* we read that, "Wisdom is a defense. * * * Wisdom strengtheneth the wise man more than ten mighty men. * * * Wisdom is better than strength," etc.[4] When we have attained his Wisdom we have learned the lesson of the 9th letter and are ready to face the Great Initiator.

---

[3] *Judges,* xiv, 5-9. [4] vii, 19.

THE 9TH TAROT CARD

THE HERMIT

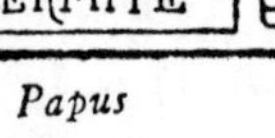

Papus

MEDIEVAL

Papus

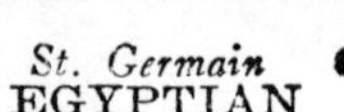

St. Germain
EGYPTIAN

Smith
MODERN

THE 9TH TAROT CARD, *The Hermit.*

The 9th card of the Tarot is called the Hermit. In it we find expressed all the ideas of Initiation, for here we have a picture of an old man who, in spite of the fact that as he walks he leans upon a Staff, nevertheless is strong and upright, with eyes wide open and undimmed, looking steadily ahead. He is wrapped in a long Mantle and in his uplifted right hand carries a Lantern.

The symbology of this card is plain. The age of the Hermit denotes not senility, but the strength and vigor of maturity, hence experience, discretion and Wisdom. The Staff upon which he leans is the Staff of the Patriarchs or that divine strength upon which he has learned to lean. It is the power of the 1 Life which every Initiate must gain through complete mastery of the forces of nature. It is also the Magic Wand with which he performs his miracles and by whose use he proves to the world that he has passed the Great Initiation of number 9. It is the power of the 1 Life like a staff running through and supporting all. It is Aaron's Rod of Power which will never fail him, Aaron symbolizing the priestly attributes through which the Initiate serves before the throne of the Great Law. It is the Shepherd's Crook with which he can guide the straying and uplift the fallen. It is that which he has tested and proved, for during all his long and toilsome journey to the gate of Initiation, which now stands open before him, it has never failed him.

The Rod has 7 knots or rings which are the 7 steps of purification. The lighted Lamp he holds high above his head is the Light of Knowledge, the Lamp of Truth or the "Word," *i. e.*, "Thy word shall be a light to my path, and a lamp unto my feet." It is the inner illumination of 1 who has come off victor. Just as in his earlier steps the Light shone above him as the Star of Initiation, which he had to follow over deserts, morasses and desolate regions without losing sight of it, even though at times the dark mists of earth hid it from view, so it is still the Light from the 1 Master, his own Immortal Self, of which we read: "The light from the *One Master,* the one unfading light of Spirit, shoots its effulgent beams on the Disciple from the very first. Its rays thread through the thick dark clouds of matter. Now here, now there, these rays illumine it, like sun-sparks light the earth through the thick foliage of the jungle growth. But, O Disciple, unless the flesh is passive, head cool, the Soul as firm and pure as flaming diamond, the radiance will not reach the chamber (the center of Spiritual Consciousness), its sunlight will not warm the heart."[5] The Hermit has let the Light reach the chamber of his heart. He has also made it shine in the chamber or center of Spiritual Consciousness. Hence the symbol of the Light being placed in the lantern, *i. e.,* no longer fitful like a distant star, but in his conscious grasp, ready to guide him every step of the way.

The Mantle which envelops him and partially hides the lighted Lamp is the Mantle of Discretion with which the Initiate must enwrap himself and shield the full Light of his Lamp from the eyes of the profane. For every Soul must find the Light within himself ere he can recognize it in another or even bear its full effulgence.

This card balances the 7th and 8th cards, the Victor in his chariot and the Mother-power of Love which holds the scales of Justice. It expresses the protection of the Initiates who, altho few in numbers as compared with the great mass of humanity, are still the Protectors of Humanity. They stand like a guardian wall

[5] *The Voice of the Silence.*

around mankind. Like watchmen in a tower, their Lamps held high, they are ready to fly to help and succor every child of man who cries out for Light and help, if the light and help are really needed. But even this help is given wisely, for there are cases in which it is best that the child should learn to help itself, even as a loving mother may wisely allow her babe to cry itself to sleep, rather than fly to it when she knows that it needs nothing but sleep. They remain upon the hilltops throughout the long nights of spiritual darkness, like faithful shepherds watching over their sleeping sheep, with their Staff ever ready to reach out to 1 who is slipping and falling, its crook ready to lift 1 who is torn and bleeding, and their Mantle of Charity ready to enwrap those who are suffering from the bitter storms of passion and desire. But dear student, they are ever wrapped in the Mantle of Discretion, hence only those who Dare, Do and Keep Silent can ever see the Light of the Hermit's Lamp.

THE 9TH COMMANDMENT.

> 9. "Thou shalt not bear false witness against thy neighbor."—*Exodus,* xx, 16.

Since 9 is the Number of Initiation, 2 pertinent questions at once arise concerning the esoteric interpretation of this Commandment: 1st, who is "thy neighbor?" 2nd, what relation does false witness bear to Initiation? The *Bible* description of the man who fell among thieves and was rescued by the Samaritan answers the 1st question. "Thy neighbor" is anyone whom the Great Law brings directly into your Path who can be helped by you if you are willing to take note of his needs.

The question as to what false witness has to do with Initiation will bear careful analysis. The Soul is ready to bear the Great Initiation only when it can face itself and see all things in their true relations. Over the 1st gateway to the Path there is written in letters of gold, "Man, Know Thyself," and when the outward comprehension of this injunction has been gained, at the very last Gate the Neophyte once more faces the same sentence, but now written in letters of living fire within his quivering flesh, "Man, Know Thyself."

If we would meet the final test of Initiation unappalled, we must accept this precept and strive diligently to obey it. As the disciples and servants of the True Self, our senses must be trained not to bear false witness. To do this we must not accept as final the reports of our senses until they have been checked up and verified by our reason, experience, judgment and discrimination, illumined by our intuition. Few persons can bear to have the searchlight of Truth turned upon their own lives, within themselves. They are wont to bear false witness by making excuses and blaming conditions or other persons for the results of their own shortcomings. At 1 extreme they bear false witness in the form of exaggerated humility, scourging themselves with the scorpion whips of self-condemnation, looking upon themselves as worms of the dust unworthy or incapable of lofty attainments. At the other extreme are those who live in a perfect glamor of the senses, accepting as right and proper whatever report the senses make. They forever focus the lime-light of self-approval and admiration upon themselves. They are ever posing, dwelling on their good points, flattering themselves to themselves, excusing every shortcoming with some flattering delusion. They interpret every phase of life as a stage-setting to bring them into more favorable notice. In fact, they are forever acting a part which they have assumed so long that they almost believe in it themselves and vainly hope that the world believes it to be their true character. All this is bearing false witness to the Truth.

If by any chance such persons should demand to be brought into the Hall of Initiation, there to be confronted with the personality they are really manifesting, they would be appalled at the sight and refuse to admit that it was their own creation. For the 1st time they would awake to find their pose revealed, the show over and no audience present but themselves and their Great Initiator, with all glamor of the senses stripped from the reality and standing face to face with the self they have manifested. These are the ones who fly shrieking in madness from the sight of their Dweller. This is the truth back of the many tales of the terrifying experiences encountered during Initiation. For ere this step can be taken the Soul must face that which it has created by its "witnessing," whether true or false, in everyday life.

That we may not bear false witness against our neighbor we need to reach the point where we do not bear false witness against ourselves. Then we are able to see clearly and consequently can help our neighbor. While we should not contemplate or dwell upon them, to shut our eyes to truths that are unpleasant or to imperfections within ourselves which we know exist, is refusing to recognize Truth, hence is bearing false witness. While we should mention, emphasize and dwell upon the good in our brothers and sisters, it is surely bearing false witness to shut our eyes to their shortcomings and say that all in them is Good. That we may bear no false witness we must learn to seek out the true motives, both in ourselves and in others. Then we will find that we will no longer condemn others, because we will realize how much we ourselves fall short of manifesting the ideals we have chosen. We will see that every Soul is upon some step of the Path, some of which we may have passed. And if we have trained our senses not to bear false witness we will know what motive was back of the effect which our senses report. And by thus working from the underlying cause, rather than from the effect, we will be able to remedy any failure in ourselves and be a help to others. Thus the 9th Commandment is given as a preparation for Initiation.

Strive always to see clearly and bear true witness. Then when you face your Great Initiation there will be nothing in yourself that has been hidden, denied or covered up, hence there will be nothing that can affright you. For as the Great Initiator holds out the Rod of Power he cries with a mighty voice: "Thou shalt not bear false witness either against thyself or thy neighbor." And only as we are able to meet this test can we grasp that Magic Rod.

CHAPTER 37

THE NUMBER 10.

"It is from this Number, 10, or Creative Nature, the Mother (the Occult cypher, or '0,' ever procreating and multiplying in union with the unit '1,' or the Spirit of Life), that the whole Universe proceeds."

—*The Secret Doctrine,* Blavatsky, I, 121.

"The ineffable Sephiroth are Ten, so are the Numbers: * * * ten and not nine, ten and not eleven. Understand this wisdom, and be wise in the perception."

—*Sepher Yetzirah,* 15.

Number 10 is the Number of Completion or Perfection through completion; the assembling of the completed parts. It is the grand summit of numbers and their completion. It is the number which expresses the completion of creation as mentioned in *Genesis* (i, 31): "And God saw everything that he had made, and, behold, it was very good." For number 10 contains all the digits or creations and returns them once more to unity, thus, 1+2+3+4+5+6+7+8+9+10 =55=10=1. Hence Number 10 cannot be surpassed. In it we again meet the ○ of unmanifested force with which we started, and whose emanations we have watched evolve through the 9 digits, but now the 1st differentiation, number 1, stands at the right of the circle ready to begin a new series of manifestation in a higher cycle of evolution.

In other words, the ○ in the beginning contained all those things which were put aside and left unconquered and unredeemed during a previous cycle of evolution, waiting until the strength and wisdom of number 9 had been attained to consciously take them up and from them evolve a new series of numbers (powers). The 1st number 1 was but a foreshadowing and prophecy of that which it should become at the close of its cycle, just as the "primitive streak" in the embryo is a prophecy of the man to be.

In 10 the ○ is no longer a Chaos of undifferentiated matter, nor a mass of left-overs from a past world period awaiting the outpouring of the Divine Creative Force of the 1 Life to start it into evolution, but has now expressed itself in the perfection of nature and man. Man, now become the Initiate, has grasped the Rod of Power (number 1) and separated it from the overshadowing ○ of number 9 and, having identified himself with the 1 Life, stands at the right hand of the now manifested forces of the ○, ready in his turn to become the creator or director of the forces which are to be manifested during the succeeding cycle. Here man as a creator must consciously say "Let there be light," with a full understanding of all it implies, and by the power of the 1 Life play an active part in the downpouring of the Light during the new day-period about to dawn. The initiated Man now stands as a responsible co-worker with the Divine. It is as though during the cycle of 1 to 10 God had held the hand of His child and guided it in carving the statue or model of the Man to be, the Initiate, while now the chisel is left in the hand of the matured youth, and he must create from the materials given him in the beginning the perfect statue whose ideal was set before him by the Master Sculptor. In other words, the Man must now accomplish for himself, by consciously utilizing the strength and power of the 1 Life, which during the period from 1 to 9 was evolving him to this point. Here he must not only redeem his own left-overs, but as an Initiate he must take his place with the more advanced Masters in the guardian wall around humanity and begin, consciously and voluntarily and because of his great love and compassion, to bear the burden of the world's suffering and aid in its redemption.

While the word *decad* comes from the Greek word *deka,* meaning 10, it was applied by the Pythagoreans to the quarternary, an elementary number denoting a factor of the Cosmos. And since 1+2+3+4=10, the word is correctly used in that connection. "X is our sign for TEN, named in the Greek D-EC-a, naming the 'God Cross' whose name is X, and who named the whole 'D-EC-I-MAL' system, which is built of TENs."[1]

> "This Decad, representing the Universe and its evolution out of Silence and the Unknown Depths of the Spiritual Soul, or Anima Mundi, presented two sides or aspects to the student. It could be, and was at first, applied to the Macrocosm, after which it descended to the Microcosm, or man. There was, then, the purely intellectual and metaphysical, or the 'Inner Science,' and the as purely materialistic or 'surface science,' both of which could be expounded by and contained in the Decad. It could be studied, in short, both by the deductive method of Plato, and the inductive method of Aristotle. The former started from a divine comprehension, when the plurality proceeded from unity, or the digits of the Decad appeared, only to be finally reabsorbed, lost in the infinite Circle. The latter depended on sensuous perception alone, when the Decad could be regarded either as the unity that multiplies, or matter which differentiates; its study being limited to the plane surface, to the cross, or the *seven* which proceeds from the *ten,* or the perfect number, on Earth as in Heaven. This dual system was brought, together with the Decad, by Pythagoras from India."[2]

The Pythagoreans made each quarter of the Cosmos complete, and argued its completeness from the fact

---

[1] *The Jarvis Letters,* v.

[2] *S. D.,* II, 605.

that 4, being the quartenary and equal to 10, made what they called the "all complete." They were apt to give extravagant terms to this number in an effort to express its perfection. For instance, they are quoted as comparing it to heaven, because in it all the digits are indrawn for a period of rest, swallowed up as it were in Eternity, symbolized by the ○, while the 1 Life stands beside it ready to begin a new cycle of evolution in the 10.

They also called number 10 Eternity which, having neither beginning nor end, is usually symbolized by the ○ alone. It was also called the Sun, for just as the sun rises on a new day after a night of darkness, the new day bringing with it all the experiences and continuing the work of the previous day, so does number 10 begin for the Soul a new outpouring of divine Light, Love and Power with which to accomplish in the new cycle. It is also called the Cosmos, because, as we have shown, the evolution of the Cosmos and man is set forth in the digits from 1 to 9, all of which are swallowed up in 10. Aristotle says that "some philosophers hold that ideas and numbers are of the same nature and amount to 10 in all."

According to the kabalistic meaning of each number we have a beautiful conception of the cycle of 10 and what it should mean in man's unfoldment. In number 1, which they call the "Crown," Spirit descends into matter and offers to man a Crown of Life, but he can attain this Crown only as he unfolds and manifests the qualities expressed in each of the digits, as follows: 2 is called "Wisdom," 3 "Understanding," 4 "Mercy," 5 "Strength," 6 "Beauty," 7 "Victory," 8 "Splendor," 9 "Foundation." Therefore, only when we can express all these qualities can we complete number 10, called the "Kingdom." Here we find a corroboration of the teaching of Christian Mysticism that while the

Father has crowned us as his heirs, we are not gods or Christs in our present undeveloped state. Only as we grow and unfold and *express* the powers of the 9 digits can we attain and rule over our "Kingdom" in number 10.

Another appellation given by some mystics to number 10 is "the Hand of God." This is explained by the fact that "The Great Law manifests in two great divisions, positive and negative, referred to in this instance as the right hand and the left. The right hand represents the Great Law working toward perfection in perfect harmony and without opposition, while the left represents the Shadow of the Law working apparently in opposition to Good, but in reality a servant of God (good) which through suffering is bringing ultimate good out of evil. This latter manifestation is termed by some the burnings of Karma, by others the fires of hell, etc., but in reality it is but the left hand of the Great Law bringing out of all disobedience, mistake, rebellion and selfishness lessons which shall ultimately bring to perfection and redeem all that is in both man and Nature. From another viewpoint the Great Law with its right hand pours forth all blessings and with its left corrects, adjusts and teaches the best use of those blessings; or with its right hand it sows the wheat and with the left pulls up the weeds."[3] Also while man needs 2 hands with 5 fingers on each to accomplish that which he designs, God, holding within Himself the dual forces expressed by man and woman, needs but 1 hand, mighty of accomplishment, and represented with 10 fingers instead of 5. The same idea is expressed in many Hindu statues which have 2 or more pairs of hands denoting powers. Another phase of the same idea is represented in the Greek Titan, Briareus, who had 100 hands.

Still another expression of the power of the Hand

---

[3] See lesson *The Ancient of Days.*

of God is a great hand with the 2nd and 3rd fingers lifted and the thumb folded in the palm. From this ancient and mystical idea the position of the fingers of the Pope's hand while giving the pontifical blessing has been derived. The raised 2nd and 3rd fingers symbolize God and perfected Man pouring out their blessing. Yet, like all forces manifesting in the physical world, this blessing may become a curse according to the desire and will of the officiating pontiff. A remarkable thing in connection with this position of the hand is that its shadow resembles the head and horns of the goat Baphomet, the symbol of Black Magic. The use of the "shadow of the blessing" was supposed to be a legitimate power possessed by the Pope, and was most terribly exercised during the Dark Ages, in the Inquisition, etc., and woe to him upon whom the "shadow of the blessing" fell. We still see pictures of this hand with the word "Benedictionen" upon it, while upon the shadow is the word "Maledictus."

Plotinus taught that number 10 was the Fountain of Life or the Fountain of Eternal Nature, the stream of the 1 Life forever flowing forth in 2 currents as it touched the earth. He also spoke of it as mundane, representing the world receiving from the Divine the potencies and powers of the Divine through the 9 digits. For instance, its 2 halves represent man and woman (5+5=10), while nature (4) with The Christ-life (6) pulsating through it is represented by 4+6=10. The manifestation of the Trinity and Perfection is represented by 3+7=10, while duality in its evolution toward equilibrium or balance is represented by 2+8=10. And finally, Initiation attained through the power of the 1 Life is expressed by 9+1=10.

> "The Pillar and Circle (IO), which with Pythagoras was the perfect number, contained the Tet-

> raktys, became later a *pre-eminently phallic* number * * * amongst the Jews, foremost of all, with whom it is the male and female Jehovah. * * * 'This idea of connecting the picture of the circle and its diameter line, that is, the number 10, with the signification of the reproductive organs, and the Most Holy Place * * * was carried out constructively in the King's Chamber, or Holy of Holies, of the great Pyramid, in the Tabernacle of Moses, and in the Holy of Holies of the Temple of Solomon. * * * It is *the picture of a double womb,* for in Hebrew the letter Hé (ה) is at the same time the number 5, and the symbol of the womb, and twice 5 is 10, or the phallic number.' This 'double womb' also shows the duality of the idea carried from the highest spiritual down to the lowest or terrestrial plane. 'But the signification is that it is androgyne or hermaphrodite, that is, phallus and yoni combined, the number 10, the Hebrew letter *Yod* (י), the containment of Jehovah'."[4]

Number 10 was given to man as a covenant of strength, for if man was given Will alone, without the Power to conquer, he would be but the shadow of God and not His image. "As there are in man 5 fingers over against 5, so over them is established a covenant of strength, by word of mouth, and by circumcision of the flesh."[5]

In the allegory of Abram and Sarai when Abram was 99 years old, that is, when he had passed his Great Initiation (99=18=9) and was ready to enter upon the new cycle of 10, the Lord or the Great Law said unto him, "walk before me, and be thou perfect [the 1 before the 0 equals the perfect 10]. And I will make my covenant between me and thee, and will multiply thee exceedingly."[6] That is, number 10 or the new cycle is to bring forth a new progeny, is to multiply exceedingly (that is by tens) and by it are all the nations of the earth to be blessed. Continuing

[4] *S. D.*, II, 486; I, 421.
[5] *Sepher Yetzirah*, 17.
[6] *Genesis*, xvii, 1-2.

the allegory, number 10 becomes the "Father of many nations" or cycles of human evolution, each 10 starting a new cycle or nation and bringing it back to unity again. This covenant was ratified when Sarai bore him a son when she was 90 and "well stricken in years," *i. e.,* when she had passed through all the digits up to 9 she brought forth the 1 which completed the cycle of 10. More remarkable still, in the Hebrew, Sarai is written SRI and has a numerical value of 235=10. In the Hebrew SRI is the wife of Abram and in the Hindu SRI is the wife of Vishnu. In both cases she is the personification of the Feminine Principle of the Godhead and is connected with water, gestation and the moon. But she could not bring forth until the letter H or 5 had been added to her name making it Sarah and increasing it to 2355=15=6. Thus Sarai (10) had to be fructified by The Christ-force (6) ere she could bring forth and become the mother of mankind. This is corroborated by the fact that the letter H or Hé represents Heva, Eve and the womb. H also represents a "householder," the esoteric meaning of which is to bring forth. Therefore both Abram and Sarai must gain the power of the letter H or the power of Eve, ere they can "multiply exceedingly" and bring forth the Children of Israel or humanity. With the addition of the H Abram becomes Abraham and Sarai becomes Sarah, thus completing the symbology of a true covenant between God and man, *i. e.,* the 10 manifesting on earth as 2 fives, male and female, and bringing forth a Son, the 1 in whom all mankind shall be blessed.

CHAPTER 38

THE NUMBER 10—*(Continued)*.

> "Every cosmogony began with a circle, a point, a triangle and a square up to number 9, when it was synthesized by the first line and circle."
> —*The Secret Doctrine*, Blavatsky, I, 341.

Apuleius, a Platonic philosopher who traveled extensively through the East seeking Initiation into the Mysteries, has left many useful hints pertaining to various ceremonies; in fact, he won for himself the name of "The Evening Star of Platonic Philosophy and the Morning Star of the Neo-Platonic." He is authority for the statements as to the great importance placed upon numbers by the Egyptian priests, especially number 10, as representing man's fitness for the priesthood.

> "*The Books of Hermes* are the oldest repositories of numerical Symbology in Western Occultism. In them we find that number *ten* is the Mother of the Soul, Life and Light being therein united. For as the sacred anagram Teruph shows in the *Book of Keys* (Numbers), the number 1 is born from Spirit, and the number 10 from Matter; 'the unity has made the ten, the ten, the unity.' "[1]

An Egyptian priest not only had to have absolute control over his passions and physical appetites, but had also to be learned in the sciences and be an Initiate into the Mysteries. Before offering the sacrifice he was obliged to fast for 10 days, during which he had to conform to a most rigid discipline.

Among the ancients the zodiac was represented exoterically with but 10 signs instead of 12 as at present.

[1] *S. D.*, III, 100.

The signs Virgo, Libra and Scorpio were united in 1 sign, combining in 1 sign the masculine (Scorpio) and feminine (Virgo) united by the sex attraction (Libra) balancing the 2.

That early zodiac represented man before the separation of the sexes, when the androgynous man of course combined the 3 now separate expressions of life in 1. This is corroborated by the myth of Phaethon, son of Phoebus, who found the Scorpion stretching over 2 signs of the zodiac.[2]

Among the Gnostics only 10 Orders of Angelic Hierarchies are mentioned as necessary to bring about perfection, the 11th and 12th not being mentioned since they pertain to the coming forth of the new cycle, just as 10 signs really complete the evolutionary cycle of the zodiac, while Aquarius and Pisces prepare for the coming forth of a new cycle of the sun in Aries.

> "The author of the *Source of Measures* says that the foundation of the Kabalah and of all its mystic books is made to rest upon the *ten* Sephiroth; which is a fundamental truth. He shows there Ten Sephiroth or the 10 Numbers, as follows:"[3]

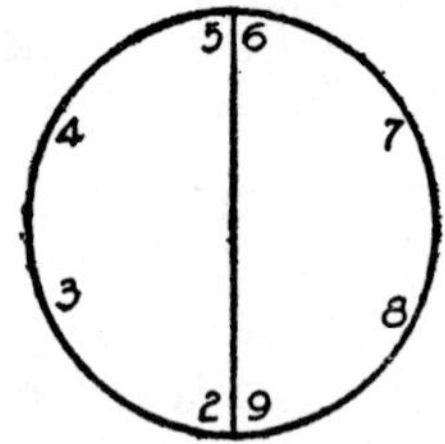

This diagram plainly shows 1st the ○ of the Unmanifested with the 1 Life like a ray of Light cutting it into halves. This illustrates in a most simple way why, as we have so often said, everything manifesting in the mundane sphere must fall under the Law of Polarity or Pairs of Opposites. For it will be seen

[2] See page 253.

[3] *S. D.*, II, 40.

at a glance that the descent of the 1 Life into manifestation must cleave the homogeneous sphere of the Divine and make it 2 or mundane. Meditation on this diagram will solve many perplexing questions, especially the 1 so often asked: Does sex inhere in the Soul? If we let the circle represent the unmanifested Soul, 1 with God or the ◯, and the vertical line the Ray of Divinity (Atma), descending into that unmanifested germ, dividing it into the 2 expressions of the 1 (*Buddhi,* negative; *Manas,* Positive), it clearly illustrates the law that *there can be no manifestation on any plane* of differentiation except through the union of the positive and negative Principles manifested by the Soul through the 2 sexes. As the Soul is the reservoir for all the experiences which must be completed and garnered on earth, only as we experience, blend and lift up the lower experiences of the Soul as the mind reports them in the separated sexes, can we register them in either the positive or the negative aspects of the Soul or Higher Self.

This diagram also explains the idea of the Group Soul, for each Divine Ray animates such a circle of unmanifested humanity, and ere number 10 can be evolved from it and the 1 (Son) stand at the right hand of the cipher (Father) all the numerals in the separated halves of the circle must each be evolved and then indrawn.

That which is true of the Higher Self is correspondingly true of the lower personality. Each personality is such a circle or cipher and must unfold all the numerals in itself as qualities, etc. For ere man can become number 10 or the perfect "all-complete," the circle must stand on his left hand while with his right hand he grasps the Staff of the Patriarchs or number 1, the 1 Life with which he shall consciously evolve the new cycle. In other words, he must so truly have lost his idea of separateness that he is 1 with the world (◯) and with all that is, his personality swallowed up and the new ◯ become the workshop in which he is to create and bring forth.

The injunction to overcome the sense of separateness is apt to bring confusion to many minds, but the idea is that while we must realize our oneness with all that is, this sense of oneness can be attained only by entering into the consciousness of the Higher Self. We must be intensely and completely ourselves ere we can become 1 with all. Then we are no longer like a grain of sand tossed hither and thither by every wind that blows, lost in a monotonous sameness of shape and characteristics, or 1 of a mass of humanity swayed by thought waves not their own, but have become like a star or planet steadily circling in our appointed orbit; consciously expressing our God-given powers with a full appreciation of our position; shedding our Light, help and influence on all because we know our position as an integral part of the 1 Life. But since man today is but an imperfect reflection of the Higher Self we must reverse the numbers in the circle, thus:

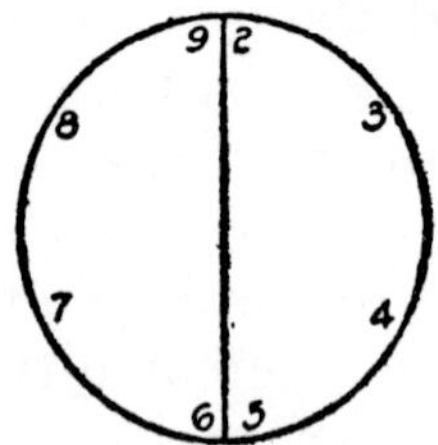

Let us consider physical man as the circle and the ray from the Higher Self as the animating Principle, 1st appearing as a Dot in the center, then extending above and below until it separates the sphere into 2 halves. These halves we will call the personality and the Individuality, within which are the potentialities of all the digits. Beginning with 2, the 1st mundane number, we evolve inside 1 half until we reach 5 or manhood. At this point we become aware of the Higher Self (1) and The Christ-force (6) and begin to reach upward in evolution until we attain our Great Initiation in number 9. Then once more we recognize, but in a far wider sense, that while we are man we have become more than man, just as man is an animal, but more than an animal. In short, that as man we have within us 2 currents of force fighting for mastery, the personality and the Higher Self. From this point onward there is no progress save as we grasp with our enlightened Will the Rod of Power and consciously work with the 1 Law, which we now see not as a line of separation but as the 1 Life common to both the personality and the Individuality. Henceforth there is no more separation either from our Higher Selves or from all that is. Then will the now more than man (what the Kabalah calls the 2nd Hé) send forth his creative Ray and repeat the process. This drama is enacted before our eyes daily in the unfolding and evolution of the seed and the hatching of the egg. Let us open our eyes to see and our hearts to understand.

The circle of the nought or cipher is often alluded to as the "Crown" or the "Crown of Ineffable Glory," while the 9 digits are represented as brilliant jewels or stars in this crown. This is the "crown of life" spoken of in *Revelation* (ii, 10), "Be ye faithful unto death (*i. e.*, Initiation), and I (the 1 Life) will give thee a crown of life." In the most famous book on the Kabalah, called the *Zohar* or *Light*, we find that:

> "When He [the Infinite O] assumed the form (of the crown, or the first Sephira), He caused 9 splendid lights to emanate from it, shining through it, diffused a bright light in all direc-

> tions. That is, these 9 with his one (which was the origin * * * of the 9), together made the 10, that is ⦶, or ⊗, or the sacred Ten * * * and these numbers were 'the Light.'"[4]

Among the Hindus number 10 is referred to as a magic power. The cipher represents the vast field of man's as yet unmanifested nature and powers, which are nothing to him except as by his attainment and use of the Rod of Power he brings them into manifestation and gives them their proper place in 10.

Among the Masons number 10 is a sign of union and good faith, expressed by the joined hands or the Master-grip, the fingers of the 2 hands making 10.

There are 10 double numbers which add up to 10, the 1st digits of each increasing from 1 to 9, the 2nd digits decreasing from 9 to 1, thus: 10, 19, 28, 37, 46, 55, 64, 73, 82, 91.

THE 10 LEPERS.

> "And as he entered into a certain village, there met him ten men that were lepers * * * and it came to pass that, as they went, they were cleansed. * * * And one of them * * * turned back, and with a loud voice glorified God. * * * And Jesus answering said, Were there not ten cleansed? but where are the nine?"—*St. Luke,* xvii, 11-19.

In the parable of the 10 men who were lepers, there is a mystical reference to number 10 as a complete number. There were 10 who were cleansed, *i. e.,* mankind in their evolution have passed through the cycle of the 9 digits and lo they were lepers or were joined unto death. When the complete number 10 is reached The Christ commands these 9 digits that they show themselves to the priests, *i. e.,* to the priestly power of the illumined intellect, which must now scan all the experiences of the life—represented by the digits—and

[4] *S. D.,* II, 42.

decide if all the leprous tendencies which bound them to death have been healed and the sting of death swallowed up in Victory. When this is done they are healed.

But there remained only 1 who returned to give thanks, hence the question "where are the 9?" was not a question of reproach, but a most pertinent 1 calling attention to the fact of the 9 being swallowed up in the 1 or 10; the fact that the Great Initiation was complete. For it is as 1 that the cycle of the 9 digits returns to give thanks and to start out on a new cycle. Again, this 1 who returned was a stranger, a Samaritan. The meaning of Samaria is "to guard," hence this 1 is the guardian or the manifestor of the experience of the cycle of the 9 digits.

> "The 'Boundless Circle,' the Zero, becomes a number only when one of the other nine figures precedes it, and thus manifests its value and potency."[5]

While every number 10 is a return to unity, still every time it thus returns it brings a new experience, which is expressed by the digit which is manifesting in the 10, thus:

Number 1 in 10 is the 1st manifestation of the Light. In the 1st day of creation "God said, Let there be light; and there was light. And God saw the light [the 1], that it was good" or 10.

Number 2 in 20 is the separation into the positive and negative; the descent of the Light into matter; the creation of heaven and earth; the firmament which "divided the waters which were under the firmament from the waters which were above the firmament. * * * and God saw that it was good" or 10.

Number 3 in 30 marks the manifestation of the Trinity reaching down into matter and expressing and

[5] *S. D.*, I, 125.

bringing forth. It was on the 3rd day that the earth brought forth. "And God saw that it was good" or 10.

Number 4 in 40 marks the completion of the physical creation. In this cycle the whole path of the earth's evolution is marked out and the Foundation Stone laid. "And God saw that it was good" or 10.

Number 5 in 50 marks the perfection of all living things. Even man as a perfect animal type is here perfected. "And God saw that it was good" or 10.

Number 6 in 60. In this cycle The Christ-force completes the informing or animating of all things. Animal man becomes the image of God and is given dominion over the earth. "And God saw everything that he had made and behold it was very good" or a perfect 10.

Number 7 in 70. On the 7th day God rested and handed over to man, now made in His image and hence responsible for his future evolution, the reins of government. Henceforth man himself, with everything made for him and placed in the Garden of Eden, must tend and cultivate that Garden and rule its animals. God saw that this day was perfect or 10, so He blessed and hallowed it. Man was not handicapped in any way, for all that God had prepared for him was perfect.

During the cycles beginning with number 8 in 80 we have to deal with the future of man. For God rests, yet watches over His creations, always ready to respond to every sincere cry for help. But from 8 onward man is held accountable for his dominion over the earth. In this cycle he must hold the scales, and in them must weigh and balance all things; for only thus can his evolution be accomplished. And when God sees that there is a just balance and good, he will bless it and make it perfect and complete or 10.

Number 9 in 90. When this number is reached man, having been weighed in the balance and not found wanting, must meet the Great Initiator and wrest from him his power. And God, knowing that this is man's heritage and that man has reached out and touched His robe, has eaten of the Tree of Life and "become as one of us," will then pronounce it good and bless it and call it perfect, or a complete 10.

This explanation of the days of creation is so obvious that the only wonder is that man can be so blinded and waste so much time and fruitless theological discussion in the effort to build up such a dogma as "original sin," with all its attendant evils, hopeless confusion and discouragements.

The *Bible* is a most wonderful occult treatise, full of cryptic utterances, each sentence expressing volumes, yet so very clear, once the mind has thrown off the shackles of prejudice and the misconceptions due to materialistic interpretations and is willing to read with open eyes, the while listening to the Still Small Voice of the Spirit for the spiritual interpretation—the "Spirit who is with thee always, even to the end of the world, will bring all things to thy remembrance."

CHAPTER 39

THE 10TH LETTER, *Yod* (י).

"He produced Yod, predominant in work, crowned it, combined and formed with it Virgo in the Universe, Elul (Sept.) in the Year, and the left hand of Man."—*Sepher Yetzirah,* 24.

While Yod is 1 of the 12 simple letters it is 1 of the most important, corresponding to the English letters I and Y.[1] Its meaning is "the origin of all things," for by and from Yod were all the other letters created. Its hieroglyph is "the finger of man," pointing upward, the sign of aspiration and also of command.

Yod represents humanity in its entirety, the 2 expressions, male and female (2×5) in the 1. It expresses all the potencies of the Father (1), but now fully expressed in number 10. Here we find the 1 no longer piercing the circle of undifferentiated substance and starting into evolution all the potencies resting in the darkness, but out of the mysterious depths of this universe of unmanifested life, the ○, all the numbers have now evolved. Hence the 1 has taken its stand at the right hand of the ○.

Yod, representing the Active Principle of all life manifestations, symbolically stands for the Reincarnating Ego. Just as the 10 recurs again and again in its multiples, each 10 symbolizing a cycle of evolution and experience, so does the Ego add experience to experience throughout the cycles of evolution on its journey of unfoldment—its great "Cycle of Necessity." And just as each time a 10 is reached its value is raised by the power of its new digit (20, 30, 40, etc.)

[1] See *V. of I.*, 127-130-1.

while its greater cycles are indicated by the addition of ciphers (100, 1,000, 10,000, etc.), so does the Ego pass through its minor incarnations, each dominated by a special phase of development comparable to an added digit. Then at certain cyclic periods it reaches decisive or major incarnations in which, like the 10, it takes upon itself a continuation of its great and original mission in manifestation. This is a new and higher cycle, during which it unfolds or adds greater and higher aspects of manifestation to its experience, just as the number 1 adds more ciphers. Each such new cipher means that the Soul has entered upon a new and as yet unmanifested experience, a higher phase of the old experiences which it has passed and successfully expressed. Just as a boy passes and successfully manifests all that childhood holds of experience for him, then enters upon the experiences of manhood, etc., so in a far greater degree does the Real Self add cipher to cipher throughout all eternity. And like the 1, the Ego expresses these powers in its life and manifestation, so that no 1 can mistake an advanced Ego for a primitive 1, any more than he could mistake a 100 for a 10.

Just as the individual passes through minor and major incarnations or cycles, so humanity as a whole passes through minor cycles of unfoldment corresponding to the digits, and then has its decisive or major cycles in which a perfect manifestation of the Divine Man or 10 is expressed in the world in the person of an Avatar. While the periodic falling away from previous religious teachings and principles among subraces and nations may seem like a lapse and a return to the barbaric and selfish principle that "might is right," still such periods of war and barbarism are but the burning up of the chaff of the old cycle, or the indrawing of the digits into the O.

Every Avatar is the embodiment and expression of, and brings to the world, a new cycle or a new ○ of unmanifested Truth which the nations of the ensuing cycle must unfold and manifest to the best of their ability. Thus, while all Avatars are perfect and complete, as number 10 is perfect and complete, still each comes with an added cipher. This is why no nation, society or individual can really progress while they cling to precedent and the traditions of the past. Each new age is a new ○ which can be developed only through the Light of The Christ Dot in that ○, which manifests through the inspired teachings of that age, couched in the terms of its race thought and including its most advanced discoveries. In the individual life each new step is such a ○ whose guiding Light is Intuition.

Many critics look upon the Christian religion as a failure because most of the so-called Christian nations are now not exemplifying its principles in their dealings with each other, yet it has been and is lived out and manifested today by millions of its followers, who are the golden grain or the harvest of its cycle. But since the burning of the chaff makes a dense black smoke, a superficial observer is apt to overlook the fact that the harvest of that cycle has been gathered, and may think that the field itself is being destroyed and that no future crops can be raised, yet in truth the burning is but a preparation for the new cycle.

In the Kabalah the sacred word Yod-He-Vau-He represents Jehovah, also God *and* man, the Higher Self and the personal self united by the "bridge" and bringing forth the next creation or the 2nd Hé. Yod represents the Higher Self, Hé or number 5 represents the human personality and Vau (6) the link that unites the 2. This sacred word therefore expresses all that we have said about number 10. Being an expression of cyclic law, it embodies the recognition of the divinity of man, through the union of the personality with the divine Higher Self, the 1 Life flowing unimpeded through both and making Man a true representative of the 7 fold Elohim, for the "likeness" has now evolved into the "image."

The 10th Sephira unfolds naturally from the 9th and thus completes the cycle of The Mystic Rose, as well as the decad of the numbers. It is called in the Kabalah, Malkuth, the Kingdom, also The Queen, Matrona or the Inferior Mother, The Bride, also Shekinah, and is represented by the divine name "Adonai," and among the Angelic hosts by the name Kerubim.

THE 10TH TAROT CARD

THE WHEEL OF LIFE

Papus

MEDIEVAL

Papus

St. Germain
EGYPTIAN

Smith
MODERN

THE 10TH TAROT CARD, *The Wheel of Life.*

The 10th card of the Tarot depicts a wheel, called the Wheel of Life or the Wheel of Fortune. The word *tarot* itself means a wheel or something that rotates, its beginning and end in 1, or endless time in eternity. "The importance of the picture of the Orb which named all wheels is further shown in the fact that human language was made on this Ball, Circle and Wheel. Thus ORB-IT names 'the going of the Orb', and even the rut in the road made by the wheel is called 'Orbita' because the rut shows the route, rute, ruis or way, or road of the Wheel. Any schoolboy can understand the general plan for the making of words on the Sun. The Rota or Wheel, named everything Rotary and going in rota-t-ion, and that which was attributed to the action or causings of the Sun, such as rolling, rotting, roasting." [2]

This Wheel or ○ is pivoted upon the upper end of the upright 1 while at the base are 2 entwined serpents, representing the 1 Life manifesting as duality upon earth. This Wheel is sometimes represented as suspended between 2 uprights expressing the same symbology, but more crudely, for the Wheel of Life to be a perfect number 10 must be supported by the 1 Life, yet must find its base supported in the balanced pair of opposites, the 2 serpents.

Poised with outspread wings above the top of the Wheel is the Sphinx, the sign of calm, equilibrated Wisdom and Perfect Justice. The figure has the paws of a lion and holds a sword in its right paw. It is crowned with the symbol of Venus. On the right side of the wheel we see Anubis, the Egyptian dog-faced god—the symbol of good—ascending, bearing in his right paw the Caduceus and having on his head the symbol of Mercury. On the left side of the wheel

[2] *The Jarvis Letters,* xi.

we see Typhon, the Egyptian god of evil and destruction, descending with a trident in his hand. These 2 figures on the Wheel indicate that good is ever aspiring and ascending, while evil is ever fleeing before it and descending into darkness and disintegration.

The balanced and reclining sphinx represents the supremacy and command which Wisdom has over both good and evil. Anubis and Typhon represent the opposition of good and evil and indicate that evil must descend and be disintegrated that its force may rise and manifest as good at the next upward turn of the Wheel. It also presents the idea that good must triumph through aspiration and incessant equilibration. The Wheel is the original ○ which we considered in the beginning as the Garden of Eden in which infant humanity started out on its "Cycle of Necessity." But now the Wheel has become the Law as *Karma,* "The wheel of the good law which grinds by night and day."

THE 10TH COMMANDMENT.

> 10. "Thou shalt not covet thy neighbor's house, thou shalt not covet thy neighbor's wife, nor his manservant, nor his maidservant, nor his ox, nor his ass, nor anything that is thy neighbor's."—*Exodus,* xx, 17.

Moses was given 10 Commandments to bring down from the mountain for man's guidance. But they were written upon 2 tables of stone,[3] again the perfect 10 separated into its 2 fives, man and woman.

As number 10 is the Number of Completion, it is the ingathering of all experiences into the ○ of fulfillment. Therefore if we have really reached number 10 there will be nothing of another's to covet, for all things will be ours. The thing above all others that will hold us back from complete realization of our oneness, both with the unmanifested Dot within the circle which is

---

[3] See *V. of I.,* Chapter xxv. *The Two Tables of Stone.*

ever ready to unfold new and more wonderful fields of experience and also with the ingathered experiences of the past cycle—symbolized by the 1 which now stands at the right hand of the ○—is to covet anything. Even when we have reached the point where we are 1 with all that is, this oneness does not mean that we as individual Souls shall have every experience and pass through every condition, but that we shall have just that which belongs to us and is needed to round out our experience and fit us for our own place in the whole where we will enjoy the fruits of the experiences of all the others. To covet that which is another's is to lust after it, and as long as we lust after anything we are not and cannot be complete or at 1 with it.

This, however, does not mean that we are never to seek after, desire or aspire to greater and higher attainments. There is a great difference between seeking and finding that which is necessary for our growth, and lusting after or coveting something that belongs to another, and which we are by no means sure is best for us. We are told to grow as the flower grows. This means that as we evolve through the 9 digits we are to create around ourselves an aura comparable to the circle in the 10 and realize that our Real Self is the Dot within this aura which must bring all its potentialities into manifestation by the time number 10 is reached. Number 1 may be likened to a gardener standing in the midst of a circular field and scattering his seeds, while in number 10 the seeds have sprung up thickly and borne fruit, leaving no room for the gardener, so he now takes his stand beside the fruitful field. Within the circle of our aura are the seeds of everything needed for our completeness, even though as yet unmanifested. Just as the seeds of the future world rested in potentiality in the darkness of the ○

in the beginning, so have we all within our ○. And as the gods said over the ○ of unmanifested world-stuff in the beginning, so must we say: "Let there be light." For we have recognized the radiant Star of Initiation as the center of our ○ and it is now our task to bring into manifestation that which we know is within us, be it something necessary for the little 1 which stands beside the ○ or for the unfolding of the Star which shines in the center.

By the time we have reached the number 10 we are no longer children to ask even God for our daily bread, for we have passed our Initiation in number 9 and must stand alone and consciously create through the power of the Dot which we have unfolded within us. Jesus standing at this step said: "I have bread to eat that ye know not of." We must no longer draw to us that which has been manifested by another, even though we think we can draw it from the source of Divine Supply, for the Great Mother has ceased to feed us at her breast, since we have outgrown that kind of nourishment. When we were babes we drew our supply from that which our mother had gathered, eaten and furnished us in the form of milk, but when we grow up we must minister to our own needs through the exercise of our own powers. Just so when we are no longer children spiritually. We must minister to our needs by bringing into manifestation, through the power within us, the supply which is always present potentially in our aura. To do otherwise is to covet that which belongs to another, lusting after that which is not our own. For we are demanding that another furnish us with that which we have the power to manifest for ourselves.

We must train our minds to realize that we have within the ○ of our aura just those forces whose manifestation is needed for our unfoldment, and that we have the creative power of thought and will by means of which we can and must bring into being, from out the seeming nothingness of our ○, that which we need both for the physical conditions and for our spiritual perfection. Many pupils in despair cry out: "If the Masters are so powerful and can see how hard I am trying and how hampered I am by poverty, why do They not give me that which I need so sorely? They must know that I desire it only that I may do Their work unhampered." But the Masters are wise and loving as well as powerful, and would rather endure the reproachful complainings of their children than take away the very test which above all others they need to complete their strength, quicken their faith and awaken in them the knowledge that they also have within them the power to become Masters if they will. Others more orthodox cry: "I have prayed to God. I have lived daily with Christ. I have striven to use everything I possess for His glory, yet why am I still poor, sick, lonely, unloved and forsaken?" The best answer the Church can give is: "'Whom the Lord loveth he chasteneth.' The more you suffer in this life the greater your reward in heaven," etc. All this is false witness against the loving Christ, and has done more to hold back the perfection of the Race than many things called sins. The next natural question is, If each Soul has an ample supply for all its needs within its own aura, why does not that supply automatically manifest itself as it is needed? Because the perfection of the Soul means that it must learn how consciously to use its powers. Hence only as we are able to manifest them can we be trusted with their use. It is much as though an ignorant maid-servant were offered every up-to-date contrivance to make her work easy, every convenience and every comfort, and her mistress should offer to explain them 1 by 1, saying: "Whenever you need help just ask me to explain the thing you are using; for if I tried to explain the use of all at the same time I would only confuse and discourage you." And suppose the maid, instead of learning to use 1 at a time tucked them all away in some dark closet and went on working in the same old, hard way. Could the mistress prevent the maid from experiencing the unnecessary toil and suffering her refusal to learn entailed? Yet this is just what many, many complaining Souls are doing in their spiritual households.

The way to make use of our possibilities and experience the comforts which our loving Father-in-heaven has provided for us, is 1st to say, over and over again until we realize it, that all that is needed is already ours *in potentiality* and that it is our present task to show our appreciation of our heavenly Father's care by bringing out the various powers and forces and learning to use them to bring into manifestation our supply. We must 1st make a mental picture of just what we want and repeat it until we see it clearly, saying: "I want to bring this thing out of my dark closet and put it to work." If it is money we need, we must make a visual picture of it coming to us, not from someone else, but from out our own storehouse. We must not see it coming to us from another or wait for it to be given to us or we will be bitterly disappointed. We must see it coming from within our own ○ as a result of the diligent use of all our powers. By so doing we will never be tempted to covet that which belongs to another, for we will know that our Father has placed plenty for us in the dark storehouse of the unmanifested and that it is all ours for the bringing out into the Light. Therefore, just as we would make every effort in hunting for a long buried treasure in a dark cellar, so must we turn on the Light within ourselves, that the possibility and the means of our attaining it may be revealed to us. That is, just as the Light which entered the dark ○ of Chaos in the beginning created a world—not out of nothing, but out of the material already present in the darkness—so must the Light within the center of our ○, "The star whose ray thou art," reveal to us all that we need to create our world and start out on a new cycle of manifestation. Only thus can we complete number 10. Until then, once we have turned from the lights of the world, the Star of Initiation and the Sun of Righteousness will be apt to dazzle our eyes and make the darkness of the unmanifested seem more profound, while through the darkness the muttering thunder will continually rumble the warning, "Thou shalt not covet."

CHAPTER 40

THE JOY OF COMPLETION.

"Make a joyful noise unto the Lord, all ye lands. Serve the Lord with gladness: come before his presence with singing. * * * For the Lord is good; his mercy is everlasting; and his truth endureth to all generations."—*Psalms*, i, 25.

"Believe thou not that sitting in dark forests, in proud seclusion and apart from men; believe thou not that life on roots and plants, that thirst assuaged with snow from the great Range—believe thou not, O Devotee, that this will lead thee to the goal of final liberation."

—*The Voice of Silence,* Blavatsky, 30.

Since number 10 is Completion it is well to close this volume on the 1st cycle of the digits with some definite thoughts on the characteristics of Completion and how they should be related to our individual lives.

The attributes of Completion are, 1st, Peace, the struggle of accomplishment is over; 2nd, Harmony, all the conflicting elements have found their proper places and hence work harmoniously together; 3rd, Joy, the joy of achievement, of attainment; the vibration of ecstasy that comes when the creation or outer manifestation expresses the ideal. Job tells us that when the foundations of the physical earth were completed and the earth was ready for man, "The morning stars sang together, and all the sons of God shouted for joy."[1] This creation was accomplished in an outpouring of joy, love and harmony, just as today we find the joy and harmony in the happy songs of the birds constantly sending out harmonious vibrations which help most materially to unfold and perfect the leaves and flowers. In fact, if we are to believe the *Bible* or any

[1] *Job*, xxxviii, 7.

other Sacred Scripture, the creation of the earth was set to music of the most joyful measure, symbolized by the spoken Word. The very rhythm of the earth, even the rock strata proclaim it, as well as the persistent joyousness of all Nature which ever returns to smiles after tears. No matter how devastating the storm, or how appalling the catastrophe, Nature will in a few short months or years heal the ugly wounds and cover the scars with living verdure. After the tempest and shipwreck, how beautifully the sunlight dances upon the waters! After the storm how green the leaves, how glad the songs of the birds!

Joy is the keynote of creation ever proclaiming to man God's Divine Plan of peace, harmony and perfection. It is Nature's voice proclaiming the utter fallacy of the belief in the supremacy of error or evil, telling man that only through joy and peace and harmony can completion be reached; that all which is apart and cannot vibrate to this joy and harmony is ephemeral, to be swept aside as a mere passing phase of existence. It is the grand Psalm of Life speaking of the unswerving on-going of The Lord of Hosts, *i. e.*, the Law of the hosts of the air, the water, the earth, and the fire, who has looked upon His works and proclaimed them good.

"And thou shalt rejoice in every good thing which the Lord thy God hath given thee." (*Deut.*, xxvi, 11). In spite of all that man can do to mar Nature by his evil thoughts, his inharmonies, his vile emanations, his wars, etc., we still find her persistently smiling, persistently calling the children of men to rest upon her bosom.

Geologists tell us that the earth was created during 4 great eras called the Eozoic, Paleozoic, Mesozoic and Cenozoic, thus confirming the occult teaching that 4 is Nature's Foundation Stone upon which the Completion of number 10 is to be erected (1+2+3+4=10). Through all these long ages while the physical earth was passing through its evolution toward Completion in number 10, there were terrible upheavals, changes and what man might call evils, yet the Sons of God spoken of by Job, were not overcome with sorrow for that which was swept away to make room for the new, but instead they shouted for joy, knowing full well that change must succeed change until the completion of number 10, because it contains the achievements of all the digits, not 1 thing being lost.

The evolution of the planet has taught us that out of imperfection is perfection builded up and brought forth, hence there is nothing to grieve over or regret if an experience has tended toward our perfection and completion, for the earth today is of the same substance as that which was breathed out as fire-mist in the beginning, but under a different phase of expression. We still find that it contains all things for man's well being, not only food, clothing, healing herbs, etc., but all things needed to build his cities, to carry on his commerce and to light and cheer him on his way. We also find Nature always beautiful and gracious, with ever a mystical and magic power to charm.

While the earth as a dwelling place for man reached the completion of the 1st expression of number 10 in 4, man, being septenary, must pass through the cycles of evolution indicated by the digits up to 7 to reach his 1st cycle of completion. Thus the earth reaches its completion in 4 periods (1+2+3+4=10), man reaches his completion in 7 (1+2+3+4+5+6+7=28=10) and Super-Man in 10 periods (1+2+3+4+5+6+7+8+9+10=55=10). Since Nature has passed her 1st cycle she becomes for man a completed Book of the Law, "written with the finger of God," in which every step of man's evolution is exemplified; for on his higher spiral he must pass through the steps corresponding to those which brought Completion to the Earth. Hence in Nature there is worked out and displayed before man an answer to every problem to be met with in his evolution, even though, until man realizes his oneness with Nature and his power to affect her, he is continually casting the reflection of his own inharmonies upon her.

One of the great lessons written on every page of the Book of Nature, and which runs as a golden thread through every expression of the 1 Life manifesting in her, is the lesson of the joy and gladness and the eternal peace and harmony in life; the ever reverting back to joy and harmony after each disturbance of her equilibrium, together with the ephemeral and transitory nature of all inharmony. This is man's great lesson. And until he learns it he will be like the planet while forming, *i. e.*, subject to terrible storms, cataclysms and disasters.

Through an almost universal misconception of all spiritual teachings, man has been and is inclined to lay great stress on the necessity of suffering; in fact, this phase of spiritual teaching has been carried to such great extremes that it has been looked upon as meritorious to suffer. Man has even used his intellect and will to devise tortures for his body and for his mind, thus deliberately setting himself up as critic and judge of that which God has created, forgetting that man is made in God's image and that man's physical body is necessary to complete God's expression in matter. Just as a physical planet was needed to give God a field of action on the physical plane, and just as God made the physical planet beautiful, harmonious and complete, so must man's body be beautiful, harmonious and complete ere he can be said to have laid the physical foundation on which the Super-Man can begin his evolution.

Remember that even the highest and purest inspiration must be interpreted by the brain of the 1 giving it out, hence only that which is found written in, and can be proved by, the great Book of Nature, can be absolutely depended upon. This Book of Nature each Soul must ultimately learn to read for himself. No matter how high or advanced the Teacher, the only perfect teaching is to show man how to decipher and interpret the Book of Nature for himself. If this were done there could not be such a wide gulf between science and religion. Hence in our contemplation of number 10 we wish to turn from the interpretation of the Book of Life as sorrow and suffering and emphasize the gospel of Joy; to reiterate again and again that as long as we dwell in the thought of sorrow or permit ourselves to believe that the only way to evolve God-ward is to trample on His gifts, to insult Him with the idea that all the beauty and perfection and joy of life have been evolved through ages of growth, not to make man's pathway through these lower levels o evolution more joyful and to teach him of the grandeur and goodness of the wonderful overflowing graciousness of Divine Love "that would not that any perish but all have eternal life," but that all this wonderful stage setting was elaborated merely as a temptation; to hold man back; to make his struggles harder that we must expect to suffer, etc.

As long as the teachers of religion make it living a dark, hopeless sacrifice, telling man he must give up all joy, all ease and comfort—all that God had so carefully and bountifully prepared for the happiness of his children—and must spend the rest of his life in scourgings, either of the flesh or of the mind, they are demanding somethin which is not in the scheme of God's Law; something not necessary but inimical to man's Completion; something not written in the Book of Nature. Hence it is natural for the whole mind and inner consciousness of man to rebel.

Because man for a time believes what is taught him, he is overcome with a sense of his utter unworthiness, but later on when he finds that he cannot easily kill out the joy of life which is innate in him, he turns away from the gloomy picture of religion as a sacrifice, and pushes aside what he is taught are the demands of his Soul, until he has enjoyed the beautiful world and has listened to the natural cry of his senses for a time. Because he is taught that all the beauty and enjoyment of life are wrong, he separates Divine Love from life; separates life from God, looks upon joy as evil. The world of beauty he is taught to consider a temptation, a field in which he can revel only as a traitor to his divine nature, a field in which to express only his lower instincts. So with his higher nature pushed back he goes forth to indulge his lower nature and its appetites, to kill and slaughter birds, animals and his fellow men; to spread death and disaster wherever his foot has trodden. Because he is taught that the gold and wealth stored up for his use are inherently evil, are put there but to tempt his greed and avarice, he turns his back on the good that the wealth of nature was intended to bring about and tries to grasp all he can; tries to enjoy in his own selfish way all that wealth and power can give him. But the Law is inexorable and everything that interferes with the peaceful and harmonious joy of life and with evolution must be ruthlessly swept aside and Nature allowed to return again to smiles.

So man's misguided religious teaching and selfishness, which have turned the gifts of God into instruments of self indulgence, must be swept away. This is done by war, famine, pestilence and all manner of evils. Who dare say, however, that these are intended as part of God's plan, and are necessary to man's Completion? They are only the inevitable result of man's own perversion of God's laws and gifts. Who shall say that those well meaning teachers whom Jesus called "blind leaders of the blind," who have impressed on the world for so many long ages the desirability of suffering and have made religion such a dark picture that man has rebelled, are entirely blameless?

The humanity of the world as a whole will never reach Completion in number 10 until the leaders and teachers permit The Christ to anoint their eyes, that they may be healed of their blindness and look in Nature's Book for the interpretation of the inspiration given them, and learn to read with the open eye of Spirit. Once this is done they will teach man the gospel of Joy; teach him to look for the 1 Life, the Spark of spiritual oneness in all things; teach him that man is made in God's image, hence all things in him are expressions of the Divine, when put to their proper uses; that religion is seeing the Divine back of all and manifesting it in the life; that nothing that is selfish is in reality joyous, nor can it endure, but that real joy is the enduring reality of vibrating in harmony with the divine ideal. Then Number 10 for man will bring beauty, joy, peace, harmony, love, understanding, discretion, wisdom, realization and Completion. Then with the Sons of God man can shout for joy and sing understandingly the hymn he now sings with little real appreciation:

"Joy to the world; the Lord has come.
Let earth receive her King,
Let every heart prepare him room,
And heaven and nature sing."

"Blessed shalt thou be in the city, and blessed shalt thou be in the field, blessed shalt be the fruit of thy body, and the fruit of thy ground, and the fruit of thy cattle; the increase of thy kine, and the flocks of thy sheep; blessed shall be thy basket and thy store, blessed shalt thou be when thou comest in, and blessed shalt thou be when thou goest out, the Lord shall cause thine enemies that rise up against thee to be smitten before thy face; they shall come out against thee one way, and flee before thee seven ways. The Lord shall command the blessing upon thee in thy store-houses, and in all that thou settest thine hand unto."[2]

"The man of sorrow and acquainted with grief" must be crucified that the Divine Christ, the Son of God, may manifest in Completion and sit forever at the right hand of his Father, where he is lifted up and shines as the Spiritual Sun in the divine world, drawing all men unto him. "Weeping may endure for a night but joy cometh in the morning." *(Psalms,* xxx, 5.)

The subject of this volume will be found completed in its sequel, *The Key of Destiny,* Curtiss.

[2] *Deuteronomy,* xxviii, 3.

Prayers of *The Order of Christian Mystics.*

Prayer for Light

O Christ! Light Thou within my heart
The Flame of Divine Love and Wisdom,
That I may dwell forever in the radiance of Thy countenance
And rest in the Light of Thy smile!

Morning Prayer

I have within me the power of the Christ!
I can conquer all that comes to me today!
I am strong enough to bear every trial
And accept every joy
And to say
Thy will be done!

Healing Prayer

O thou loving and helpful Master Jesus!
Thou who gavest to Thy disciples power to heal the sick!
We, recognizing Thee, and realizing Thy divine Presence with us,
Ask Thee to lay Thy hands (powers) upon us in healing Love.
Cleanse US from all OUR sins, and by the divine power of Omnipotent Life,
Drive out the atoms of inharmony and disease, and
Fill our bodies full to overflowing with Life and Love and Purity.

Prayer of Protection

O Christ! Surround and fill me and Thy Order with the Flame of Divine Love and Wisdom,
That it may purify, illumine and guide us in all things.
May its Spiritual Fire form a rampart of Living Flame around me and Thy Order,
To protect us from all harm.
May it radiate to every heart, consuming all evil and intensifying all good.
In the name of the Living Christ! Amen.

Prayer of Demonstration

I am a child of the Living God!
I have within me the all-creating power of the Christ!
It radiates from me and blesses all I contact.
It is my Health, my Strength, my Courage,
My Patience, my Peace, my Poise,
My Power, my Wisdom, my Understanding,
My Joy, my Inspiration, and my Abundant Supply.
Unto this great Power I entrust all my problems,
Knowing they will be solved in Love and Justice.
(Mention all problems connected with your worldly affairs, visualize each and conclude with the following words)
O Lord Christ! I have laid upon Thy altar all my wants and desires.
I know Thy Love, Thy Wisdom, Thy Power and Thy Graciousness.
In Thee I peacefully rest, knowing that all is well.
For Thy will is my will. Amen.

Prayer to the Divine Indweller

Come, O Lord of Life and Love and Beauty!
Thou who art myself and yet art God!
And dwell in this body of flesh,
Radiating all the beauty of holiness and perfection,
That the flesh may out-picture all that Thou art within!
Even so, come, O Lord. Amen.

Prayer to the Divine Mother

O Divine Mother!
Illumine me with Divine Wisdom,
Vivify me with Divine Life and
Purify me with Divine Love,
That in all I think and say and do
I may be more and more Thy child. Amen.

Grace Before Meals

I am a creator.
By the power of my spiritualized Will
I consciously gather all the forces from this food,
And use them to create health, strength and harmony
In all my bodies (physical, astral and mental).

APPENDIX

In response to the many inquiries received since the First Edition was published in regard to our teachings as to the "other and higher uses" (page 35) of the Creative Force besides that of procreation, we would say that it must be remembered that the Creative Force is the Divine Creative Power of the Godhead, "that fructifying and vivifying Power through whose action *all things.* are brought into manifestation," and that it becomes sex-force *only when focused in and acting through* the sex centers. When acting through other centers, for instance through the brain or hands in literary or musical composition, planning a building, painting a picture, modeling in clay, designing a dress or any other form of *creative* work—not mere physical exercise—it is still the Divine Creative Force that is being used, but it is not sex-force because it is not functioning through those centers. Keep this fundamental conception in mind.

The main object of our teaching has always been to help the great mass of married people who are advancing spiritually and who desire to live as highly a spiritual life as possible, yet who are neither advanced enough nor strong enough to live a strictly celibate life without sexual intercourse. Hence the teachings aim to show how to take the simpler steps before attempting the more advanced. The *first step* is to eradicate the idea that there is anything impure or evil about the sex relation itself (See 283). It becomes impure and evil only when thought of as impure and used merely to minister to lust and not as an expression of pure love between lawfully married couples. When we say lawfully married, we mean made one in the sight of both God and man. For while the mere repetition of a marriage ceremony, differing as it does in many countries, is not of itself a true marriage—and by true marriage we mean "a true marriage of the Soul, not mere union of the sexes" (84)—and granting a true marriage to be one of divine complementation, nevertheless it is not a true marriage *on earth* until solemnized and recognized and legalized according to the laws of whatever country the couple may be living in (See 106). Only under such circumstances is a sexual union permissible. And even under such conditions, if impure thoughts concerning it are held by one or both of the parties, especially during the union, it becomes impure. Our aim is therefore to teach those who are not ready for the more advanced steps to purify and uplift their union by holding thoughts of purity, love, peace and harmony concerning it.

The *second step* is to teach them to moderate and control it and transmute it, as long as they feel that they need its expression. It may be limited to procreation by those who have so controlled it that they can limit its expression to once in two or three years, naturally and without sense of repression and without creating inharmony and perhaps breaking up the home and family life. For those who cannot thus limit it naturally and harmoniously, it *can be transmuted* and used on the higher planes—through the directing power of thought and high ideals—to create in the higher realms the mental and spiritual qualities and bring forth the ideals they most desire to manifest in their lives. This is not using sex-force for spiritual development, but is using the Divine Creative force. This, together with the exchanging and balancing of the positive and negative magnetic and psychic currents, etc., is what we mean by saying that it has "other and higher uses" than procreation; for we have seen the "procreation only" doctrine break up many otherwise happy families and cause untold misery among others, all of which is unnecessary. Even if one of the two is unwilling to join in the ideals of transmutation, the other alone can accomplish a great deal by holding those ideals, not in rebellion but in love and harmony, during the union.

For the unmarried or those who for any reason, karmic or otherwise, are temporarily separated from their complementary mates, transmutation through the other channels mentioned above is, of course, the only method of expression open to them. Very often because one has refused to listen to the inner guiding Voice or because passion or worldly ends have blinded them to the inner guidance, they find themselves married in a merely earthly sense to one whom they realize is not their true mate, and later find in another, one whom they recognize as the true mate. Such a mistake can in no wise excuse a violation of their marriage vow—certain modern doctrines of so-called "freedom" in this respect we regard as false and most pernicious—in fact such a recognition makes more binding the law of the land; for since such couples are joined *only by the law of man* and not by divine harmony and love, and since they have voluntarily submitted to it, they must be true to its mandates until the same law sets them free. *On this point we admit no latitude whatever.* Transmutation can be accomplished alone, but it is much slower and more difficult than when each has the help of the other. The method of this transmutation is fully dealt with in the chapter on "The Sex Problem" in our *Letters from the Teacher.*

The *third step* can be reached only by the comparatively few, the stage in which the force is not merely controlled and purified, but in which even the *desire* for physical union is transcended or outgrown; not merely repressed and denied with great struggle, but is *no longer felt, i. e.,* it is truly *mastered.* Here the desire for physical union has been transmuted into aspiration or desire for union with the Divine, the Higher Self. When this stage is reached all the necessary exchange of magnetism can be attained by mere social contact with each other. Even here great discretion must be used and each must be faithful to his or her true mate, for when magnetism has become the vehicle for the exchange of the positive and negative forces it is just as much adultery to mix magnetism promiscuously as it would be on the lower plane to mix sex-force.

When this stage is reached all the forces can be used in the higher realms without feeling any call from, hence without denying or repressing, the sex centers. And since there is *no desire* for physical union, there is no suppression or repression and no inharmony arises, and both work as normally together in this higher relation and both are as fully satisfied by this relationship as they were in the lower stages while attaining it. At this stage it must be firmly understood that "Whom God hat joined together, let no man put asunder." For when two Souls have reached *this stage* of oneness there can be no more putting asunder or divorce.

To teach indiscriminately to the *spiritually undeveloped* that they must refuse the natural demands of their lawfully wedded mate—in many cases brought to our attention, the demands *of the wife* have been as insistent as those supposed to be made only by men—before their mate understands what it is all about or is willing to accept it and still desires the usual normal relations and is not ready for their transmutation or regeneration, such teaching, we repeat, in our experience is the cause of greater inharmony and evil than that which it is designed to correct. The effect on the average husband is either to cause the greatest inharmony and unhappiness or to cause a separation, in many cases driving him outside the family for what he considers "his rights," or it completely breaks up the otherwise happy family through divorce. The effect on the woman, since in most cases her denial merely results in suppression unless *really transmuted,* is to fill her mind and entire outlook upon life with thoughts of sex when she should be turning her mind away from it. Even the very effort to avoid it is but focusing her mind upon the subject and so saturating her aura with it that she becomes a greater attraction for and an easy prey to obsessing entities from the astral world, who are ever seeking just such gratification, thus depleting her physically as well as astrally and magnetically. Of this we have had ample evidence from the cases who apply to us personally for help in nearly every city in which we have lectured, and by letter from almost every part of the world. Therefore we say there can be no hard and fast rule or forcible denial for all stages of development, except the rule of purity, normality, moderation, harmony and love, any more than we can expect the same standard of conduct from children of all ages, except in the fundamentals. We therefore maintain that there must be at least three stages in the mastery of this force: First, *Purification* of body *and mind;* second, *Transmutation* or diversion from the lower centers by use through the higher; and third, *Regeneration* or the conscious and harmonious use of the forces by both in the higher realms. This is not sex worship or phallicism.

To endeavor to kill out or suppress this function or so to fear it that the very sight of the opposite sex precipitates the thoughts to the sex and passion level is not the way to Mastery. True Mastery or Regeneration can only be attained by two Souls working in unison and harmony, both desiring only the higher uses of the Creative Force and working toward it without strain and without striving to force themselves beyond their normal stage of development, as evidenced by the character of their desires.

In reply to many questions we would say that we do not approve of Dr. Stockham's book, "Karezza," because its conclusion is unnatural and abnormal and in many cases has simply become a means of ministering to indulgence, since the mind and thought is concentrated on the act instead of being centered above the physical union so that the act and the union itself is forgotten in the concentration on the higher ideals.

In conclusion, our main plea is, *first,* be natural and normal but *pure and wholesome* in your relations; *second,* purify and uplift your *mind and thought* concerning those relations until the mere physical expression is no longer necessary *or desired.* Only then are you ready for a higher step.

Page 23: Numbers may be . . . In the ancient Jewish Law called the Talmud, the rabbis theorized that the body was made of 248 parts. To redeem oneself, and to find eternal bliss, each one of those 248 parts had to be sanctified by holy acts. According to some that process took a minimum of 3 reincarnations. *In the Bible . . .* These are reflective numbers which commemorate actions of the Almighty. Greatest stress, however, is placed upon the number one, which at times is the Name of the Lord; it needs no reflection, and is impossible of division.

Page 24: This is recognized . . . See the apodoctic nature of Exodus 20, Leviticus 19, and Deuteronomy 5. The rhythmic nature of those chapters is proof of their revelatory basis. *This is recognized . . .* For this reason prayers are most effective if the ears hear what the lips say. In this idea is the secret of "speaking in tongues." *The nerves are . . .* Note how the single point in theory takes up no space. The line is composed of two parts, the triangle 3, and the square 4. The circle is made of infinite points, and in theory cannot be drawn!

Page 27: Son of God . . . All this is a commentary on Genesis 1:2: "The spirit of God hovered upon the face of the deep." Here "face" equals form, while "deep" refers to the formless. Thus we have the first proof of that fundamental axiom "extremes meet." In this beginning form and formless, finite and infinite have touched.

Page 28: But when the . . . How aptly the ○ defines our being. It is essential nothingness, emptiness. In order to find that saving grace, and call to the Lord, we must be, like the circle, empty. God can work within us only when we are emptied of Ego.

Page 29: The circle also . . . Here that aspect of smoothness, found in every circle, becomes evident. The ○ is the only 2 dimensional geometrical design without points or roughness. Every point on the circumference of a circle teaches about every other point. The Garden of Eden, like the circle, contained no roughness—no points. All reflected God; goodness, all worked to the health of Adam and Eve.

Page 30: A circle formed . . . Clearly this is alluded to in Genesis 3, where the snake, "symbolizing unending life and immortality," is wrapped around the Tree of Life. *The serpent therefore . . .* Man's fall came when he focused on the Great Creative Force in conjunction with the sex organs. The snake, a symbol of good, became bad.

Page 40: While the egg . . . The egg, like the circle, is complete in its roundness. But the egg further contains new life and possibility of reproduction—the germinal center which is common to all bodies.

Page 41: The sea foam . . . The Great Deep is Primordial Egg while chaos is pre-Christian germinal center. *He is that* . . . Note the close parallel between this system and the ancient scheme of Kabala. Themis represents Gevurah while Anteros is Chesed.

Page 42: Thus does life . . . The esoteric concept of tzimtzum was never better described. A constant condition of affirmation—denial is impregnated in all creation. This is a world that proves and denies God's existence at all times.

Page 61: Yang is associated . . . In the great prayer P'Tach Eliyahu, God is described as "One to which there is no number 2." Here the strength and divinity of the first odd number shines forth.

Page 62: The Monad, or the 1 God . . . The Hebrew for One is e'had. Three letters, each representing a number, make up e'had. Aleph equals one—there is but one God in the Universe. Heth stands for 8. God rules this earth and the seven heavens. Daleth represents 4. God rules the four corners of the world. In sum, the One leaves little room for power other than His.

Page 63: It also symbolizes . . . The light of creation represents the sublime manifestation of thought. Therefore, like the number 1, the primordial light which breaks through the darkness of ignorance has no opposite. Where light shines there can never again be darkness

Page 64: The number 1 . . . Adam Kadmon is not a physical person but a description of the creative process. Adam Kadmon is the macrocosm, and man is a microcosm of the same order of creation.

Page 67: The seven double letters . . . 7 also refers to the seven heavens. The Zeir Anpin, representing the first 3 sephiroth, finds expressed in this world through the Zeir Arickin and Malchoth, compromising the last 7 sephiroth.

Page 68: Nevertheless, the letters . . . Thus by certain combinations and permutations, the Kabbalah is able to awaken certain cosmic forces—even to the extent of hastening the End of Days. By the use of this Gematria the Maharal of Prague was able to create the Golom. *Like number 1* . . . This is so because Aleph is silent, and, like soft breathing, cannot be heard.

Page 70: Since Aleph is . . . Yod, equaling ten in gematria, is reduced to 1 in gematria Katana. Thus the 10 becomes 1 as the sound becomes silent.

Page 72: Every god which . . . The earth was formless and void . . . and the Lord said: "Let there be light." Out of the paradox where earth existed and did not exist, God created One, light, Divine Wisdom. Meaning is brought into Chaos.

Page 82: It is the Number of Polarity . . . Polarity, or Ying Yang, holds that all existence has an opposite. To good there is bad; to happiness there is sadness;

to life there is death. God, as noted above, has no opposite. Thus it must be or the living God would reflect the dying God.

Page 83: Many philosophers teach . . . According to the Kabbalah, one cannot "see" God unless he or she is married. In this case, 2 mystically makes a higher a 1. *In fact such* . . . First Adam was a construction of the Divinity manifesting in the universe. 2 represents the physical Adam and Eve who are our ancestors!

Page 84: Beginning of evil . . . For the place of opposites in the word, see Ecclesiastes III, Verse 1, and following "To every season there is a time."

Page 85: 2 in the Binary . . . Maimonides states that God cannot be defined by words of this world. Adjectives by definition are opposed to the 1 meaning.

Page 89: The great lesson for earth . . . Thus the ultimate polarity. The etrnal soul is forced to live in the impure body. Earthly life is a combination of both opposites.

Page 90: The 2nd Hebrew letter . . . The Hebrew letter Beth corresponds either to the English letters b or v. Rules of grammar determine pronunciation.

Page 91: The Beth represents . . . Significantly, according to the ancient Hebrew Tradition, the world was created with the letter Beth. Many esoteric and mystic teachings delve into the forces of the simple B sound through which God created all from nothing.

Page 107: Hence the sacredness . . . Kabbalah divides the sephiroth into three categories, all of which must be in balance for the Messiah to bring the end of days. *As they advance* . . . Maimonides, St. Thomas, and Aristotle refer to this balance as the Golden Mean. Most correct behavior can be judged by that Golden Mean. In like manner, *Magid Maysharim* says that none can inherit the world to come, save by 3 reincarnations.

Page 108: The only real satisfaction . . . That ray is primordial light of creation which is participation with the divine minds through proper deeds and thoughts. *As man and woman* . . . Thus in the first chapter of Genesis God told man to have dominion over the earth and to subdue it. Divine intention was not to hurt and kill, but to redeem.

Page 109: They realize that in . . . Ancient Kabbalists recognized that only through marriage can one evolve sufficiently to find God.

Page 110: In such cases . . . The ancient law holds that our actions determine our mates. With correct living we shall find our divinely ordained spouse. Improper actions will have an opposite affect.

Page 116: It is the Comforter . . . In one Kabbalistic system the first of the sephiroth, hochmah, refers to man. The second, binah, refers to woman. The lower sphere, Tifereth, draws on the characteristics of the upper sephiroth.

Page 117: All life is . . . In politics and science the triad is force, counterforce, and revolution. In psychology it is ego, id, and superego.

Page 120: The idea of water . . . The three patriarchs, and three of the matriarchs, were buried in the cave of Machpelah at Hebron. *In the Kabalistic Trinity* . . . Kether, being the most eternal, is at times not considered in the schematic of the sephira. Chabad Kabbalists replace Da'at for Kether in their trinity. *The solar lives* . . . By this system every soul participates in the universe at one time. From highest to lowest, the four worlds of the universe are Aziluth, Breyeh, Yitzirah, and Asiyahu.

Page 124: But is also apparent . . . The Hebrew ceremony, Blessing of the Sun, occurs every 28 years when the sun completes its cycle. Also Ko'ah, or strength, referred to in mystic writing equals 28 in Gametria. 28 itself stands for 18 (life) plus 10 (the Ten Commandments) according to Kabbalistic speculation. The seven couplets of Seher Yetzirah is actually a series of letters numbering 14. Thus by reducing the 14 to 7 couplets, each couplet equals 7; each individual letter equals 3-1/2.

Page 125: The third letter is . . . Gimel, according to the Talmud, corresponds to acts of lovingkindness especially done for the poor.

Page 131: This name or signature . . . The ancient Hebrew did not pronounce the Tetragramaton mentioned in the 3rd Commandment. They feared that capturing God's name would also permit them to control God's attributes. *This is the* . . . In Kabbalah God's names have numerical values that can be used to better understand God's place in this world.

Page 133: Therefore, while causing . . . Some say that every word of the Bible is another expression of God's name. Indeed the Hassidim say that the Book of Proverbs teaches but one lesson: God exists. Each sentence is geared to another intelligence so that all humanity can learn of God's existence from that one book.

Page 139: or Thor's Hammer . . . Dr. Curtiss wrote *The Key to the Universe* in 1917, well before World War II. Events of that period have made impure the purity of Thor's Hammer. Indeed, the Law of Karma can be analyzed through the spiritual developments of the Swastika.

Page 141: By thus working with . . . See also Psalm 118:22, which reads: "The stone which the builders have rejected has become the cornerstone." *Living the higher life* . . . The force of this lesson is demonstrated by Jacob who, before striving with an angel of God, chose a foundation stone on which to rest his weary body in order to soar heavenward.

Page 144: The fourth wind . . . See also Ecclesiastes 1:6

Page 148: In all these cases . . . The mystical name of God, only recited by the High Priest, and only on Yom Kippur, is made of but 4 letters, Yod, Hay, Vau, Hay, called the Tetragramaton. Although pronounced Jehovah in English, in truth the pronounciation has been lost. *Number 5 being* . . . The less mystical name Elohim is composed of five Hebrew letters. Elohim also can mean human judges or giants.

Page 150: The number 4 . . . There is a question if the watches of the night are of 3 or 4 hours in duration. Those who say 3, and posit four watches, hold that King David had a harp that by God's word began to play at midnight so that he could distinguish between the 2nd and 3rd watch.

Page 154: There are four . . . *Ethics of the Fathers* reports: There are 4 types of persons: One who says mine is mine, and yours is yours. This is the ordinary man (but some say he is a man of Sodom). One who says what is mine is yours, and yours is mine. This is a boor. One who says Mine is yours and yours is yours. This is a saint. One who says yours is mine and mine is mine. This is a wicked man. *While this is* . . . Tractate Sanhedrin says: "God used one stamp (Adam) to make all mankind and thus to teach the law 'Unity is diversity.' "

Page 158: Hence, in the fourth letter . . . Daleth actually means door in Hebrew. *Therefore Daleth is* . . . In early creations the human being was two people: Man was welded to woman and shared the same backbone.

Page 162: This is man's . . . Of the two tablets of the Decalogue, the right tablet contained but 4 commandments, this being the last. *Remember the sabbath* . . . This is the only ritual commandment in the Decalogue—but look for its higher and more esoteric worth.

Page 169: The Sabbath day . . . Sabbath teaches mankind to sanctify time, the one aspect of life man cannot control.

Page 173: Number 5 is called . . . In the esoteric Hebrew numerology, gematria k'tanah, the word for Love, equals 5. (By similar calcuations eesh—man—also equals 5.)

Page 174: Thus the division . . . The first question asked by the heavenly court is: "Were you fair in business? Were all affairs given a just balance?"

Page 182: Since the pentacle . . . Thus 5, the pairless number, is used to make the good evil; the white black. In Zohar God, like 5, is pairless. Yet God's backward reflection, like that of the upside down pentacle, is the Sitra Ahra (or all that is evil in the universe).

Page 184: Let number 5 . . . The fifth of the *sephiroth* also represents *Tifereth,* which balances all of the Divine Attributes of the other *sephiroth* and passes them to *Malchuth,* and then to this world. The structure of the *sephiroth* corresponds to the structure of man and is a macrocosm similar to the microcosm of man.

Page 186: Hence Hé is not . . . Hé is an aspirant. In a very real sense it is the mortal sound of breathing. Yet hé also holds the name of God and is the only letter twice mentioned in the tetragramaton, God's lost name.

Page 187: Hé is also called . . . The Hé is made of a Daleth to the right, and an inverted Vau to the left. The space between the Daleth and Vau is referred to as a divine window since Vau hé is itself a name of God.

Page 189: come mental difficulties . . . The final hé of the tetragramaton stands for the Sepher Malchuth, and brings manifestations of the Divine into this otherwise godless world.

Page 191: Honor thy father . . . This is one of two times in the Old Testament where man is promised long life as a reward for obeying a commandment.

Page 193: The "land" which . . . This, indeed, is a spritual commandment calling together obedience to parents and to the Divine One. Land is a watchful hint to the resurrection when all who have kept this law will be called to life again in a renewed world.

Page 198: Even today man . . . Race is not used in the sense of bigotry, but of development. All humanity, at some time enters the 6th Race through proper understanding and meditation.

Page 207: According to the Kabalah . . . The Macroprosopus, on the one hand, is so sublime and esoteric that it cannot be understood by the human mind. On the other hand, it is made of more concrete emanations of the Godhead out of which love, mercy, justice, and strictness find their basis. *Tipherath* is a tetragramaton and is God's holy name through which Moses found God. Tipherath was unknown to Abraham and to the other patriarchs.

Page 209: Number 6 is . . . Mystically, esoteric Hebrew tradition reports that when one visits and prays for the sickly, 1/60 of the illness is removed. A second visitor would remove 1/60 of the remainder, and so on (of course certain prayer can remove *all* illness. Ordinary prayer, however, will remove at least .0166).

Page 211: The 6th letter . . . More correctly the sixth letter is spelled Vau *Is an 'eye'* . . . In Hebrew the Ayin (16th letter) means eye. Vau means hook.

Page 213: Vau being the . . . Vau, when used as a prefix to another word, does mean "and" and is itself the uniting principle between ideas and principle. In Kabbalah Vau ties together the Macroprosopus wth the Sephira Malchuth through the Microprosopus.

Page 216: Therefore anything that we . . . The 6th through 8th commandments constitute a negative trinity showing man how he must not act in ordinary affairs with others.

Page 217: It is said . . . Thus to kill is more than to just deprive another of life—it is to deprive the world of Divine Love and life through all acts that diminish another.

Page 220: blending of the 7 . . . Seven also refers to the number of heavens that exist above us. Each is separated by a distance of 500 years, and each is more sublime than its predecessor.

Page 221: The 7 great . . . The seven Creative Rays are the seven sephiroth between Binah and earth. Each ray is progressively less concentrated so that with Malchuth, Earth can humbly accept God's divine gift of love.

Page 222: The 7 virtues . . . Before entry to Israel, Moses was commanded to destroy the seven nations. Mystically these nations refer to pernicious human attributes.

Page 223: Since each manifesting . . . In Kabbalah the highest sephira of a lower world becomes the lowest sehpira of an upper world, thus completing and beginning God's scales of creation.

Page 228: The menstrual functions . . . Psalms state "The number of man's years are 70 . . ." Psalm 45 adds: "Hypocrites will not live our half of their years . . ." (i.e., they will die before age 35 or 5 times 7).

Page 232: There are 7 functions . . . The Kabbalists point out that man is born of the rehem (womb) which in gematria ketana equals 14 (a new being coming from the binding of man and woman—7 + 7). 14 also equals 5 which is the most human number, and represents the new being. Herem, or excommunication, also equals 14 equals 5. 5 represents the loss to humanity of one person.

Page 233: Number 7 is . . . The sun completes its orbit around earth once every 28 years. In such a manner 28 = 10 = 1 points to the unity of all creation.

Page 237: 3 as the number . . . Lurianic Kabbalah holds that the 3 souls of the human being participate in the four worlds of creation simultaneously (□ + △).

Page 241: There are 7 gifts . . . *Ethics of the Fathers* holds that 7 things were created before the 7th day of the world in order to complete creation.

Page 246: We do not teach . . . The candlesticks of the ancient Temple held 7 candles. Until God brings the resurrection and rebuilding, such candlesticks are shunned by certain religious communities who wait for reappearance of seven to demonstrate the advent of the end of days.

Page 249: A star with . . . The unity of God is found in the Hebrew echad. Aleph, the first letter, equals one and stands for 1 God. Heth, the second letter, equals 8 and stands for 1 earth and 7 heavens—giving 8-fold power. Daleth stands for 4 and represents the four corners of the earth.

Page 256: It may be compared . . . Resurrection will entail a second joining of the dense physical body with the sublime lightness of the spirit.

Page 259: janitor takes charge . . . According to the Ari, all creatures that move, possess animal souls. However, higher bodies' lives are determined by more sophisticated souls as long as they keep an open and correct communication with the divine.

Page 262: The 1st great battle . . . The Spiritual Mind or Yetzer Hatov is in constant battle with the Animal soul or Yetzer Harah. Unfortunately the battle lines are not equally drawn. The Spiritual Mind with love as a weapon must bring arms against the animal soul armed with lust. Only by fortification through study of Divine Principles can the Spiritual Mind succeed.

Page 266: The Spiritual Soul . . . At night the spiritual mind journeys heavenward to be refreshed from the aura of spiritual souls. Those trained in esoteric thought, understand this principle through the story of Jacob's ladder. *This is called* . . . Kabbalists call this ray Kether as it is too sublime to ever quantify.

Page 272: For it has been . . . The sages also realized that the stars have deep souls, and are life forms far more exalted than our own. Only future scientific advances can affirm this fact scientific thought refuses to admit.

Page 277: Thus Zain is the . . . Aleph Zain together spell the mystical word Az, which at one and the same time refers to past and future, creation and redemption. Az is the mystical vocabulary to define the allusion of time. Kabalistically Az equals 8, which is fulfillment or perfection.

Page 278: And until at least . . . Speaking is the act of bringing spiritual ideas into this profane and animal world. For that reason wasted speech by all religions is considered sinful.

Page 282: Since we know . . . Significantly, 7 refers to the Hebrew letter Zain, which at time, means the masculine phallus.

Page 283: Only thus can . . . Thus Talmud states: "The greater the man, the greater his sexual urge." While he must work hard to control that urge, the resulting energy still continues and does seek creative fruition.

Page 285: Number 8 is . . . Therefore the Jewish people circumcise their sons on their 8th day of life. Therefore the Christian peoples celebrate New Years Day on the eighth day after the birth of Jesus.

Page 286: For evolution means . . . "Then they will say . . ." The time of Messiah has come. *Then* in Hebrew equals 8.

Page 287: Since evolution can . . . Mystics say that there is building which is destruction and destruction which is building.

Page 288: For number 4 we . . . The Hebrew word for dead, dying, death is Mayt, which in gematria Ketana equals 8.

Page 292: For only as . . . In 8 is the constant tension and pain of the Ying Yang. Every idea and act reflect opposites. There can be no laughing without crying, no youth without old age, no mortality without immortality, no life without death.

Page 294: Do not demand . . . 8 says accept that which comes, and recognize that all happenings bring with them their opposite. Do not be excited by either. As Kipling said: "If you can meet with triumph and disaster and treat those two imposters just the same."

Page 296: Only when through . . . The word Hath in Hebrew means sin. The allusion is clear. One must beat one's sword into a plowshoe "for victory." Any other "victory" is pyrrhic and just a compromise with the animal soul.

Page 303: Evolution is retarded . . . Thus the two most important commandments: a) "Love thy neighbor as thyself"; b) "You should love the Lord your God with all your heart and all your soul." *Each soul is* . . . Note this is panantheism which holds that God is all and more than all. It is not pantheism which only holds that God is all.

Page 305: Under the oppression . . . A karma is a spiritualization of that great Roman principal "Lex talionis" or "measure for measure." Nothing goes unpunished or unrewarded in the universe.

Page 307: This Rose is represented . . . Nine is the final male order of God's emanation—called Sephira *Yesod.* From *Yesod* God's emanation goes to *Malchuth* to become indwelling in the word as we know it.

Page 308: The Initiates are the Sons . . . Each of the four worlds repeat, at different levels of intensity, all the sephiroth. Emanations go from Kether to Yesod (sephira number 9), enter the world through Malchuth which then becomes Kether in the next world or the process repeats.

Page 310: For response to this need . . . All of these hours were not based upon our scheme of the day, but upon a division of daylight into 12 parts and of night into 12 parts. Therefore, days of summer would be longer than 12 of our hours of duration. Winter, conversely, would be shorter. Real time can be noted with the use of a sundial.

Page 312: For some number 9 . . . Words spoken limit the imagination and power of meditation, because words are guided by principles of physics and biology. Thoughts are not and may reach the sephers of heaven.

Page 314: Life brings these tests . . . God, however, never tests man with travail so mighty that man cannot overcome it.

Page 327: The actual meaning of . . . The serpent was used to beguile Eve because it was the most subtle of all beasts of the earth. It's skin could be cast off without change to it's nature.

Page 330: Leo the Lion . . . Of the lion who must become tame, the prophets say: "If the lion roars, who will not be afraid." "Who" are those lacking in strength of spirit.

Page 331: The 9th letter . . . Proverbs, a book written by King Solomon in Middle Age (Ecclesiastes was composed by him in old age) states: "The beginning of wisdom is the fear of the Lord."

Page 336: Over the 1st gateway . . . As Laertes said to Polonius in Hamlet: "This above all to thine own self be true, and it must follow as the night the day, thou cannot then be false to any man."

Page 337: All this is . . . Truth in Hebrew (Emeth) is made by joining the first, middle and last Hebrew letters together. Thus truth encompasses all.

Page 340: For 10 the 0 . . . 10 is not chaos undifferentiated but it is differentiation. It is separation, and as separation grows, we grow farther from unity and farther from God. *Here man as* . . . That light is the healing light of understanding which brings unity into all things.

Page 342: They also called . . . In Hebrew 10 is known as world. *It is also* . . . Sun (Shemesh) in gemantria ketanah equals 10.

Page 343: Only as we grow . . . Those 9 qualities refer directly to God's emanations called sephiroth kingdom or Malchuth is the 10th sepher, but actually acts only as a receiver for the emanations above it.

Page 351: Then will the now . . . The second hé stands for Malchuth, the 10th sepher and the first sepher in the world beneath it. Clearly this is the trinity: creation, revelation, redemption all at one time.

Page 355: The Bible is . . . Biblical numbers must be understood as digits and according to powers multiplied and divided by 10. Every word is a number that reveals esoteric secrets only to the initiate.

Page 356: Its meaning is . . . Indeed Yod does mean hand which in gematria ketanah equals 5, and two hands naturally equal 10.

Page 358: Being an expression . . . Yod is the smallest letter, yet stands for God's name! Oddly, as a suffix, it means my, and refers to man.

Page 362: But they were written . . . Maimonides calls the oral and written law together the Yod (Hand) because it is the completion of all the law and understanding which man can fathom.

Page 363: This, however, does . . . Only with regard to spiritual attainments, and esoteric teachings is coveting and jealously permitted because coveting can cause us to study and reach divine heights.

Page 364: I have bread . . . Thus it is written: "I was young, now I am old, but I have never seen the righteous (saintly) lacking bread."

Antony W. Lee, B.A., M.A., D.D.
Editor of *Notes and Esoterica*

A

B